5

# motivation
# SCIENCE

TEKS–Based Alignment to STAAR®

## student edition

Critical Thinking for Life!
Mentoring Minds

**Publisher**
Michael L. Lujan, M.Ed.

**Editorial Director**
Teresa Sherman, B.S.E.

**Production Coordinator**
Kim Barnes, B.B.A.

**Digital Production Artists**
Judy Bankhead, M.F.A.
Sarah Poff, B.S.
Ashley Francis, A.A.

**Illustrators**
Judy Bankhead, M.F.A.
Gabriel Urbina, A.A.S.

**Content Development Team**
Karen Lane, M.Ed.
Janna Najera, B.S.I.S.
Angela Peyton, M.Ed.
Stephanie Rieper, B.S.I.S.
Beatrice L. Taylor, Ph.D.

**Content Editorial Team**
Karen Lane, M.Ed.
Erica Miller, B.S.E.
Allison Wiley, B.S.E.
Jennifer Mallios, B.A.

# Critical Thinking for Life!™
### Mentoring Minds

PO Box 8843 · Tyler, TX 75711

[p] 800.585.5258 · [f] 800.838.8186

For other great products from Mentoring Minds,
please visit our website at:

mentoring**minds**.com

ISBN: 978-1-935123-26-2

Dear Student,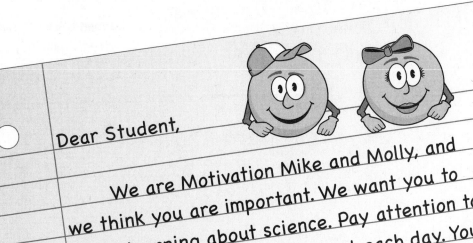

   We are Motivation Mike and Molly, and we think you are important. We want you to enjoy learning about science. Pay attention to your teachers and do your best each day. You will learn many new and interesting things to help you become successful in school and in life. Here are some tips to help you be the best possible student.

# You Can Do It!

Your friends,
Motivation Mike and Molly

- Listen to your parents.
- Follow school rules.
- Listen to your teacher.
- Ask your teacher questions if you do not understand.
- Apply what you learn to your everyday life.
- Find friends who like school, and study with your friends.
- Get enough sleep each night.
- Eat proper meals, drink plenty of water, and exercise.
- Be positive.
- Never give up.

# motivation**science**™
## Table of Contents

**Motivation Station: Mike's Cool Science Fact**

Did you know pumpkins float in water? Even though pumpkins can be large and heavy, the inside is mostly hollow. This makes the density of the pumpkin less than the density of water.

## After this lesson I will be able to:

- **Classify** matter based on physical properties, including mass, magnetism, physical state (solid, liquid, and gas), relative density (sinking and floating), solubility in water, and the ability to conduct or insulate thermal energy or electric energy.

## Comparative Investigations

**Activity 1:** Can you Classify? The Property of Mass

1. Find objects in the classroom to complete the chart below.

2. Use a triple beam balance to check the results by finding the actual mass of the objects.

3. Record your answers in the data table.

| Find an object that has... | Name of Object | Mass of Object |
|---|---|---|
| more mass than a pencil | | |
| less mass than a crayon | | |
| more mass than a pair of scissors | | |
| less mass than a ruler | | |
| more mass than an eraser | | |

## Activity 2: Physical Properties of Matter

1. Classify the objects listed in the data table according to their physical properties.

2. Test each object to determine the properties of magnetism, physical state, density, solubility, and whether it is a conductor or insulator.

3. Record your findings in the table below.

### Physical Properties of Matter

| Object | Magnetism (Yes or No) | Physical State | Density: Sink or Float? | Soluble in Water (Yes or No) | Conductor or Insulator? |
|--------|-----------------------|----------------|-------------------------|------------------------------|-------------------------|
| Wood | No | Solid | Float | No | Insulator |
| Spoon | | | | | |
| Nickel | | | | | |
| Salt | | | | | |
| Sugar | | | | | |
| Paper | | | | | |
| Iron Nail | | | | | |
| Penny | | | | | |
| Oil | | | | | |

What did you learn about objects that conduct electricity? Cite evidence to support your answer.

_____

_____

_____

Is oil soluble in water? Why or why not?

_____

_____

_____

**1** Which physical property is used to identify matter based on solubility?

Ⓐ Ability to evaporate

Ⓑ Volume

Ⓒ Ability to dissolve

Ⓓ Mass

**2** A student tries to dissolve 25 grams of sugar in a beaker containing 300 mL of water. The student proposes the following question:

> What factor would result in sugar dissolving faster in water?

Which change would most likely cause sugar to dissolve the fastest?   **5.2(B)**

Ⓕ Decreasing the temperature of the water

Ⓖ Using larger pieces of sugar

Ⓗ Stirring the mixture rapidly

Ⓙ Using less water

**3** A student conducts an investigation to learn how materials conduct heat. The student places a wooden spoon and a metal spoon in identical containers of hot water. Then, the student takes the temperature of the water in each container to make sure both are the same temperature. What is the variable in the student's investigation? **5.2(A)**

Ⓐ The temperature of the water

Ⓑ The type of container

Ⓒ The length of time the student leaves the spoons in the water

Ⓓ The type of spoon

**4** Which tool is used to measure the property of temperature?

Ⓕ Celsius thermometer

Ⓖ Stopwatch

Ⓗ Pan balance

Ⓙ Meter stick

**5** According to the picture, what is the mass of the object? Record and bubble your answer in the box below.   **5.2(C)**

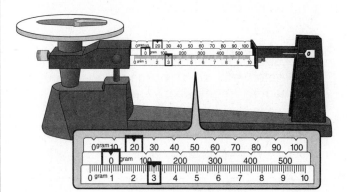

| | | | . |
|---|---|---|---|
| ⓪ | ⓪ | ⓪ | |
| ① | ① | ① | |
| ② | ② | ② | |
| ③ | ③ | ③ | |
| ④ | ④ | ④ | |
| ⑤ | ⑤ | ⑤ | |
| ⑥ | ⑥ | ⑥ | |
| ⑦ | ⑦ | ⑦ | |
| ⑧ | ⑧ | ⑧ | |
| ⑨ | ⑨ | ⑨ | |

**6** What evidence in the picture proves ice has less density than water?

Ⓕ The water has more buoyancy than the ice cubes.

Ⓖ The ice cubes are floating in the water.

Ⓗ The ice cubes are resting at the bottom of the glass.

Ⓙ The ice cubes are melting and becoming a liquid.

**Unit 1** Check for Understanding

**1** Which of these materials would **NOT** be a good insulator of electricity?

Ⓐ Metal  Ⓒ Glass

Ⓑ Plastic  Ⓓ Wood

**2** A material that has definite volume but no definite shape is classified as a —

Ⓕ solid  Ⓗ gas

Ⓖ liquid  Ⓙ not here

**3** Students are working to find the mass of a hand lens. Which of the following tools should students use to measure mass?

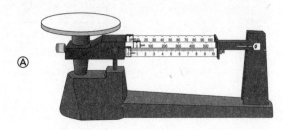

Ⓐ

Ⓑ

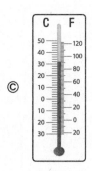

Ⓒ

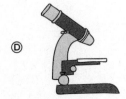

Ⓓ

**4** The objects have all of the following properties in common **EXCEPT** —

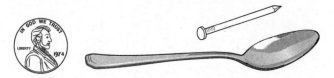

Ⓕ they all conduct electricity

Ⓖ they all sink in water

Ⓗ they are all magnetic

Ⓙ they are all solids

**5** Which objects below would be classified as having the greatest density?

Ⓐ Ping-pong ball

Ⓑ Penny

Ⓒ Water

Ⓓ Duck

**6** Which substance is NOT soluble in water?

Ⓕ Powdered drink mix

Ⓖ Sugar

Ⓗ Salt

Ⓙ Sand

 motivation**science**™ LEVEL 5

| Scientific Investigation and Reasoning Skills: Questions 7–14 |
| :---: |

**7** During an indoor science investigation, students mix unknown substances to determine which substances are soluble in water. Which safety procedure should the students follow?  **5.4(B)**

   Ⓐ Observe the outdoor area for any possible dangers

   Ⓑ Wash their hands before working with substances

   Ⓒ Wear safety goggles and gloves when working with substances

   Ⓓ Complete the investigation before the teacher instructs them to do so

**8** Students have two blocks that are the same size. They drop each block into a beaker of water. Why does Block 1 float and Block 2 sink?  **5.2(D)**

   Ⓕ Block 1 is made of a different material than Block 2.

   Ⓖ Block 1 is smaller than Block 2.

   Ⓗ Block 2 absorbs more water than Block 1.

   Ⓙ Block 2 has less mass than Block 1.

**9** Four students sort materials into two groups – Conductors and Insulators.

**Student Results**

| Student | Conductors | Insulators |
| :---: | :--- | :--- |
| 1 | Rock, rubber band | Iron nail, paper clip, wooden stick |
| 2 | Iron nail, paper clip | Rock, rubber band, wooden stick |
| 3 | Paper clip | Rock, iron nail, rubber band |
| 4 | Iron nail, wooden stick | Rock, rubber band, paper clip |

Which student correctly sorted the materials?  **5.2(G)**

   Ⓐ Student 1

   Ⓑ Student 2

   Ⓒ Student 3

   Ⓓ Student 4

**10** Which tool can be used to compare the mass of a large rock to the mass of two wooden blocks?  **5.4(A)**

   Ⓕ Graduated cylinder

   Ⓖ Thermometer

   Ⓗ Spring scale

   Ⓙ Pan balance

**11** During a science investigation, a student determined how objects could be classified.

| Object | Physical State | Attracted to Magnet | Soluble in Water |
|--------|----------------|---------------------|------------------|
| A | Solid | Yes | No |
| B | Solid | No | Yes |
| C | Solid | No | No |

Based on the properties, which of the following materials has the same physical properties as Object B?   **5.2(D)**

Ⓐ Iron nail

Ⓑ Salt

Ⓒ Sand

Ⓓ Penny

**12** The table shows how a student sorted objects by properties.

**Data Table**

| Group 1 | Group 2 |
|---------|---------|
| Paper clip | Candle |
| Iron nail | Pencil |
| Copper penny | Craft stick |

Based on the information collected for both groups, which is the best title for Group 1? **5.2(G)**

Ⓕ Objects that Conduct Electricity

Ⓖ Objects that Make Good Insulators

Ⓗ Objects that are Magnetic

Ⓙ Objects that Float

**13** After performing a lab investigation about solubility, which of these procedures is an appropriate choice for conserving resources?   **5.1(B)**

Ⓐ Throw dirty beakers in the trash after completing the investigation

Ⓑ Wash and store beakers for future use

Ⓒ Save any unused food products to eat during lunch

Ⓓ Leave all lab materials for other group members to put away

**14** Two students record the mass of four objects, as shown below.

**Student 1**

15, 25, 45, 60

**Student 2**

| Object | Mass |
|--------|------|
| Plastic block | 15 grams |
| Wood block | 25 grams |
| Glass block | 45 grams |
| Steel block | 60 grams |

Which student did a more accurate job of recording the data?   **5.2(C)**

Ⓕ Student 1, because the data shows the unit of measurement

Ⓖ Student 1, because the measurements are listed from least to greatest

Ⓗ Student 2, because the information is organized and measurements are labeled

Ⓙ Student 2, because the objects are listed in alphabetical order

## Identifying Unknown Substances

Imagine you have been given two pieces of metal that look identical. One is a magnet, and one is not. How can you determine which piece of metal is a magnet?

_____

_____

_____

_____

_____

You are given two similar substances. One is powdered chalk. The other is powdered sugar. How can you use the property of solubility to determine the identity of each substance?

_____

_____

_____

_____

_____

## Formative Assessment

Some physical properties of matter can be tested or observed. Other physical properties are measured. Complete the graphic organizer to compare and contrast physical properties that can be tested or observed with those that can be measured.

### Physical Properties

| Properties that are Tested or Observed | Properties that are Measured |
|---|---|
|  |  |
|  |  |
|  |  |
|  |  |

**Science Journal**

Design an invention to keep a candy bar from melting. Use your knowledge of conductors and insulators to reach a solution. Draw and label the design in the space below.

Explain how the invention works.

_____

_____

_____

_____

_____

_____

_____

_____

_____

_____

_____

_____

_____

_____

_____

_____

_____

## Science Vocabulary Builder

Place each word from the box below in the column that describes your knowledge of the word. Summarize what you know about the word.

> mass    magnetism    physical state    density
> soluble    thermal energy    electric energy

|  | Brand New Word | I have seen the word, but I do not know the meaning. | I think I know the meaning. | I know the meaning. |
|---|---|---|---|---|
| **Word** |  |  |  |  |
| **Summary** |  |  |  |  |
| **Word** |  |  |  |  |
| **Summary** |  |  |  |  |
| **Word** |  |  |  |  |
| **Summary** |  |  |  |  |
| **Word** |  |  |  |  |
| **Summary** |  |  |  |  |
| **Word** |  |  |  |  |
| **Summary** |  |  |  |  |
| **Word** |  |  |  |  |
| **Summary** |  |  |  |  |
| **Word** |  |  |  |  |
| **Summary** |  |  |  |  |

## Investigating Solubility

**Obtain parent permission before conducting this investigation.**

Find common household objects to test solubility. Stir a spoonful of each substance into a cup of water. Record the results in the table below.

| Substance | Prediction | Observations | Soluble in Water? (Yes or No) |
|---|---|---|---|
| Salt | | | |
| Sugar | | | |
| Flour | | | |
| Oil | | | |
| Cornstarch | | | |

✁ - - - - - - - - - - - - - - - - - - - - - - - - - - - - - - - - - - - - - - - - - - - - - - - - - - - - -

## Parent Activities

1. Fill a large container or bathtub with water. Test a variety of objects to see if they sink or float.

2. Water at room temperature is a liquid. When water freezes, it turns into a solid. If water is heated, it turns into water vapor. Find another substance at home and try to change its physical state (e.g., butter).

3. Gather a variety of objects and classify them based on the ability to conduct or insulate thermal (heat) energy.

       motivation**science**™ LEVEL 5

**After this lesson I will be able to:**

- **Identify** the boiling and freezing/melting points of water on the Celsius scale.

## Experimental and Descriptive Investigations

**Activity 1:** Melting/Freezing Point

### Question

What effect does salt have on the melting/freezing point of water?

### Hypothesis

The temperature of ice and water will be _____°C.

The temperature of ice, water, and salt will be _____°C.

### Procedure

Obtain a beaker containing ice and water and a beaker containing ice, salt, and water. Gently stir each mixture with a thermometer, and record the temperature every four minutes.

**Ice and Water**

| Time | Temperature |
|------------|-------------|
| 4 minutes | |
| 8 minutes | |
| 12 minutes | |
| 16 minutes | |

**Ice, Water, and Salt**

| Time | Temperature |
|------------|-------------|
| 4 minutes | |
| 8 minutes | |
| 12 minutes | |
| 16 minutes | |

### Observations

_____

_____

### Conclusion

_____

_____

# Unit 2 Introduction

## Activity 2: Investigating Boiling Point

Watch as your teacher performs a demonstration about the boiling point of water. In the frames below, design a comic strip showing each step of the demonstration. Share your creation with the class.

**Title** _____

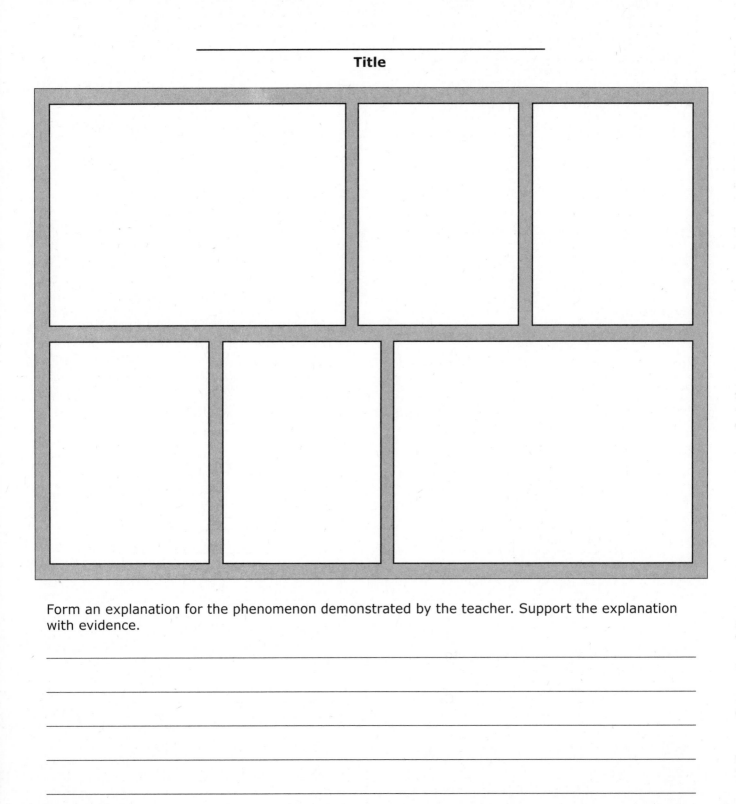

Form an explanation for the phenomenon demonstrated by the teacher. Support the explanation with evidence.

_____

_____

_____

_____

1  What unit of measurement is used when recording the temperature of boiling water?  **5.2(C)**

Ⓐ  Milliliter

Ⓑ  Degrees Celsius

Ⓒ  Gram

Ⓓ  Millimeter

2  A glass beaker is placed on a hot plate. Five hundred milliliters of room temperature water are added to the beaker. If the temperature continues to increase, the water in the beaker will most likely —

Ⓕ  turn into a solid

Ⓖ  become more dense

Ⓗ  turn into a gas

Ⓙ  show no change in temperature

3  Each of the following scenarios demonstrate freezing point **EXCEPT** —

Ⓐ  a liquid changing into a solid

Ⓑ  the temperature reaching 100° Celsius

Ⓒ  liquid precipitation turning into freezing rain

Ⓓ  the temperature reaching 0° Celsius

4  What can be inferred as the change that occurs between 1:00 P.M. and 1:20 P.M.?  **5.2(D)**

Beaker at 1:00 P.M.

Beaker at 1:20 P.M.

Ⓕ  Freezing          Ⓗ  Condensing

Ⓖ  Melting           Ⓙ  Evaporating

5  An ice cube is placed in a plastic cup on the lab table. Students record the mass of the ice cube and the plastic cup as 5 grams. One hour later the ice cube completely melts, turning into liquid water. Then, the students record the mass of the water and the cup. What is the mass of the water and the plastic cup? Record and bubble in your answer to the nearest gram.  **5.4(A)**

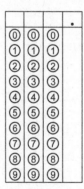

6  Water changes its state of matter when heat is added or taken away. When water reaches its boiling point the particles —

Ⓕ  are closer together

Ⓖ  stay the same

Ⓗ  are moving more rapidly

Ⓙ  are moving more slowly

**Unit 2** Check for Understanding

**1** Which thermometer shows the temperature, in Celsius, that water freezes?

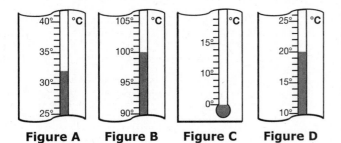

| Figure A | Figure B | Figure C | Figure D |

Ⓐ Figure A     Ⓒ Figure C

Ⓑ Figure B     Ⓓ Figure D

**2** Which of the following is an example of water reaching its melting point?

Ⓕ A cup of water sitting outside on a sunny day

Ⓖ Water simmering on a hot stovetop

Ⓗ An ice cube left on the counter

Ⓙ A cup of water placed in the refrigerator

**3** Does the temperature on the thermometer show the melting, freezing, or boiling point of water?

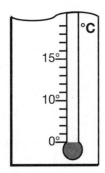

Ⓐ Freezing point

Ⓑ Melting point

Ⓒ Boiling point

Ⓓ Both freezing point and melting point

**4** Students complete this chart during an experiment. They heat water to find the boiling point.

**Time it Takes for Water to Change State**

| Beginning temp (°C) | After 1 minute (°C) | After 3 minutes (°C) | After 4 minutes (°C) | After 5 minutes (°C) |
|---|---|---|---|---|
| 20 | 42 | 87 | 100 | 100 |

According to this chart, when did the water begin to boil?

Ⓕ After 1 minute

Ⓖ After 5 minutes

Ⓗ After 4 minutes

Ⓙ After 3 minutes

**5** The temperature of water in a beaker measures 87°C. How many more degrees must the temperature increase to reach the boiling point?

Ⓐ 23°C     Ⓒ 212°C

Ⓑ 13°C     Ⓓ 100°C

**6** A science class performs a temperature experiment. Groups measure the temperatures of items in cups. If the temperature of a cup of water measures 100°C, which statement correctly describes the water?

Ⓕ The water is boiling.

Ⓖ The water is cool.

Ⓗ The water is freezing.

Ⓙ The water is warm.

## Scientific Investigation and Reasoning Skills: Questions 7–14

**7** Students make ice cream to investigate matter and its properties. The students add salt to the ice cream maker so that the mixture will change from a liquid to a solid. Which conclusion provides the most important reason salt is used to make the ice cream solidify?   **5.2(F)**

Ⓐ Salt dissolves in water.

Ⓑ Salt adds flavor to the ice cream.

Ⓒ Salt evaporates in water.

Ⓓ Salt lowers the freezing point of water.

**8** Which question can be used to make an inference based on the picture?   **5.2(B)**

Ⓕ What is the dissolving point of water?

Ⓖ What is the boiling point of water?

Ⓗ What is the melting point of water?

Ⓙ What is the freezing point of water?

**9** Four students investigate the boiling point of water.

**Measuring Boiling Point of Water**

| Student | Tools Needed |
|---------|--------------|
| A | Thermometer, beaker, timer, goggles, hot plate |
| B | Hot plate, goggles, thermometer, tongs |
| C | Tongs, hot plate, timer, graduated cylinder |
| D | Beaker, pan balance, goggles, thermometer |

Which student gathers the correct tools for determining the boiling point of water? **5.2(B)**

Ⓐ Student A

Ⓑ Student B

Ⓒ Student C

Ⓓ Student D

**10** Which safety precaution must be taken when investigating the boiling point of water?   **5.1(A)**

Ⓕ Report any changes in temperature

Ⓖ Make sure to record your data

Ⓗ Always wear goggles

Ⓙ Only use gloves and an apron

**11** Students test the freezing/melting point of water. Students record the time and temperature every 2 minutes for 6 minutes using a thermometer and a timer. What is the best way to report the results of this experiment? **5.2(G)**

Ⓐ A table

Ⓑ A pie graph

Ⓒ A sketch

Ⓓ A list

**12** A student places a cup of water in the freezer and leaves it there overnight. The next morning the student observes that the water in the cup has changed to ice. Which of the following statements best concludes why the water changes to ice? **5.2(F)**

Ⓕ The water gains energy.

Ⓖ The water reaches its boiling point.

Ⓗ The volume of the water decreases.

Ⓙ Heat is taken away from the water.

**13** A glass of water is placed in a very cold freezer. Every 5 minutes the temperature of the water is measured and recorded.

| Time Elapsed | Temperature (°C) |
|---|---|
| 5 minutes | 18 |
| 10 minutes | 12 |
| 15 minutes | 6 |
| 20 minutes | ? |

If the pattern continues, which statement correctly describes the water after 20 minutes? **5.2(D)**

Ⓐ The water temperature is 2°C, and the water is still liquid.

Ⓑ The water temperature is 1°C, and the water is still liquid.

Ⓒ The water temperature is 1°C, and the water is freezing.

Ⓓ The water temperature is 0°C, and the water is freezing.

**14** A student is given an unknown liquid to test in the laboratory. The student thinks the liquid is water. Which of the following is most helpful to determine if the liquid is water? **5.2(D)**

Ⓕ Boiling point of liquid

Ⓖ Color of liquid

Ⓗ Mass of liquid

Ⓙ All of the above

 motivation**science**™ LEVEL 5 ©2011–2014 mentoring**minds**.com

## Does Volume Affect the Boiling Point?

**Complete this activity with adult supervision.**

Pour 50 mL of water in a glass beaker. Heat the beaker on a hot plate. Record the temperature at which the water begins to boil– _____°C. Continue recording the temperature every 2 minutes for 6 minutes.

Pour 100 mL of water in a glass beaker. Heat the beaker on a hot plate. Record the temperature at which the water begins to boil– _____°C. Continue recording the temperature every 2 minutes for 6 minutes. Plot the findings on the line graph to show results.

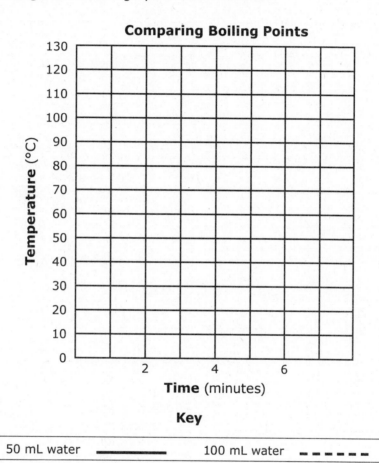

**Comparing Boiling Points**

**Key**

50 mL water ————— 100 mL water – – – – – –

## Formative Assessment

Explain the boiling point of water based on the Celsius scale. Use evidence from the unit investigations to support your answer.

_____

_____

_____

_____

**Science Journal**

Think about a time when you placed something in the freezer and noticed a change. How did the substance change? What did it look like when you removed it from the freezer?

_____

_____

_____

_____

_____

_____

_____

_____

_____

_____

_____

_____

_____

_____

_____

_____

_____

_____

_____

_____

_____

_____

_____

     motivation**science**™LEVEL 5

### Science Vocabulary Builder

Fill in the blanks with the appropriate answer. Write answers using the Celsius scale.

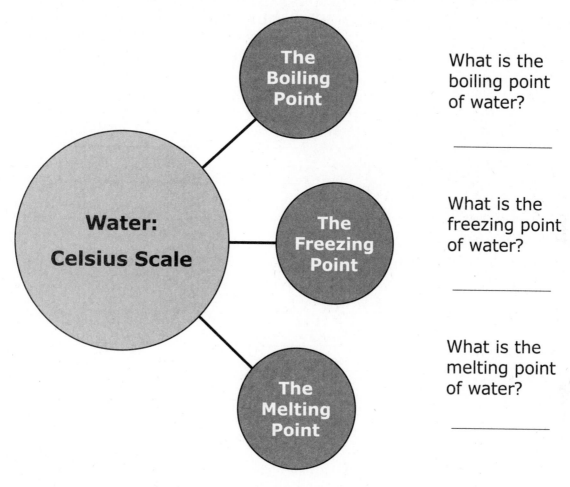

What is the boiling point of water?

_____

What is the freezing point of water?

_____

What is the melting point of water?

_____

Use pictures to draw representations of boiling point, freezing point, and melting point.

## Unit 2 Homework

**Temperature Tests**

**Obtain parent permission before conducting this investigation. Adult supervision required.**

Place a pan of room temperature water on a stovetop. Record the time it takes the water to begin boiling. Repeat using cold water and hot water. Place containers of room temperature water, hot water, and cold water into the freezer. Investigate the length of time it takes each container of water to freeze.

|  | Boil | Freeze |
|---|---|---|
| Room temperature water |  |  |
| Cold water |  |  |
| Hot water |  |  |

1. Which sample (room temperature water, cold water, or hot water) boiled in the shortest amount of time? Why?

   _____

   _____

2. Which sample took longest to freeze? Why? _____

   _____

   _____

3. Did room temperature water boil faster than hot water? _____

4. Did hot water freeze faster than cold water? _____

   _____

5. Did cold water take more time to freeze or boil? _____

- - - - - - - - - - - - - - - - - - - - - - - - - - - - - - - - - - - - - - - - - -

**Parent Activities**

1. Help your child with the above activity.
2. Take a piece of ice out of the freezer. Place it on a plate and set on a table or cabinet. Record the time it takes for the ice to begin melting.
3. Fill up an ice cube tray with water. Record the time it takes for the water to freeze. Try freezing another liquid such as lemonade. Which one freezes faster?

 motivation**science**™LEVEL 5 ©2011–2014 mentoring**minds**.com

**Motivation Station: Mike's Cool Science Fact**

Have you ever heard of GORP? What about Smhogle? GORP stands for good ol' raisins and peanuts: aka, trail mix. Smhogle is a word for trail mix used in places such as New Zealand and Australia. Trail mix is a type of mixture that can be easily separated.

## After this lesson I will be able to:

- **Demonstrate** that some mixtures maintain physical properties of their ingredients such as iron filings and sand.

## Experimental Investigations

**Activity 1:** Mixture Madness

Create a plan to separate a mixture of wood chips, gravel, iron filings, and sand.

| What tools are needed? | How can we separate our mixture? |
|---|---|
| | |
| **Hypothesis: What do we think will happen?** | **What does our mixture look like?** |
| | |

Other questions or observations:

_____

_____

_____

**Activity 2:** Do Oil and Water Mix?

**Cup 1:** Fill half full with water. Add 3 drops of food coloring and stir. Record your observation.

_____

_____

**Cup 2:** Fill half full with water. Add 50 mL cooking oil. Record your observation.

_____

_____

Stir the water and oil. Wait a moment. Record your observation.

_____

_____

**Cup 3:** Fill half full with water. Add enough cooking oil to form a layer 5 cm thick. Add 3 drops of food coloring. Do not stir. Record your observation.

_____

_____

Stir the oil, water, and food coloring mixture. Record your observation.

_____

_____

What happens to the tiny drops of color?

_____

**Cup 4:** Fill half full with water. Add enough cooking oil to form a layer 5 cm thick. Add 3 drops of food coloring. Add 15 mL dishwashing soap and stir vigorously. What is different this time? Record your observation.

_____

_____

Notice the color of the oil layer. Is it the same as the water layer? _____

What happens when an oil tanker spills oil into the ocean?

_____

_____

**1** Which substances, when mixed together, maintain their original physical properties?

Ⓐ Gravel, sugar, water

Ⓑ Wood chips, water, sand

Ⓒ Sand, sugar, water

Ⓓ Water, pepper, sugar

**2** A student conducts an investigation on mixtures using water, sand, and gravel. While stirring the mixture into the container of water, the sand and water mixture accidentally splashes into the student's eyes. What safety precaution should the student have followed? **5.1(A)**

Ⓕ Wash hands before investigating

Ⓖ Wait for the other students before starting the investigation

Ⓗ Wear safety goggles

Ⓙ Use a spoon to stir the mixture

**3** A student stirs a mixture of sand, iron filings, and water and observes that eventually the sand and iron filings sink to the bottom of the container. How can the student separate the mixture?

Ⓐ Slowly pour the mixture in another container, making sure the sand does not flow out with the water. Pick the iron out with tweezers.

Ⓑ Pour the mixture into a pot and heat one minute. Spoon the sand from the water. Use a magnet to remove the iron.

Ⓒ Pour the mixture through a coffee filter, leaving only the sand and iron in the filter. Separate the sand and iron with a magnet.

Ⓓ Use a spoon and scoop out as much sand as possible. Drag a magnet through the water to remove the iron.

**4** A student makes a garden salad by stirring lettuce, tomatoes, carrots, and croutons together in a bowl. Why is the garden salad a mixture?

Ⓕ The student cut the vegetables into equally sized pieces.

Ⓖ The vegetables are combined but maintain their physical properties.

Ⓗ The croutons cannot be taken out of the salad.

Ⓙ The salad grew from a garden.

**5** All of the following are examples of containers filled with mixtures **EXCEPT —**

Ⓐ a jar filled with trail mix

Ⓑ a glass filled with water

Ⓒ a bowl of cereal with milk

Ⓓ a cup of fruit salad

**6** A mixture of oil and water is placed in a glass beaker and stirred. Which picture depicts what is most likely to happen after the beaker sits for 3 minutes? **5.2(D)**

Ⓕ  Droplets of oil, suspended in water

Ⓖ 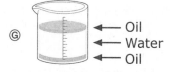 Oil
Water
Oil

Ⓗ 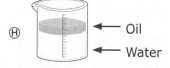 Oil
Water

Ⓙ 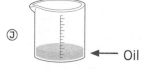 Oil

## Unit 3 Check for Understanding

**1** A mixture of iron filings and chalk dust is placed on a plate. Which of the following could be done to gather the iron filings?

Ⓐ Pour the mixture into a funnel

Ⓑ Put the mixture in a pot on the stove

Ⓒ Run a magnet over the mixture

Ⓓ Filter the mixture through a strainer

**2** A packet of trail mix has raisins, nuts, granola, and cranberries. Which statement correctly describes the trail mix?

Ⓕ The trail mix is a mixture because it contains an equal number of nuts and raisins.

Ⓖ The trail mix is a mixture because the ingredients dissolve in water.

Ⓗ The trail mix is a mixture because the ingredients cannot be separated.

Ⓙ The trail mix is a mixture because the ingredients can be separated easily.

**3** A cup of orange juice with pulp is poured into a glass. Which of these procedures could be done to separate the juice from the pulp?

Ⓐ Pour the juice through a coffee filter

Ⓑ Heat the juice in a pot until boiling

Ⓒ Pour the juice into another cup

Ⓓ Allow the mixture to settle, leaving the pulp at the bottom of the glass

**4** Which of the following mixtures can be separated using a magnet?

Ⓕ Sand and salt

Ⓖ Sand and iron filings

Ⓗ Sugar and water

Ⓙ Saltwater

**5** All of these can be separated easily **EXCEPT** —

Ⓐ nuts, bolts, and screws

Ⓑ powdered drink mix, sugar, and water

Ⓒ sand and water

Ⓓ iron filings and sand

**6** Which mixture can be separated using a filter?

Ⓕ Sand and iron filings

Ⓖ Saltwater

Ⓗ Sand and water

Ⓙ None of the above

 motivation**science**™ LEVEL 5 ©2011–2014 mentoring**minds**.com

## Scientific Investigation and Reasoning Skills: Questions 7–14

**7** Which tools are best for separating a mixture of sand, iron filings, and water? **5.4(A)**

Ⓐ Hot plate and filter

Ⓑ Tweezers and filter

Ⓒ Filter and magnet

Ⓓ Magnet and hot plate

**8** Which is the appropriate tool to use when recording the steps in separating a mixture? **5.2(B)**

Ⓕ

Ⓖ

Ⓗ

Ⓙ

**9** A new student has joined the science class. The student was not present when the class investigated mixtures and solutions. Which activity would be a good way for the class to help the student learn about mixtures and solutions? **5.3(A)**

Ⓐ Develop a model representing mixtures and solutions

Ⓑ Take the student to the library, and research mixtures and solutions

Ⓒ Draw an illustration of mixtures and solutions

Ⓓ All of the above

**10** When separating saltwater using a hot plate, what precaution should students use? **5.1(A)**

Ⓕ Unplug the hot plate if water splashes on the cord

Ⓖ Follow the teacher's instructions, and put on safety goggles

Ⓗ Leave the hot plate plugged in after the investigation is complete

Ⓙ Follow the teacher's instructions to record results in a science notebook

**11** Following an experiment testing mixtures, which would be the best conclusion about simple mixtures?  **5.2(F)**

Ⓐ After mixing, ingredients in a simple mixture develop new properties.

Ⓑ Stirring a simple mixture changes the properties of its ingredients.

Ⓒ A simple mixture can be easily separated.

Ⓓ A simple mixture dissolves in water.

**12** Students are investigating a mixture of oil and water. They notice when the mixture is stirred vigorously it appears to mix evenly, but after letting the mixture rest, the oil floats on top of the water. The students are making —  **5.2(C)**

Ⓕ an inference

Ⓖ a conclusion

Ⓗ an observation

Ⓙ a prediction

**Use the diagram below and your knowledge of science to answer questions 13 and 14.**

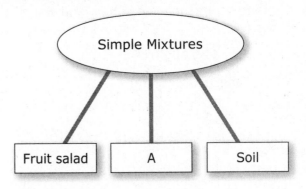

**13** Which of the following belongs in rectangle A of the diagram?  **5.2(G)**

Ⓐ Assorted nuts

Ⓑ Strawberry gelatin

Ⓒ Baked bread

Ⓓ Shelled peanuts

**14** All of the following could complete rectangle A in the diagram **EXCEPT** —  **5.2(G)**

Ⓕ trail mix

Ⓖ sandwich

Ⓗ peas and carrots

Ⓙ lemonade

     motivation**science**™LEVEL 5

## Hot Diggity Dog

- A company is creating a brand new mixture of dog food. Design an advertisement for the sale of the new product.
- Include why this product is different from others, a description of the product, the price, and a name for the product.
- Use the space below to brainstorm and create a draft for the advertisement.
- Recreate the advertisement on a piece of butcher paper or manila paper to present to the class.
- Take a class vote on which product they would purchase.

## Formative Assessment

Determine if the combinations described in the table are mixtures. Use reasoning to justify your answer.

| Combination | Is It a Mixture? | Justification |
|---|---|---|
| Water and ice cubes | | |
| Sand and gravel | | |
| Oil and water | | |

**Science Journal**

Create a list of the different mixtures seen in everyday life. Choose several mixtures and describe the properties that allow them to be classified as mixtures.

_____

_____

_____

_____

_____

_____

_____

_____

_____

_____

_____

_____

_____

_____

_____

_____

_____

_____

_____

_____

_____

_____

_____

_____

## Science Vocabulary Builder

Define and illustrate the following words using pictures and words.

**Mixture**

**Magnetism**

**Combine**

**Separate**

**Iron filings**

**Physical property**

**Unit 3** Homework

## Mixtures at Home

Complete the following table. List different mixtures found in your home. List the substances that make up the mixture. Explain how each mixture can be separated.

| Mixture | Substance 1 | Substance 2 | Substance 3 | Substance 4 | How can I separate them? |
|---------|-------------|-------------|-------------|-------------|--------------------------|
|  |  |  |  |  |  |
|  |  |  |  |  |  |
|  |  |  |  |  |  |
|  |  |  |  |  |  |
|  |  |  |  |  |  |
|  |  |  |  |  |  |

## Parent Activities

1. Make trail mix with cereal, peanuts, raisins, M&M's®, cheese crackers, or other bite-sized items. Discuss the properties of each ingredient. Did the taste or shape change after mixing?

2. Go on a scavenger hunt for mixtures in your house. Make a list of all the mixtures you find.

3. Discuss the properties of the mixtures. Can you separate the substances within the mixture?

4. Brainstorm ways mixtures can be separated.

 motivation**science**™LEVEL 5

**Motivation Station: Molly's Cool Science Fact**

Did you know a solution can be made from gases? Air is a solution. Oxygen and other gases dissolved in nitrogen gas combine to make air.

**After this lesson I will be able to:**

- **Identify** changes that can occur in the physical properties of the ingredients of solutions such as dissolving salt in water or adding lemon juice to water.

## Comparative Investigations

**Activity 1:** Creating Special Mixtures–Sugar and Water Solutions

1. What will happen if you combine sugar and water? Record your hypothesis in the box below.

2. Pour 2–3 drops of food coloring into the beaker of water and stir.

3. Pour the sugar into the colored water and stir.

4. Record observations.

| Hypothesis: What do we think will happen? | What does our special mixture look like? |
|---|---|
| 200 mL water    100 mL sugar <br><br> + = ? <br><br><br><br><br> | |
| | **Conclusion: What did we learn?** |
| | |

Name _____

Supporting Standard 5.5(D)

**Activity 2:** Creating Special Mixtures–Salt and Water Solutions

1. Measure 10 grams of salt in a cup. Record the mass of the cup and salt in the table below.

2. Create a solution of salt and water. Record the mass of the cup of saltwater.

3. Set the cup in a safe area. Place a "Science Experiment in Progress" sign next to the solution.

4. Allow time for the water to evaporate. Observe daily, and record the results in the table.

5. Compare the before and after results of the solution.

6. Draw a picture on a piece of paper to illustrate the changes.

| Day | Mass of Salt (in cup) | Saltwater (in cup) |
|-----|----------------------|--------------------|
| 1 | | |
| 20 | | |

| Day | Mass (of Solution) | Observations |
|-----|--------------------|--------------|
| 1 | | |
| 2 | | |
| 3 | | |
| 4 | | |
| 5 | | |
| 6 | | |
| 7 | | |
| 8 | | |
| 9 | | |
| 10 | | |
| 11 | | |
| 12 | | |
| 13 | | |
| 14 | | |
| 15 | | |
| 16 | | |
| 17 | | |
| 18 | | |
| 19 | | |
| 20 | | |

 motivation**science**™LEVEL 5

**1** Which statement about solutions is correct?

Ⓐ All solutions contain more than two substances.

Ⓑ A solution can only be created from liquids.

Ⓒ All mixtures are solutions.

Ⓓ All solutions are mixtures.

**2** Students prepare an experiment to determine the difference between a mixture and a solution. Before the experiment starts, one student says, "I think the chicken broth is a solution." This statement is an example of — **5.2(B)**

Ⓕ a conclusion

Ⓖ an observation

Ⓗ an inference

Ⓙ a hypothesis

**3** According to the diagram, what happened to the salt and water?

Salt crystals + Water = Solution

Ⓐ They combined physically to form a special mixture.

Ⓑ The salt and water evaporated.

Ⓒ The salt and water separated, forming layers.

Ⓓ The salt melted the water.

**4** A student dissolves 20 grams of salt in a pan of 200 milliliters of water. The student places the pan on a hot stove. How much salt is left after all the water evaporates?

Ⓕ There is no salt left because it evaporates with the water.

Ⓖ Twenty grams of salt are left after all the water evaporates.

Ⓗ Ten grams of salt evaporate, leaving ten grams in the pan.

Ⓙ None of the above

**5** A student makes a drink stirring lemon juice and sugar into a glass of water. Why is this drink considered a solution?

Ⓐ The lemon juice and sugar change the taste of the water.

Ⓑ The water changes color.

Ⓒ The lemon juice and sugar dissolve in the water.

Ⓓ The student stirs the mixture.

**6** Observe the nutritional label of chicken noodle soup.

| Nutrition Facts | Chicken Noodle Soup |
|---|---|
| Servings Per Container 4 | |
| Amount Per Serving 307g | **Nutrition Grade B\*** |
| Calories 91    Calories from Fat 12 | \*Based on a 2000 Calorie diet |
| % Daily Value | |
| Total Fat ¼g    2% | **Ingredients:** onion, chicken, |
| Cholesterol 19mg    6% | salt, sugar, chicken bouillon, |
| Sodium 34mg    1% | mixed vegetables, pepper, |
| Total Carbohydrates 16.7g    6% | chives, parsley, poultry |
| Dietary Fiber 1.0g    4% | seasoning, egg noodles |
| Protein 3.0g | |
| Vitamin A 1%    Vitamin C 1% | |
| Calcium 2%    Iron 3% | |

Which of the following are dissolved ingredients in the soup? **5.3(B)**

Ⓕ Egg noodles, chicken bouillon, and mixed vegetables

Ⓖ Salt, egg noodles, and mixed vegetables

Ⓗ Chicken bouillon, salt, and sugar

Ⓙ Pepper, salt, and sugar

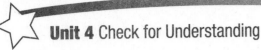

## Unit 4 Check for Understanding

**1** A beaker contains a mixture of salt, sand, gravel, and iron filings. Which substance is soluble in water?

Ⓐ Salt

Ⓑ Sand

Ⓒ Iron filings

Ⓓ Gravel

**2** What causes sugar to dissolve faster in hot water than in cold water?

Ⓕ Cold water takes up less space than hot water.

Ⓖ Cold water has faster moving particles than hot water.

Ⓗ Hot water has faster moving particles than cold water.

Ⓙ Hot water takes up more space than cold water.

**3** Which of the following has the greatest effect on the ability of a substance to dissolve in water?

Ⓐ Color

Ⓑ Volume

Ⓒ Buoyancy

Ⓓ Solubility

**4** Students are classifying substances. Which of the following substances is a solution?

Ⓕ Sand and water

Ⓖ Sugar and water

Ⓗ Spaghetti and meatballs

Ⓙ Soil and water

**5** The part of the mixture in which other substances are dissolved is called the —

Ⓐ solute

Ⓑ solvent

Ⓒ variable

Ⓓ mixture

**6** During an experiment in class, several students make statements about solutions. Which statement is **NOT** true?

Ⓕ When sugar dissolves in water, the sugar is evenly distributed throughout the solution.

Ⓖ Solutions can be classified as mixtures.

Ⓗ Heating the water first causes salt to dissolve quicker.

Ⓙ When salt is dissolved in water, parts of the solution taste saltier than others.

 motivation**science**™ LEVEL 5

## Scientific Investigation and Reasoning Skills: Questions 7–14

**7** Students test different substances to determine which are soluble. The ingredients include lemon juice, sand, salt, and sugar. After repeated tests of each substance, the students conclude all of the following have the ability to dissolve **EXCEPT** — **5.2(F)**

Ⓐ lemon juice

Ⓑ sand

Ⓒ salt

Ⓓ sugar

**8** The diagram below shows a solution.

Saltwater

Which of the following pieces of equipment should be used to separate this mixture? **5.4(A)**

Ⓕ Hot plate

Ⓖ Magnet

Ⓗ Pan balance

Ⓙ Filter

**9** Based on the information in the table, which substances could be sugar? **5.2(D)**

| Substance | Physical Properties | Soluble? |
|-----------|---------------------|----------|
| 1 | • solid<br>• sweet<br>• grainy | Yes |
| 2 | • solid<br>• grainy<br>• mineral | No |
| 3 | • solid<br>• white<br>• grainy | Yes |
| 4 | • liquid<br>• sour<br>• colorless | Yes |

Ⓐ 1 and 2

Ⓑ 2 and 4

Ⓒ 1 and 3

Ⓓ 2 and 3

**10** What is one advantage of using repeated investigations to determine the solubility of lemon juice, sand, salt, and sugar? **5.2(E)**

Ⓕ To decrease the reliability of results

Ⓖ To increase the reliability of results

Ⓗ To organize collection of data

Ⓙ To formulate testable hypotheses

**11** After creating a solution of sugar water, students are instructed to clean their work areas and dispose of all materials properly. Which student makes the best choice in disposing of the solution?   **5.1(B)**

Ⓐ Student A throws the solution in the trash can.

Ⓑ Student B drinks the solution of sugar and water.

Ⓒ Student C pours the solution down the drain and rinses the sink.

Ⓓ Student D leaves the solution and materials on the table.

**12** In science class, students combine materials to create solutions. In one experiment, students add 250 milliliters hot water to 25 milliliters sugar and record the time it takes the sugar to dissolve. Then, they add 250 milliliters room temperature water to 25 milliliters sugar and record the time it takes to dissolve. What is the variable in this experiment?   **5.2(A)**

Ⓕ The amount of sugar used

Ⓖ The amount of water used

Ⓗ The temperature of the water

Ⓙ The time of day the students are performing the experiment

**13** In an investigation, sand and sugar are mixed together in equal parts.

> **Hypothesis:** The sand cannot be separated from the sugar.
>
> **Procedure:** Pour mixture into a beaker. Add water to dissolve sugar. Filter mixture to remove sand. Evaporate the remaining liquid. Observe the remaining substance using a microscope.
>
> **Observation:** The substance observed under the microscope is sugar.

Which conclusion can be made based on the information from the investigation?   **5.2(A)**

Ⓐ The hypothesis was proven correct because the sugar was not visible under a microscope.

Ⓑ The hypothesis was proven incorrect because the sand and sugar mixture was separated by filtering and evaporation.

Ⓒ The hypothesis was proven correct because the sand and sugar mixture could not be separated.

Ⓓ The hypothesis was proven incorrect because the sugar was dissolved in the water.

**14** Students are mixing an unknown solution. The teacher tells them to follow lab safety rules. The following practices should be observed **EXCEPT** —   **5.1(A)**

Ⓕ tasting the solution

Ⓖ wafting the air to smell the solution

Ⓗ mixing the ingredients as directed by the teacher

Ⓙ wearing protective equipment

## Naming Parts of a Solution

In a solution, a solute is the substance being dissolved. A solvent is the substance in which the solute is dissolved. Using the following solutions, determine which ingredient is the solute and which is the solvent.

- saltwater
- instant tea
- Kool-Aid®
- sugar water
- air
- chocolate milk

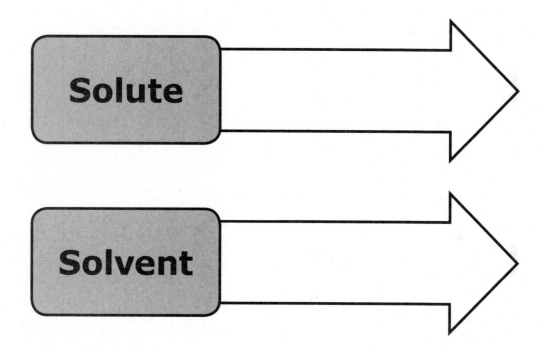

## Formative Assessment

1. Identify and describe the changes that occur when a sugar is mixed with water.

_____

_____

_____

_____

2. Create a procedure to separate a solution of sugar water.

_____

_____

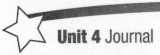
**Science Journal**

A solution is a type of mixture. What makes a solution different than other mixtures? How are the physical properties of solutions changed? Design a solution, and discuss changes that may occur in the physical properties.

_____

_____

_____

_____

_____

_____

_____

_____

_____

_____

_____

_____

_____

_____

_____

_____

_____

_____

_____

_____

_____

_____

_____

_____

## Science Vocabulary Builder

Use the spaces below to illustrate the meanings of the words.

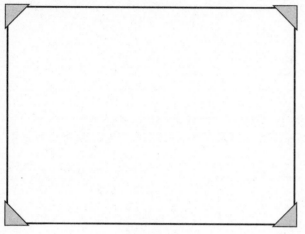

**Solution**

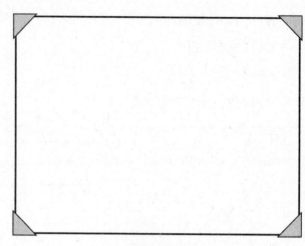

**Dissolve**

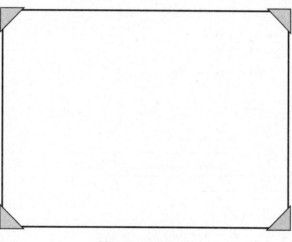

**Homogenous**

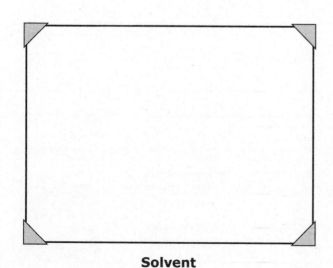

**Solvent**

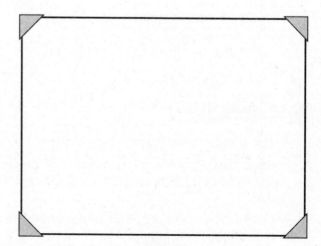

**Solute**

**Unit 4** Homework

**Solution Savvy**

Never taste materials unless directed by your teacher or parent.

Describe the changes that occur when you do the following:

1. Mix salt and water

2. Mix sugar and water

3. Add lemon juice to water

What happens to the liquid? Do the ingredients dissolve? Does the solution look clearer, cloudy, or the same? How could you speed up the mixing process? Does it smell different? Does it taste different? Record your answers in the glasses below.

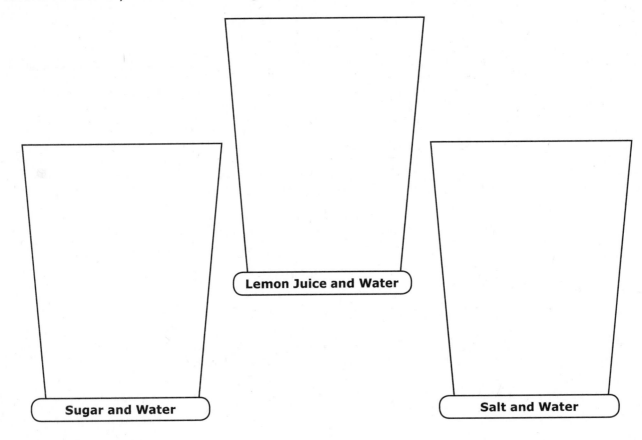

**Lemon Juice and Water**

**Sugar and Water**

**Salt and Water**

**Parent Activities**

1. At the dinner table, have your child identify solutions and mixtures he/she is eating or drinking.

2. Make a pitcher of tea with your child. Pour tea in a glass with ice, and add sugar. What happens to the sugar? Does it dissolve easily? How does the tea taste?

3. With the remaining tea, add sugar while the tea is still hot. Stir the mixture, and observe what happens to the sugar. Does it dissolve? How does the tea taste? Is the hot tea sweeter than the cold tea?

 motivation**science**™LEVEL 5

**Motivation Station: Mike's Cool Science Fact**

Have you ever had a hard time opening a pickle jar? Next time, run hot water over the jar lid. The jar becomes easier to open because heat was added. This is called thermal expansion. Cold water causes the lid to contract and become tighter and harder to open.

**After this lesson I will be able to:**

- **Predict**, **observe**, and **record** changes in the state of matter caused by heating or cooling.

## Descriptive Investigations

**Activity 1:** Changing Matter

Before completing each investigation, predict what might happen. Then, observe and illustrate how matter changes. Record your findings in the tables below.

1. What happens when you pour water into a cup?

| Predict | Observe | Record |
|---------|---------|--------|
|         |         |        |

2. What happens when the cup of water is placed in the freezer?

| Predict | Observe | Record |
|---------|---------|--------|
|         |         |        |

3. Peel away the paper cup and put the substance in a pan. What happens when the pan is heated on a hot plate?

| Predict | Observe | Record |
|---------|---------|--------|
|         |         |        |

**Unit 5** Introduction

**Activity 2:** Meltdown

Place 3–4 flavored ice cubes in a sealable bag, and close tightly. Tape the bag to a glass window or door so it receives sunlight for most of the day. Observe the ice cubes once every half hour, and record observations.

| Draw a picture of the cubes in the bag. | Prediction | What kind of change? | What caused the change? |
|---|---|---|---|
| At the start... | | | |
| 30 minutes later | | | |
| 1 hour later | | | |
| 1 $\frac{1}{2}$ hours later | | | |
| 2 hours later | | | |

Think of another substance that changes state by cooling. Draw the substance as it goes through the changes.

| Substance | Liquid ➡ Solid | What caused this change? |
|---|---|---|
| | | |

 motivation**science**™LEVEL 5 ©2011–2014 mentoring**minds**.com

**1** Which of the following can cause water to change from solid to liquid?

Ⓐ Time and temperature

Ⓑ Time and volume

Ⓒ Temperature and volume

Ⓓ Weather and volume

**2** Students tape a bag of ice cubes on a window in the classroom. After 20 minutes, students observe droplets of water forming on the outside of the bag. Which process causes the droplets of water to appear?

Ⓕ Accumulation

Ⓖ Evaporation

Ⓗ Precipitation

Ⓙ Not here

**3** An investigation is set up to explore what causes a solid to change into a liquid. Each lab group uses four ice cubes in a sealable bag. Two groups tape the bags of ice cubes on a window where sunlight will shine through. The other two groups place the bags inside a desk. Students then record their observations every half hour to determine what causes the change in state of matter. What is the variable within the experiment?  **5.2(A)**

Ⓐ Sealable bag

Ⓑ Four ice cubes

Ⓒ Sunlight

Ⓓ Length of time observed

**4** Ice cream is left out of the freezer for several hours. It changes from a solid to a liquid. This change is most likely caused by —

Ⓕ adding cool air

Ⓖ taking away heat

Ⓗ adding heat

Ⓙ an air conditioner unit

**5** Students investigate changes in states of matter caused by heating and cooling. How can the reliability of the results be increased?  **5.2(E)**

Ⓐ Repeat the investigation

Ⓑ Communicate valid conclusions

Ⓒ Organize the information

Ⓓ Create a data table

**6** According to the diagram, what change is most likely to occur in box C?

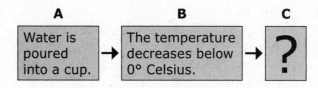

Ⓕ The water would change into a liquid.

Ⓖ The liquid would change and no longer be a form of water.

Ⓗ The water would change to a solid.

Ⓙ The water would begin to melt.

**Unit 5** Check for Understanding

**1** Ten minutes after swimming on a hot summer day, a student noticed that he no longer had water on his arms. What caused the water to evaporate?

Ⓐ The heat from the Sun warmed the water.

Ⓑ Precipitation fell from the clouds.

Ⓒ Condensation formed on the student's skin.

Ⓓ The water was cooled from the Sun.

**2** Students are experimenting with states of matter. Water is heated until it begins to boil. What will happen to the water if it continues to boil?

Ⓕ It will turn into a gas.

Ⓖ It will solidify.

Ⓗ It will thicken.

Ⓙ It will melt.

**3** Students observe the changes that occur when substances are heated. Which of the following is **NOT** an accurate observation?

Ⓐ When chocolate is heated, it melts.

Ⓑ Heating cheese causes the particles to move slower.

Ⓒ Ice melts when heated.

Ⓓ When ice is heated, the particles move to a more active state.

**4** Students are making Jell-O® in class. What will happen to the liquid when it is cooled?

Ⓕ The liquid will evaporate.

Ⓖ The physical state will change from liquid to solid.

Ⓗ The physical state will remain a liquid.

Ⓙ The physical state will change from a liquid to a gas.

**5** The change from a solid to a liquid is caused by —

Ⓐ freezing

Ⓑ evaporating

Ⓒ heating

Ⓓ cooling

**6** In the water cycle, what causes the process that takes place at stage 1?

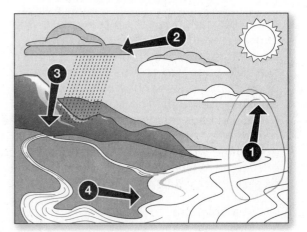

Ⓕ Cold air rising

Ⓖ Subfreezing temperature

Ⓗ Removing heat

Ⓙ Adding heat

 motivation**science**™ LEVEL 5

## Scientific Investigation and Reasoning Skills: Questions 7–14

**7** The diagram below shows a model of some particles in a liquid.

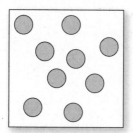

Which model shows how particles would appear if the substance was frozen? **5.3(C)**

Ⓐ 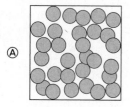　　　Ⓒ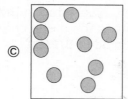

● 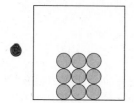　　　Ⓓ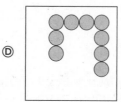

**8** A student places four different substances in separate beakers. The student places each beaker on a hot plate and heats the substances for five minutes. Which substance goes through a change in state when tested in this manner? **5.2(D)**

Ⓕ Penny

Ⓖ Craft stick

● Ice cube

Ⓙ Pebble

**9** Which question can best be answered from the picture below? **5.2(B)**

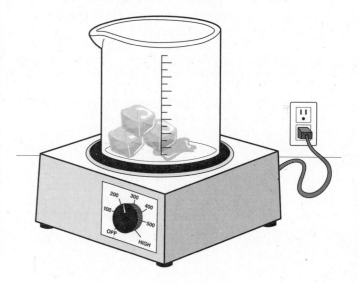

Ⓐ Do ice cubes sink or float?

● What causes changes in states of matter?

Ⓒ Do ice cubes have the ability to dissolve in water?

Ⓓ Are ice cubes conductors or insulators?

**10** All the following tools are useful when experimenting with heat **EXCEPT** — **5.4(A)**

Ⓕ hot plate

Ⓖ thermometer

Ⓗ timer

● spring scale

**Unit 5** Check for Understanding

**11** Water undergoes changes in state because temperature affects the speed of its particles. Which of the following statements best explains why water changes into a gas when heated? **5.3(A)**

Ⓐ The lower the temperature, the slower the speed of the particles.

Ⓑ Particles of liquids can move from place to place.

● The higher the temperature, the faster the speed of the particles.

Ⓓ Water takes the shape of its container.

**12** Which change is occurring at stage 2 in the diagram? **5.2(D)**

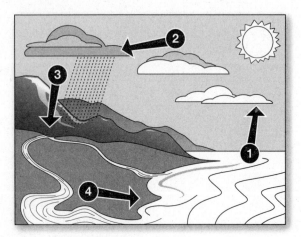

Ⓕ Solid to a gas

Ⓖ Liquid to a gas

● Gas to a liquid

Ⓙ Liquid to a solid

**13** The United States Mint makes all U.S. coins. When cutting blank coins out of strips of metal, the remaining metal is recycled to make a new coin strip, as shown in the diagram.

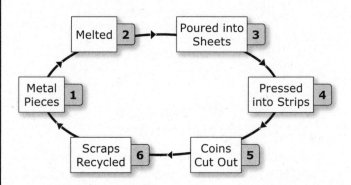

At which step in the coin-making process does the metal change from a solid to a liquid? **5.2(D)**

Ⓐ Step 1          Ⓒ Step 3

● Step 2          Ⓓ Step 4

**14** After melting chocolate chips in the Sun, a student made the following conclusion:

> Changes in physical state can be caused by heat.

Is the student's conclusion valid? **5.3(A)**

Ⓕ Yes, because the chocolate chips changed from liquid to solid.

Ⓖ No, because the chocolate chips did not go through a phase change.

● Yes, because the physical state of the chocolate chips changed after being exposed to heat from the Sun.

Ⓙ No, because heat from the Sun only causes water to change its physical state.

Supporting Standard 3.5(C)

## Going Through a Phase

Develop a model to show how particles appear in the three physical states: solid, liquid, gas.

**Solid**

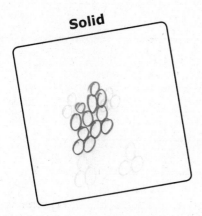

**Liquid**

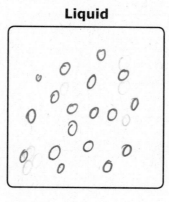

**Gas**

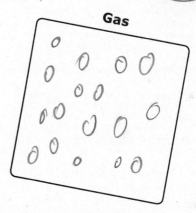

Distinguish between the behavior of particles in solids, liquids, and gases, and describe how they change as matter is heated or cooled.

_____

_____

_____

_____

_____

_____

_____

## Formative Assessment

A student places an uncovered tray of ice in the refrigerator. Predict and describe the changes most likely to occur if the tray is left undisturbed for two weeks.

_____

_____

_____

_____

Name _____

**Science Journal**

Imagine you are an ice cube in the Sun. What could you do to keep yourself from melting?

_____

_____

_____

_____

_____

_____

_____

_____

_____

_____

_____

_____

_____

_____

_____

_____

_____

_____

_____

_____

_____

_____

_____

_____

_____

_____

 motivation**science**™LEVEL 5

## Science Vocabulary Builder

In the outer ring, write the words *heating and cooling*, *freezing*, *melting*, and *evaporating*. In the second ring, write a sentence using the word(s). In the middle ring, draw an illustration depicting the word(s).

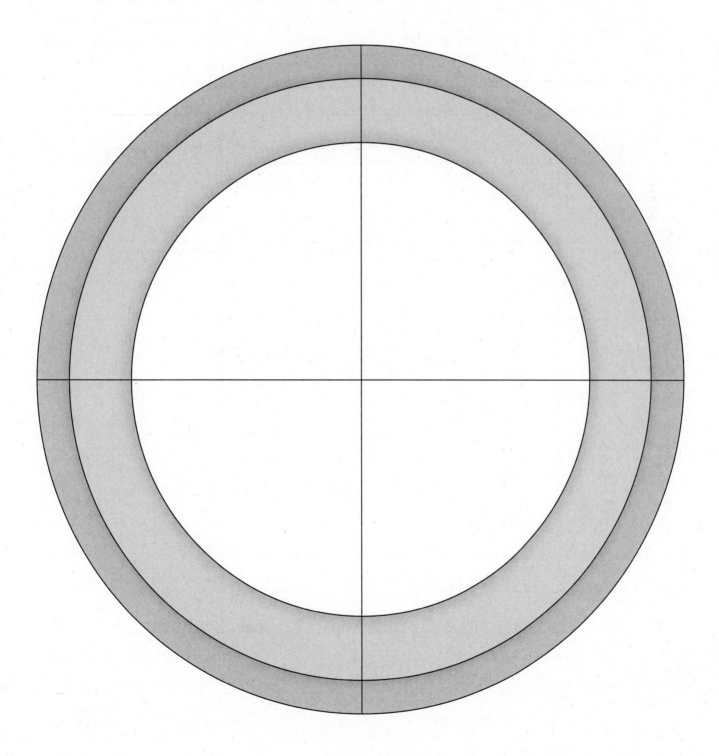

## Heating and Cooling

**Obtain parent permission before conducting this investigation.**

1. Predict what will happen if a substance is heated.

2. Heat each substance by placing it on a plate and microwaving for 20 to 30 seconds. Remove the plate using oven mitts or pot holders. Write down observations of the appearance of the substance during the heating process. Do not allow the substance to burn.

3. After the substance has been heated, record the changes that have taken place.

4. Then, cool down the material and repeat the procedure–predict, observe, and record changes.

| Substance | Prediction | Observation | Changes |
|-----------|-----------|-------------|---------|
| Cheese–heated | | | |
| Cheese–cooled down | | | |
| Butter–heated | | | |
| Butter–cooled down | | | |
| Marshmallow–heated | | | |
| Marshmallow–cooled down | | | |

✂ - - - - - - - - - - - - - - - - - - - - - - - - - - - - - - - - - - - - - - - - - - - - - - - - - - - - -

## Parent Activities

1. Help your child with the above homework activity. Discuss the changes that occurred during the experiment. Test other common objects and record the changes that occur when matter is heated or cooled.

2. Fill a plastic water bottle to the top. Twist on the lid, and place in the freezer. What happens to the bottle after freezing? Did the water expand or contract?

**1** An igloo is made of ice and snow. Which state of matter is used to make an igloo?

  Ⓐ Liquid

  Ⓑ Solid

  Ⓒ Water

  Ⓓ Gas

**2** Which thermometer accurately shows the boiling temperature of water? **5.2(C)**

Ⓕ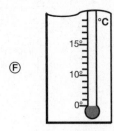

Ⓖ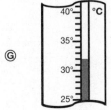

Ⓗ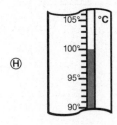

Ⓙ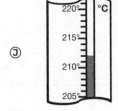

**3** Students combine sand, water, and iron filings in paper cups to learn about separating mixtures. After the investigation, how should the students properly dispose of the materials? **5.1(B)**

  Ⓐ Pour the sand, water, and iron filings down the drain, rinse the sink, and throw the paper cup in the trash.

  Ⓑ Remove the iron filings, saving them for future use. Drain the water from the sand, saving it for future use, and throw the sand and paper cup in the trash.

  Ⓒ Throw the sand, water, and iron filings in the trash. Wash hands.

  Ⓓ Empty the mixture of sand, water, and iron filings on the playground beside the school.

**4** A student leaves snow-covered boots in front of the fire for many hours. When the student comes to get them, the snow is gone, and puddles of water surround the boots. Which statement correctly describes the boots after they warm by the fire?

  Ⓕ The snow on the boots remains solid and unchanged.

  Ⓖ The snow on the boots changes from a solid to a liquid.

  Ⓗ The snow on the boots changes from a liquid to a gas.

  Ⓙ The snow on the boots becomes a solid form of water.

## Reporting Category 1 Assessment

**Use the diagram below and your knowledge of science to answer questions 5 and 6.**

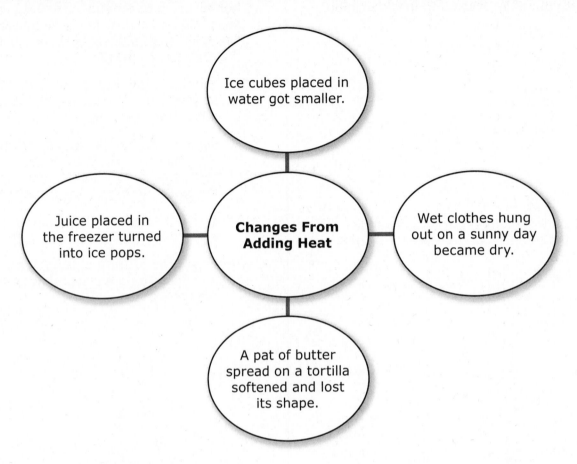

Ice cubes placed in water got smaller.

Juice placed in the freezer turned into ice pops.

**Changes From Adding Heat**

Wet clothes hung out on a sunny day became dry.

A pat of butter spread on a tortilla softened and lost its shape.

**5** A student makes a graphic organizer to brainstorm changes that occur when heat is added. Which change did the student list incorrectly? **5.2(D)**

Ⓐ Ice cubes placed in water got smaller.

Ⓑ Wet clothes hung out on a sunny day became dry.

Ⓒ A pat of butter spread on a tortilla softened and lost its shape.

Ⓓ Juice placed in the freezer turned into ice pops.

**6** Which process occurs when wet clothes are hung out to dry on a sunny day?

Ⓕ Condensing

Ⓖ Melting

Ⓗ Freezing

Ⓙ None of the above

 motivation**science**™ LEVEL 5

**7** At the end of a very hot, sunny day, which playground area will probably be too hot to touch?

Ⓐ Metal climbing tower

Ⓑ Plastic slide

Ⓒ Wooden bridge

Ⓓ Rubber bounce house

**8** A student heats a beaker of water on a hot plate and measures the temperature every 2 minutes. After 2 minutes, the water measures 30°C. After 4 minutes, the temperature is 60°C. After 6 minutes, the temperature is 100°C. At 8 minutes, the water measures 100°C. What does the data from the investigation show? **5.2(F)**

Ⓕ The water is at its boiling point after 2 minutes.

Ⓖ The water is at its boiling point after 4 minutes.

Ⓗ The water is at its boiling point after 6 minutes.

Ⓙ The water does not reach its boiling point during this investigation.

**9** Which tool is necessary when using evaporation to separate a solution? **5.2(B)**

Ⓐ

Ⓑ

Ⓒ

Ⓓ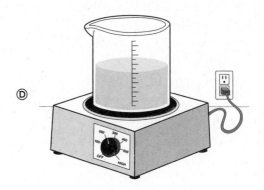

**10** Students are combining ingredients to make solutions. Which of the following is a way they could speed up the process of combining sugar and water?

Ⓕ Allow the solution to sit undisturbed

Ⓖ Heat the water

Ⓗ Add more sugar to the solution

Ⓙ All of the above

**11** Which part of an investigation did the student describe?  **5.2(A)**

---

**Density Column**

**Step 1**–Gather the following materials: graduated cylinder, dropper, corn syrup, cooking oil, and water.

**Step 2**–Pour 10 mL corn syrup into the graduated cylinder.

**Step 3**–Using the dropper, slowly add 10 mL water to the graduated cylinder.

**Step 4**–Using the dropper, slowly add 10 mL cooking oil to the graduated cylinder.

---

Ⓐ  A hypothesis

Ⓑ  A conclusion

Ⓒ  An observation

Ⓓ  A plan

**12** Which of the following statements is true?

Ⓕ  The freezing point of water is 32° Celsius.

Ⓖ  The melting point of water is 1° Celsius.

Ⓗ  The boiling point of water is 0° Celsius.

Ⓙ  The freezing point and melting point of water are both 0° Celsius.

**13** Which combination, after mixing, retains its original physical properties?

Ⓐ  Vinegar and baking soda

Ⓑ  Oil and water

Ⓒ  Salt and water

Ⓓ  Food coloring and water

**14** The substance being dissolved in a solution is called the —

Ⓕ  solute

Ⓖ  solvent

Ⓗ  variable

Ⓙ  not here

**15** The chart shows items classified using the property of magnetism.

| Attracted to Magnet | Not Attracted to Magnet |
|---|---|
| Steel wool | Wood |
| Wrought iron | Glass |
| Iron shavings | Plastic |

Based on the information in the chart, which material would **NOT** be attracted to a magnet?   **5.2(D)**

Ⓐ Steel nail

Ⓑ Cast iron skillet

Ⓒ Plastic milk jug

Ⓓ Steel screw

**16** Which physical property of water changes when it reaches its melting point?

Ⓕ Color

Ⓖ Shape

Ⓗ Volume

Ⓙ Mass

**17** A student is investigating mixtures. Which of the following is the best way to separate a mixture of gravel and sand?

Ⓐ Separate the mixture using a coffee filter.

Ⓑ Separate the mixture by evaporation.

Ⓒ Separate the mixture using a magnet.

Ⓓ Separate the mixture using a sieve.

**18** A glass of water was left outside over a period of five days.

Monday    Tuesday    Wednesday    Thursday    Friday

What caused the level of water in the glass to decrease each day?

Ⓕ Heat over time caused the water to evaporate.

Ⓖ Colder temperatures changed the water from liquid to solid.

Ⓗ Melting caused less liquid to appear in the glass.

Ⓙ The boiling point of water changed.

# Reporting Category 1 Assessment

**Use the information in the passage and your knowledge of science to answer questions 19 and 20.**

## The History of a Famous Soda

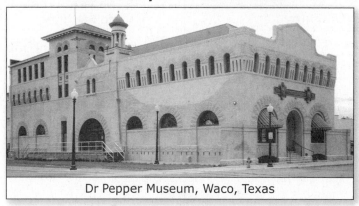

Dr Pepper Museum, Waco, Texas

In 1885, a man named Charles Alderton was working as a pharmacist at Morrison's Old Corner Drug Store in Waco, Texas. The store had a soda fountain where Alderton enjoyed creating recipes for carbonated drinks. One of his most popular recipes was named Dr Pepper® by the store owner, Mr. Morrison. Morrison, Robert Lazenby, and J.B. O'Hara began a company that later became known as the Dr Pepper Bottling Company. Alderton's concoction of over 20 fruit syrups and carbonated gas was introduced to the public at the World's Fair Exposition, held in St. Louis, Missouri, in 1904. The Dr Pepper Bottling Company remains the oldest manufacturer of soft drinks in the United States.

**19** What inventor is credited with developing the mixture, Dr Pepper? **5.3(D)**

Ⓐ Robert Lazenby

Ⓑ Charles Alderton

Ⓒ Mr. Morrison

Ⓓ Charles Pepper

**20** What characteristic of Dr Pepper makes it a solution?

Ⓕ It contains more than one ingredient.

Ⓖ It was developed using a recipe.

Ⓗ It contains dissolved fruit syrups and carbonated gas.

Ⓙ It can be separated using a filter.

 motivation**science**™ LEVEL 5

# Chart Your Success

**Color Mike or Molly *green* if your answer was correct or *red* if your answer was incorrect.**

## Properties of Matter

| Total Correct | Total Possible |
|---|---|
| | **4** |

## Boiling/Freezing/Melting Points

| Total Correct | Total Possible |
|---|---|
| | **4** |

## Mixtures

| Total Correct | Total Possible |
|---|---|
| | **4** |

## Solutions

| Total Correct | Total Possible |
|---|---|
| | **4** |

## Changes to Matter

| Total Correct | Total Possible |
|---|---|
| | **4** |

motivation**science**™ LEVEL 5

# Notes

 motivation**science**™LEVEL 5 ©2011–2014 mentoring**minds**.com

**Motivation Station: Molly's Cool Science Fact**

Light waves travel at a speed of approximately 300,000 kilometers per second. Sound waves travel much slower, at a speed 870,000 times slower than the speed of light.

**After this lesson I will be able to:**

• **Explore** the uses of energy, including mechanical, light, thermal, electrical, and sound energy.

## Descriptive, Comparative, and Experimental Investigations

### Energy Exploration

As you travel to each station, read the station directions. Complete each activity to collect data and investigate the uses of different energy forms.

**Station 1:** Light the Way and Turn up the Heat

**Teacher supervision required.**

1. Watch as the teacher lights the candle. Draw an illustration of the flame in the box.

2. What forms of energy does a burning candle produce?

_____

_____

_____

3. As the teacher toasts bread, observe what happens inside the toaster. Describe what happens.

_____

_____

_____

4. Observe butter, then spread some on warm toast. What types of energy did the toaster produce? What type of energy caused the butter to change?

_____

_____

_____

## Station 2: Thermal Thinking

Design an investigation to explore thermal energy using warm water, foam cups, paper cups, and thermometers.

In stations -6, explore the objects at each station. Identify the form of energy the objects use. Give an example of another object which uses the same form of energy as the objects at each station.

## Station 3: Moving Parts

| Type of energy being used | Object which uses the same form of energy |
| --- | --- |
|  |  |

## Station 4: Let it Shine

| Type of energy being used | Object which uses the same form of energy |
| --- | --- |
|  |  |

## Station 5: Power Cord

| Type of energy being used | Object which uses the same form of energy |
| --- | --- |
|  |  |

## Station 6: Make Some Noise

| Type of energy being used | Object which uses the same form of energy |
| --- | --- |
|  |  |

**1** Which of the following best uses mechanical energy to perform a useful task?

Ⓐ Flashlight

⬤ Pencil sharpener

Ⓒ Candle

Ⓓ Solar calculator

**2** This gumball machine has a coin handle that must be turned when dispensing a product.

Which form of energy is used to dispense the gumballs? **5.3(C)**

Ⓕ Electrical

Ⓖ Thermal

Ⓗ Sound

⬤ Mechanical

**3** What is the energy of moving particles that produces heat?

Ⓐ Mechanical energy

⬤ Thermal energy

Ⓒ Electrical energy

Ⓓ Sound energy

**4** Which is **NOT** an example of the use of sound energy?

Ⓕ Beating a drum

Ⓖ Talking

Ⓗ Playing music on the radio

⬤ Cooking hot dogs

**5** A student makes a list of ways electric energy is used at home. Which is **NOT** an object that uses electric energy?

Ⓐ Alarm clock

Ⓑ Blender

⬤ Skateboard

Ⓓ Video game player

**6** Below is a picture of an aquarium that a group of students designs as a new home for aquatic plants and fish.

Based on the picture, which forms of energy are required for the aquarium to work properly? **5.4(A)**

⬤ Electrical, thermal, light

Ⓖ Electrical, light, sound

Ⓗ Mechanical, thermal, light

Ⓙ Light, sound, mechanical

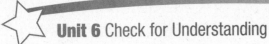

Name _____

## Unit 6 Check for Understanding

Readiness Standard 5.6(A)

1   A student plugs a hot plate into an outlet and turns on the hot plate. The student notices that the hot plate produces heat. What form of energy is used to power the heat from the hot plate?

Ⓐ   Thermal

●   Electric

Ⓒ   Mechanical

Ⓓ   Light

2   What is the best use for the energy form shown below?

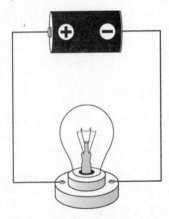

Ⓕ   To product sound energy

●   To produce solar energy

Ⓗ   To produce mechanical energy

Ⓙ   To produce electric energy

3   Which type of energy from the Sun provides sunshine and heat to Earth?

Ⓐ   Mechanical

Ⓑ   Electrical

●   Solar

Ⓓ   Sound

4   The slingshot below is made with wood and a rubber band. When a ball is placed in the sling shot and the rubber band is pulled, it forces the ball outward.

Which kind of energy is produced by pulling the rubber band back?

●   Mechanical          Ⓗ   Electrical

Ⓖ   Thermal             Ⓙ   All of the above

5   What type of energy is generated when a doorbell rings?

Ⓐ   Light              ●   Sound

Ⓑ   Thermal            Ⓓ   Solar

6   A campfire, fireworks, and a burning candle all produce —

Ⓕ   mechanical and thermal energy

Ⓖ   light and sound energy

●   light and thermal energy

Ⓙ   sound and electrical energy

68      ILLEGAL TO COPY        motivation**science**™ LEVEL 5        ©2011–2014 mentoring**minds**.com

## Scientific Investigation and Reasoning Skills: Questions 7–14

**7** Students decide to explore thermal energy used in the classroom. Which instrument should the students use? **5.4(A)**

Ⓐ Microscope

Ⓑ Thermometer

Ⓒ Timer

Ⓓ Graduated cylinder

**8** Which type of building uses the most energy of all the building types? **5.2(G)**

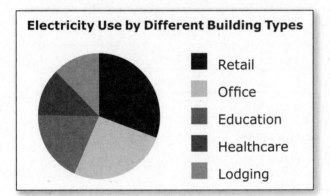

**Electricity Use by Different Building Types**

- Retail
- Office
- Education
- Healthcare
- Lodging

Ⓕ Education

Ⓖ Office

Ⓗ Retail

Ⓙ Lodging

**9** Since the 1600s, many scientists and inventors, such as Benjamin Franklin and Thomas Edison, have worked to understand the principles of electricity. It is hard to imagine what life would be like without electricity. All of the following are tasks that use electricity on a daily basis **EXCEPT** — **5.3(D)**

Ⓐ powering televisions

Ⓑ cooling homes

Ⓒ emptying the dishwasher

Ⓓ powering computers

**10** Which of the following topics can best be explored using this graphic? **5.2(D)**

Ⓕ Uses of sound energy

Ⓖ How sound energy differs from light energy

Ⓗ Materials used to make speakers

Ⓙ Comparing pitch and volume

11  A student is investigating ways to conserve electricity at school. All of the following are positive ways to impact the conservation of electricity at school **EXCEPT** —   **5.1(B)**

Ⓐ  recycling aluminum cans

Ⓑ  turning off machines when not in use

Ⓒ  replacing light bulbs with energy efficient bulbs

●  turning the thermostat up during warm months

12  The advertisement below promotes riding a bicycle.

**Ride for Life!**

Riding a bicycle improves your health and fitness. While you pedal your way to good health, you help the environment by reducing harmful air pollution.

Which form of energy is being used in the advertisement?   **5.3(B)**

Ⓕ  Thermal energy

●  Mechanical energy

Ⓗ  Sound energy

Ⓙ  Light energy

13  Which tool would be useful for learning about light energy?   **5.4(A)**

Ⓐ  Metric ruler

Ⓑ  Magnet

●  Prism

Ⓓ  Hot plate

14  In a sound activity, students ring a bell and observe the sound of the chime from different distances. They rate the loudness on a scale from 1 to 10, with 1 being the softest and 10 being the loudest.

| Chime | Distance | Loudness |
|-------|----------|----------|
| 1 | 5 feet | 10 |
| 2 | 20 feet | 8 |
| 3 | 35 feet | 5 |
| 4 | 50 feet | 2 |

Which conclusion best describes why the bell chime got quieter as the distance increased?   **5.2(F)**

Ⓕ  Sound waves lose energy as they travel because they are not very loud.

Ⓖ  Sound waves lose energy as distances decrease.

Ⓗ  Sound waves lose energy as time increases.

●  Sound waves lose energy as they travel through materials such as air.

## Energy Invention

In the space below, design a useful invention which uses at least three different energy forms (mechanical, light, thermal, electrical, or sound energy). Illustrate your invention, labeling each part and its function. Create a name for your invention. Share your invention with the class, and explain how your invention uses energy.

**My Energy Invention**

_____

## Formative Assessment

Write song lyrics persuading others to conserve energy resources. In the lyrics, give examples of ways energy resources can be conserved.

_____

_____

_____

_____

_____

_____

## Science Journal

Describe and illustrate the following forms of energy: mechanical, thermal, and sound. Then, rank each form of energy from the one you use the most to the least.

| Mechanical Energy | Thermal Energy | Sound Energy |
| --- | --- | --- |
|  |  |  |
| **Rank** | **Rank** | **Rank** |
| _____ | _____ | _____ |

## Science Vocabulary Builder

Write a vocabulary word in the top of each triangle, a definition in the middle, and examples of how the form of energy is used at the bottom. An example is done for you.

| mechanical | light | thermal | electrical | sound |
| --- | --- | --- | --- | --- |

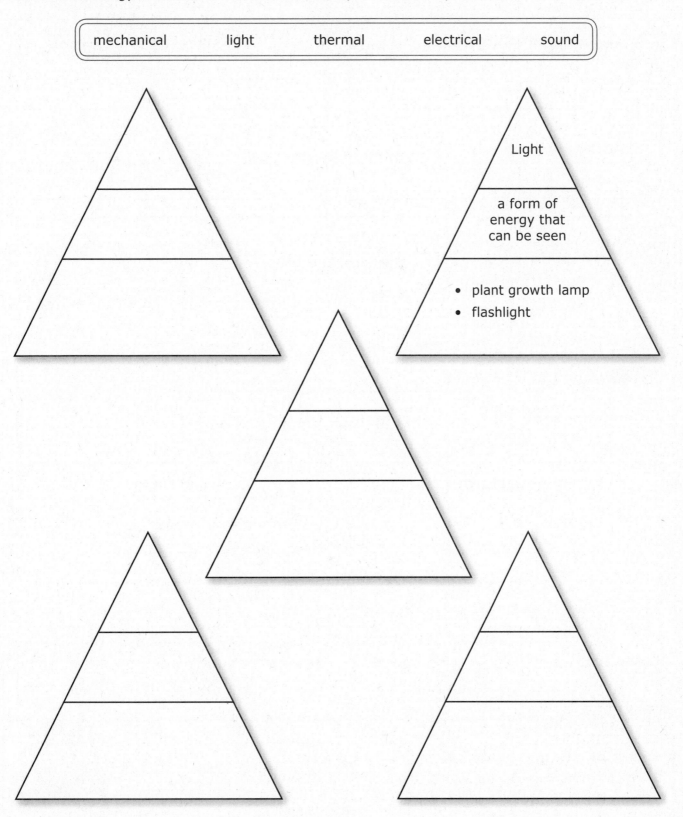

Light

a form of energy that can be seen

- plant growth lamp
- flashlight

## Scavenger Hunt

Go on a scavenger hunt at home. Find 5 examples of each energy form. Can you find more? List as many as possible, and see who finds the most.

### Mechanical Energy

1. _____
2. _____
3. _____
4. _____
5. _____

### Light Energy

1. _____
2. _____
3. _____
4. _____
5. _____

### Electrical Energy

1. _____
2. _____
3. _____
4. _____
5. _____

### Thermal Energy

1. _____
2. _____
3. _____
4. _____
5. _____

### Sound Energy

1. _____
2. _____
3. _____
4. _____
5. _____

## Parent Activities

1. Discuss ways to use energy at work, school, and home.
2. Which form of energy do you use the most?
3. How can you save energy at home?

**After this lesson I will be able to:**

- **Demonstrate** that the flow of electricity in circuits requires a complete path through which an electric current can pass and can produce light, heat, and sound.

## Experimental Investigations

**Activity:** Circuit Discovery

**Question**

Which materials can be used to demonstrate that the flow of electricity requires a complete path?

**Hypothesis**

I think the following plan to create a circuit will work to light a bulb.

(Illustrate and describe your plan below.)

_____

_____

_____

_____

## Investigate

With your team, gather materials from the table to test your plan. If your original hypothesis is proven incorrect, revise your plan, and try again.

Record your observations and discoveries in the space below.

_____

_____

What materials did your team use to make a circuit? Did some materials work better than others? Why?

_____

_____

What did you discover when making your circuit?

_____

_____

Create a chart to record which materials make a successful circuit.

### Building Circuits

| Materials That Work | Materials That Do Not Work |
| --- | --- |
|  |  |
|  |  |
|  |  |
|  |  |
|  |  |

What conclusions can you make from your investigation?

_____

_____

_____

What questions about electricity would you like to explore next?

_____

_____

**1** What is wrong with the circuit below?

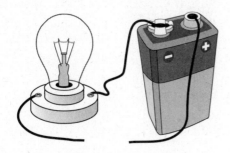

Ⓐ The light is not big enough.

Ⓑ It needs more wires.

Ⓒ The wires are not closed.

Ⓓ Another energy source is needed.

**2** Which of the objects below is **NOT** needed to test electrical conductivity?

Ⓕ Battery

Ⓖ Object powered by electricity

Ⓗ Insulated wire

Ⓙ Electrical tape

**3** The picture below shows an open circuit.

Which of the objects below can be connected to the ends of the wires to complete the circuit and make the buzzer sound?

Ⓐ Another wire    Ⓒ Battery

Ⓑ Switch    Ⓓ Lightbulb

**4** What process causes electricity to flow in a circuit, completing its path so that an electric current can pass through and produce sound?

Ⓕ Conductivity

Ⓖ Solubility

Ⓗ Insulation

Ⓙ Vibrations

**5** Students experiment with the flow of electricity in circuits. The teacher instructs them to wear rubber gloves during the experiment because — **5.4(B)**

Ⓐ rubber gloves are insulators

Ⓑ rubber gloves are conductors

Ⓒ rubber gloves keep the student dry

Ⓓ rubber gloves allow electricity to flow

**6** A group of students decides to investigate what is required to make a complete path through which an electric current can pass. The students use different objects to see if they can produce heat. They test each object but do not record their observations. Why is it important for students to repeat this investigation? **5.2(E)**

Ⓕ To formulate a new hypothesis

Ⓖ To record accurate data

Ⓗ To test additional objects

Ⓙ To communicate a written conclusion

**1** In which of the following circuits will the buzzer sound?

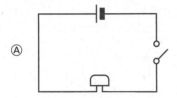

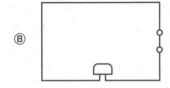

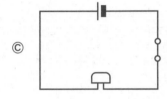

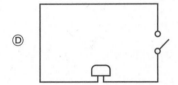

**2** A student forgets to use a plastic coated wire and notices that the wire connecting to the battery is very hot. Which statement below explains why the wire is hot?

Ⓕ The wire is not insulated and electrical energy from the wire produces heat.

Ⓖ The wire is not insulated and electrical energy flowing from the battery produces heat.

Ⓗ The wire is not insulated and electrical energy from the bulb heats the wire.

Ⓙ The wire is not insulated and electrical energy from the switch produces heat.

**3** Which part of a circuit is the energy source?

Ⓐ Wire

Ⓑ Bulb

Ⓒ Battery

Ⓓ Switch

**4** Which of these could **NOT** be used to replace a wire in a circuit?

Ⓕ Iron nail

Ⓖ Bendable straw

Ⓗ Steel spoon

Ⓙ Aluminum foil

**5** Electricity can be used to produce —

Ⓐ light

Ⓑ heat

Ⓒ sound

Ⓓ all of the above

**6** When wires are connected to a battery and a lightbulb in a circuit, the lightbulb is lit. Which types of energy are produced by the battery and lightbulb?

Ⓕ Electrical and light

Ⓖ Sound and light

Ⓗ Electrical and sound

Ⓙ Light and sound

 motivation**science**™ LEVEL 5

## Scientific Investigation and Reasoning Skills: Questions 7–14

**Use the following information and your knowledge of science to complete questions 7–10.**

Students discover how to create a circuit to light a lightbulb. The teacher records the work time for each group.

|         | Start Time | End Time   |
|---------|-----------|------------|
| Group 1 | 9:15 A.M. | 10:05 A.M. |
| Group 2 | 9:17 A.M. | 10:02 A.M. |
| Group 3 | 9:20 A.M. | 10:15 A.M. |
| Group 4 | 9:23 A.M. | 9:58 A.M.  |

**7** Which group takes the least amount of time to complete their circuit? **5.2(D)**

Ⓐ Group 1

Ⓑ Group 2

Ⓒ Group 3

Ⓓ Group 4

**8** Which accurately shows the order from shortest amount of time to longest amount of time taken to complete the experiment? **5.2(F)**

Ⓕ Group 1, Group 2, Group 3, Group 4

Ⓖ Group 4, Group 2, Group 1, Group 3

Ⓗ Group 4, Group 1, Group 2, Group 3

Ⓙ Group 3, Group 1, Group 2, Group 4

**9** Students in Group 2 completed a circuit using wire, an iron nail, and a battery to light the bulb, as shown.

According to the information in the data table, how much longer did it take Group 3 to light the bulb than Group 2? Record and bubble in your answer to the nearest minute. **5.2(G)**

| | | | . |
|---|---|---|---|
| ⓪ | ⓪ | ⓪ | |
| ① | ① | ① | |
| ② | ② | ② | |
| ③ | ③ | ③ | |
| ④ | ④ | ④ | |
| ⑤ | ⑤ | ⑤ | |
| ⑥ | ⑥ | ⑥ | |
| ⑦ | ⑦ | ⑦ | |
| ⑧ | ⑧ | ⑧ | |
| ⑨ | ⑨ | ⑨ | |

**10** The groups made observations while constructing circuits. Which of the following is an incorrect observation? **5.3(A)**

Ⓕ The path for electricity to flow must be closed.

Ⓖ Aluminum foil cannot be used as a path for electricity to flow.

Ⓗ Conductors, such as copper wire and iron nails, can be used to connect the energy source to the lightbulb.

Ⓙ Electricity does not flow through the circuit when the circuit is open.

**11** A group of students creates a circuit using 3 lightbulbs, a battery, and a switch.

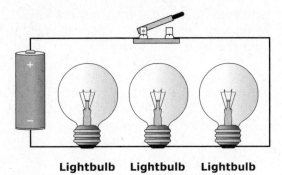

**Lightbulb 1    Lightbulb 2    Lightbulb 3**

What will the group most likely observe in this circuit?   **5.2(D)**

Ⓐ Lightbulb 1, Lightbulb 2, and Lightbulb 3 will be on.

Ⓑ Lightbulbs 1 and 2 will be on, but Lightbulb 3 will be off.

Ⓒ Lightbulb 3 will be on, but Lightbulbs 1 and 2 will be off.

Ⓓ Lightbulb 1, Lightbulb 2, and Lightbulb 3 will be off.

**12** Students were given materials to complete a circuit to turn on one light. The materials received were 2 wires, a AA battery, and various sizes of lightbulbs. What is the variable in the experiment?   **5.2(A)**

Ⓕ Wires

Ⓖ Battery

Ⓗ Size of lightbulb

Ⓙ Time of day

**13** After several attempts to turn on a light using a simple circuit, a student concludes that the circuit must be closed in order for the light to turn on. Is the student's conclusion reasonable?   **5.2(F)**

Ⓐ No, because circuits cannot turn on lights.

Ⓑ No, because the circuit needs to remain open in order for it to work.

Ⓒ Yes, because all conclusions are correct.

Ⓓ Yes, because circuits must be closed in order for the electricity to flow through them.

**14** In science class, students investigate ways to build circuits. Which items should students choose to create a working electrical circuit?   **5.2(B)**

Ⓕ One copper wire, wood chips, and a lightbulb

Ⓖ Two copper wires, a plastic straw, and a lightbulb

Ⓗ Two copper wires, a battery, and a lightbulb

Ⓙ Wood chips, iron filings, and a battery

 motivation**science**™ LEVEL 5 ©2011–2014 mentoring**minds**.com

## New Way to Create a Battery

**Teacher assistance is required with any cutting involved in the experiment.**

Did you know lemons can be used to create a battery? Choose from the materials listed, and create a battery. Experiment by using the materials in different ways. Record what works.

First, construct a lemon battery. Then, use the lemon battery and create a circuit. Try connecting several lemon batteries to produce more energy.

| **Materials for battery** | **Materials for circuit** |
| --- | --- |
| • Lemon<br>• Something made of copper, such as an old penny, piece of copper, or piece of copper wire<br>• Something made from zinc, such as a dime, zinc-coated nail, or other piece of zinc | • Lemon battery<br>• Two wires<br>• Small light such as a holiday tree light<br>• Buzzer, digital clock, compass, or voltmeter |

What needed to happen in order for the battery to work?

_____

Were any problems experienced during this experiment?

_____

How is the lemon battery circuit similar to and different from other circuits you have created?

_____

_____

## Formative Assessment

One Minute Summary: Summarize what you have learned about circuits. Write for one minute without stopping.

_____

_____

_____

_____

_____

**Science Journal**

Imagine you lived long ago when there was no electricity in homes. How would things be different? Design a tool to help you keep warm, heat food, and see in the dark. Describe the tool, what it does, and how it works. Illustrate your journal entry.

_____

_____

_____

_____

_____

_____

_____

_____

_____

_____

## Science Vocabulary Builder

Write a description and create an illustration for each vocabulary term. Use the three vocabulary terms and information in the graphic organizer to write a summary of the information learned during this unit.

| **Term** gravity | **Illustration** |
| --- | --- |
| **Description** | |

| **Term** friction | **Illustration** |
| --- | --- |
| **Description** | |

| **Term** magnetism | **Illustration** |
| --- | --- |
| **Description** | |

Summary _____

_____

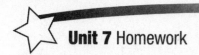
**Diagramming a Circuit**

Create a diagram in the space below that demonstrates the flow of electricity in a circuit, and label the parts. Be sure to include a battery, wires, a switch, and a light. Answer the questions that follow.

1. Why do circuits need wires? What do the wires do?

_____

_____

2. What is the significance of the switch?

_____

_____

3. What other types of energy could be created using a circuit?

_____

_____

✂ - - - - - - - - - - - - - - - - - - - - - - - - - - - - - - - - - - - - - - - - - - - - -

**Parent Activities**

**1.** Experiment with the lasting power of different brands of batteries. Which brands last the longest?

**2.** Help your child research the history of electricity.

**3.** The next time a bulb burns out, allow your child to inspect the bulb. What happened to the wires inside?

**Motivation Station: Molly's Cool Science Fact**

The archerfish has the amazing ability to catch insects by spitting a stream of water at them. A special adaptation allows the archerfish to adjust for the angle of refraction, making the fish so accurate it almost always hits its prey on the first try. That's some fish!

## After this lesson I will be able to:

- **Demonstrate** that light travels in a straight line until it strikes an object or travels through one medium to another and **demonstrate** that light can be reflected such as the use of mirrors or other shiny surfaces and refracted such as the appearance of an object when observed through water.

## Comparative Investigations

**Activity 1:** Lovely Light–KLEW

Light is very important to our everyday lives. What do you know about light? Complete the *K* section of the KLEW chart below to record your knowledge of light. The other sections will be completed as you investigate light.

| **K**<br>What do I think I know about light? | **L**<br>What am I learning about light? | **E**<br>What is my evidence about light? | **W**<br>What am I wondering about light? |
|---|---|---|---|
| | | | |

**Activity 2:** Lovely Light–Investigate

As a group, travel to each station to learn more about light energy. Record your data and observations in the boxes below. As you discover more about light, record your thinking on the KLEW chart.

| | |
|---|---|
| **Station 1:** Dancing Light<br><br>Use the materials at the station, and explore the behavior of light. Record your observations. | **Station 2:** Fun With Fences<br><br>Make a clay rope. Stick 8 toothpicks in the clay to make a fence. Place the toothpick fence on one side of the desk. Use clay to prop up a mirror on the other side, facing half of the fence at an angle. Shine a flashlight through the fence, toward the mirror. What do you observe? |
| **Station 3:** King Kong's Thumb<br><br>Put your thumb into the cup of water, and make observations. Draw what you observed.<br> | **Station 4:** Catch a Fish<br><br>Shape a fish out of clay. Drop the fish into the water. Use a pencil to spear the fish. Describe what happens. |
| **Station 5:** What's Inside?<br><br>Observe the cup on the table. What do you see?<br><br><br>Reach into the cup to see what is inside. Record your observations.<br><br><br>Replace the materials, and dry your hands on the paper towels provided. | **Station 6:** Explore Some More<br><br>Explore the behavior of light using the materials at the station. Record your observations. |

**1** What happens when light hits an object that it cannot pass through?

Ⓐ The light is refracted or absorbed.

Ⓑ The light is reflected or absorbed.

Ⓒ The light is reflected or refracted.

Ⓓ The light is scattered or curved.

**2** Sometimes it is possible to see light rays. An example is when sunlight is breaking through the clouds. Sunlight breaking through the clouds demonstrates how light rays travel in —

Ⓕ straight lines

Ⓖ curved rays

Ⓗ zigzag rays

Ⓙ circular waves

**3** When light hits different types of objects, it acts differently depending on the object.

| Transparent | Translucent | Opaque |
|---|---|---|
| Drinking glass | Wax paper | Aluminum foil |
| Sealable bag | Shower curtain | Wood |

Which object above best reflects light? **5.2(D)**

Ⓐ Sealable bag

Ⓑ Shower curtain

Ⓒ Aluminum foil

Ⓓ Drinking glass

**4** Does water refract or reflect light?

Ⓕ Refract

Ⓖ Reflect

Ⓗ Refracts and reflects

Ⓙ Not here

**5** Students perform an investigation to compare and contrast the effects of reflection and refraction. What tools are most helpful to students when conducting this investigation? **5.4(A)**

Ⓐ Magnets, mirrors

Ⓑ Prisms, hand lenses

Ⓒ Hand lenses, cameras

Ⓓ Mirrors, prisms

**6** Students construct a model of a periscope to prove light travels in a straight line. They place one of the mirrors at position A.

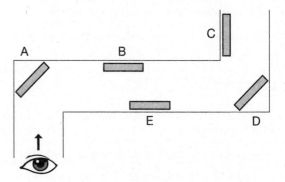

Where should they place the second mirror in order for the light to exit the opposite end of the periscope from where the students are viewing? **5.3(C)**

Ⓕ Position B

Ⓗ Position D

Ⓖ Position C

Ⓙ Position E

**Unit 8** Check for Understanding

**1** In an activity, a student floats a toy boat in an aquarium.

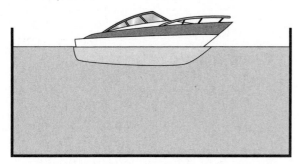

Why does the bottom of the boat appear to be larger than the top of the boat?

Ⓐ Reflection   Ⓒ Conduction

Ⓑ Absorption   Ⓓ Refraction

**2** Light travels into a camera lens to form a small, upside down image on the inside of the camera. Which of the following best describes why the lens flips and decreases the size of the image?

Ⓕ Light is refracted by the lens.

Ⓖ Light is absorbed by the lens.

Ⓗ Light is reflected by the lens.

Ⓙ Light is transmitted by the lens.

**3** What is the difference between refraction and reflection?

Ⓐ Light bends when it is reflected and bounces off when it is refracted.

Ⓑ Light bounces off when it is reflected and bends when it is refracted.

Ⓒ Light travels in curved lines when it is reflected and straight lines when it is refracted.

Ⓓ When light is refracted, it no longer travels.

**4** What happens when light strikes a dark, heavy object?

Ⓕ Light is refracted.

Ⓖ The light moves quickly through the medium.

Ⓗ Light energy is absorbed.

Ⓙ Light does not strike dark objects.

**5** Which of the following objects does **NOT** reflect light?

Ⓐ A mirror

Ⓑ A white car

Ⓒ A black shirt

Ⓓ Aluminum foil

**6** A man floating in a boat on a lake sees an image of an airplane in the water. At the same time he hears a plane and turns to see the source of the sound in the sky.

Which property of light best explains why an image of the plane appears in the water?

Ⓕ Conduction   Ⓗ Absorption

Ⓖ Reflection   Ⓙ Refraction

     motivation**science**™LEVEL 5

## Scientific Investigation and Reasoning Skills: Questions 7–14

**7** Students performed an experiment testing refraction of objects in water. First, they recorded how objects looked in hot water. Then, they used cold water to test if the appearance changed. What variable did students test in this experiment?  **5.2(A)**

Ⓐ Temperature of the water

Ⓑ The student who performed the experiment

Ⓒ Time of day the experiment was performed

Ⓓ The objects tested

**8** Before beginning an experiment, students are instructed to gather the materials necessary to classify objects with the properties of reflection or refraction. What objects can be used as materials that reflect light?  **5.2(B)**

Ⓕ Glass, water, and camera

Ⓖ Water, piece of wood, and clear plastic container

Ⓗ DVD, shiny pot, and mirror

Ⓙ Mirror, wood, and water

**9** After testing refraction of light in water, a student makes the following conclusion.

> Objects look broken when they are in water, so light is reflected in water.

Is the student's conclusion accurate?  **5.2(F)**

Ⓐ Yes, because when objects appear broken in water, they are reflected.

Ⓑ Yes, because all objects can reflect light.

Ⓒ No, because objects submerged in water do not appear broken.

Ⓓ No, because objects appear broken in water due to refraction of light.

**10** Which science tool could be used to reflect light?  **5.4(A)**

Ⓕ

Ⓖ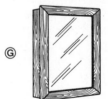

Ⓗ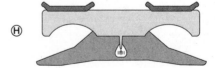

Ⓙ

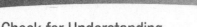
**11** While investigating whether objects reflect or refract light, a student asks when would be an appropriate time to make a conclusion. What is a good response to this question?  **5.2(E)**

Ⓐ After performing experiments one time, a reliable conclusion can be made.

Ⓑ No matter how many times an experiment is tested, you should never make a conclusion.

Ⓒ Test the experiment several times to ensure your conclusion is accurate.

Ⓓ All of the above

**12** Bifocals were invented in 1784 by a famous scientist named Benjamin Franklin. He invented bifocals to make it easier to see both up close and far away. Bifocals are a type of glasses which have two different lenses. One lens helps people to see at a distance, and the other is for seeing up close. Why can people who are both nearsighted and farsighted see better through bifocals?  **5.3(D)**

Ⓕ The bifocal lenses refract light.

Ⓖ The bifocal lenses reflect light.

Ⓗ The bifocal lenses make light less visible.

Ⓙ The bifocal lenses absorb light.

**13** When exploring light in an outdoor investigation, which safety rule should be followed?  **5.1(A)**

Ⓐ Never look directly at the Sun

Ⓑ Wear a lab coat or apron

Ⓒ Wear sandals or open-toed shoes

Ⓓ When waiting for directions, play with your friends

**14** A student holds a mirror against the letter B.

Which statement correctly explains why the B appears backward in the mirror?  **5.3(A)**

Ⓕ Light is refracted by the mirror, creating an image of the letter B.

Ⓖ Light is absorbed by the mirror, creating an image of the letter B.

Ⓗ Light is reflected by the mirror, creating an image of the letter B.

Ⓙ Light is conducted by the mirror, creating an image of the letter B.

## Reflection and Refraction Time

Remembering the meaning of reflection and refraction can be confusing because the words sound very similar.

Compose a rhyme or song to help you differentiate between reflection and refraction. Write your composition in the space below. Share your composition with the class.

## Formative Assessment

Create an explanation for the phenomenon shown in the picture below. Support your explanation with reasoning and evidence.

| Phenomenon | Explanation |
|---|---|
| White light / Prism → Red Orange Yellow Green Blue Indigo Violet | |

**Science Journal**

Light travels in a straight line until it strikes an object. Light can be reflected and refracted. Distinguish the difference between reflection and refraction. Draw examples of how light is reflected and refracted.

## Science Vocabulary Builder

Create cartoon figures to help you remember the meanings of the vocabulary words.

| light | reflection | refraction |

### Light

Name of character: _____

What does the character represent?

_____

_____

Explain how this character is a reminder of the meaning of light.

_____

_____

### Refraction

Name of character: _____

What does the character represent?

_____

_____

Explain how this character is a reminder of the meaning of refraction.

_____

_____

### Reflection

Name of character: _____

What does the character represent?

_____

_____

Explain how this character is a reminder of the meaning of reflection.

_____

_____

**Paths of Light**

Demonstrate the path light takes when traveling through the convex lens. Include an explanation of the drawing.

| **Drawing** | **Explanation** |
|---|---|
|  |  |

Illustrate how light is refracted when traveling through the concave lens. Include an explanation of the drawing.

| **Drawing** | **Explanation** |
|---|---|
|  |  |

**Parent Activities**

1. Help your child research the way light travels through convex and concave lenses to complete the homework above.

2. Look for examples of reflection and refraction around the home.

3. Build a periscope. Simple directions for construction can be found at *http://www.exploratorium.edu/science_explorer/periscope.html*

**After this lesson I will be able to:**

- **Design** an experiment that tests the effect of force on an object.

## Descriptive and Experimental Investigations

**Activity 1:** Fun with Force

Participate in a tug-of-war activity with your classmates. What happens?

_____

_____

_____

After one round, play again, but this time have one team let go. What happens?

_____

_____

_____

Which team won? What had to happen for one team to win?

_____

_____

_____

_____

What happens when both teams are pulling with the same amount of force?

_____

_____

_____

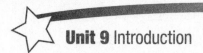
## Activity 2: Design an Experiment

There are many ways to test force on objects. Create an experiment to test force with one of the objects listed below. What type of force will you test on the object?

Circle the object to test force.

        Balloon      Marble      Rubber band      Car      Ball      Iron nail

Circle the force to be tested.

        Gravity      Magnetism      Friction

Create a drawing of your experiment.

Describe the experiment performed. Identify your variable.

_____

_____

Were there any problems encountered during the experiment? Explain.

_____

_____

What did you observe during your experiment?

_____

_____

What can you conclude about force?

_____

_____

**1** Fifth graders study force and motion. One group of students decides to repeat Galileo's famous experiment for their science project. They design an experiment to test the effects of gravity on heavier objects versus lighter objects. They drop an iron ball and a rubber ball from two flights of stairs. Three trial runs are conducted, and then data is recorded. Why do the students conduct three trial runs during the investigation? **5.2(E)**

Ⓐ To formulate a hypothesis ✗

Ⓑ To increase reliability of results ✓

Ⓒ To test more than one variable ✗

Ⓓ To impress the teacher ✗

**Use the paragraph below and your knowledge of science to answer questions 2 and 3.**

In science class, students learn that friction is the resistance to motion when two objects rub together. The students decide to design an experiment at home to compare friction on dry and icy surfaces.

**2** Which question is most beneficial for this type of investigation? **5.2(B)**

Ⓕ Is it faster to sled down an icy hill or down a rough gravel driveway? ✓

Ⓖ What is friction? ✗

Ⓗ What makes ice slippery? ✗

Ⓙ What effect does the height of the hill have on the distance an object travels? ✗

**3** What is the most appropriate tool to use when collecting data from the investigation? **5.2(G)**

Ⓐ List ✗        Ⓒ Table ✓

Ⓑ Graph ✗      Ⓓ Chart ✗

**4** When designing an experiment, why is it important to test only one variable? **5.2(A)**

Ⓕ Testing one variable explains what caused the change once data has been gathered. ✓

Ⓖ Testing one variable collects inaccurate data and repeats the investigation more than necessary. ✗

Ⓗ Testing one variable decreases the reliability of the investigation. ✗

Ⓙ It is not necessary to test only one variable. ✗

**5** Students test the effects of forces that act from a distance, causing objects to move. They discover that two forces have this effect on objects. These forces are —

Ⓐ friction and gravity ✗

Ⓑ gravity and magnetism ✗

Ⓒ magnetism and friction ✓

Ⓓ gravity and density ✗

**6** A science class completes a study on how objects move. All of the following would be considered appropriate when testing the effects of the force of motion on an object **EXCEPT** —

Ⓕ throwing a baseball ✗

Ⓖ two teams playing tug-of-war ✗

Ⓗ measuring the size of two marbles ✓

Ⓙ paddling backwards in a boat ✗

**Unit 9** Check for Understanding

**1** What is the unit of measurement for force?

Ⓐ Gram ✗

Ⓑ Newton ✓

Ⓒ Pound ✗

Ⓓ Meter ✗

**2** Students wrap a copper wire around an iron nail and connect the ends of the wire to a battery. The nail attracts other small nails and paper clips as they stick together. What force keeps the nails and paper clips attached together?

Ⓕ Gravity ✗

Ⓖ Electrical ✗

Ⓗ Magnetism

Ⓙ Friction ✗

**3** What force is being tested when an object is forced downward toward the center of Earth?

Ⓐ Gravity ✓

Ⓑ Air pressure ✗

Ⓒ Magnetism ✗

Ⓓ Friction ✗

**4** Rubbing two sticks together to make a fire is an example of —

Ⓕ gravitational force ✗

Ⓖ frictional force ✓

Ⓗ pulling force ✗

Ⓙ magnetic force ✗

**5** What is an example of a gravitational force?

Ⓐ Pushing a grocery cart ✗

Ⓑ Pulling a wagon ✗

Ⓒ Dropping a pencil on the ground ✓

Ⓓ Picking up iron filings with a magnet ✗

**6** In the picture below, one object is attracted to another by —

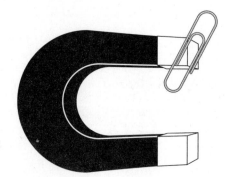

Ⓕ gravity ✗

Ⓖ friction ✗

Ⓗ air pressure ✗

Ⓙ not here ✓

motivation**science**™LEVEL 5

| **Scientific Investigation and Reasoning Skills: Questions 7–14** |

**7** Students organize their ideas in preparation for an experiment they design. Below is a list of tools needed for the experiment.

> **Tools Needed for Experiment**
> - Spring scale
> - Metric ruler
> - Calculator
> - Magnets

Based on the information above, what type of experiment do the students plan?  **5.2(B)**

Ⓐ Testing the physical properties of solutions

Ⓑ Investigating the effects of light and heat on an object

Ⓒ Testing the characteristics of conductors and insulators

Ⓓ Testing the effects of force on an object

**8** For a science project, students decide to design a model of a roller coaster to test the force of gravity. They plan to build a roller coaster track 5 m in length and use books and boards to build the hills and ramps. According to the process of designing an experiment, which of the following should be the students' next step? **5.2(A)**

Ⓕ Construct different types of roller coasters

Ⓖ Gather the materials needed to build the roller coaster

Ⓗ Create a graph to display the results

Ⓙ Draw conclusions from the results

**9** Based on the advertisement below, what can be concluded about this product?  **5.3(B)**

> **Physics Experiments** has a wealth of information about forces such as magnetism, friction, and gravity, including a variety of engaging experiments using household items.
>
> Video instructions and demos make learning science at home fun!
>
> Recommended for ages 9 and up.
>
> **Physics Experiments** *Science Fun for Kids*
>
> *Jam-packed DVD*

Ⓐ It contains information about topics related to all areas of science. ✗

Ⓑ The experiments can be conducted using materials found around the house. ✓

Ⓒ All ages will find these experiments fascinating and engaging. ✗

Ⓓ The directions are easy for anyone to understand. ✗

**10** A group of students constructs an experiment testing the effects of force on an object. Some of the materials they use are items produced from nonrenewable resources. What is the wisest choice for disposal of these materials? **5.1(B)**

Ⓕ Throw the items in the trash can

Ⓖ Place the items in a metal trash can, and burn them

Ⓗ Place the items in the recycling bin

Ⓙ Return the items to the store

**11** Which conclusion can be made from the lab report?  **5.2(F)**

---

**Lab Report**

**Hypothesis**
*A feather weighing 2 grams will take longer to fall from a distance of 6 meters than a 2-gram ball bearing.*

**Procedure**
1. Use a stopwatch to measure the amount of time it takes for a feather to fall to the floor from a distance of 6 meters.

2. Use a stopwatch to measure the amount of time it takes for a ball bearing to fall to the floor from a distance of 6 meters.

**Observation**
The hypothesis was correct. The feather took more time to fall to the floor than the ball bearing.

**Conclusion**

---

&#9398; The feather fell slower because it weighs less.

&#9399; The ball fell faster because it has more gravitational force.

&#9400; The ball fell faster because it weighs more.

&#9401; The feather fell slower because it encountered more air resistance.

**12** Which scientist is best known for explaining gravity?  **5.3(D)**

&#9403; Albert Einstein

&#9404; Isaac Newton

&#9405; Thomas Edison

&#9406; Anders Celsius

**13** Based on the notebook entry below, which experiment to test force is likely to have been tested?  **5.2(F)**

---

September 24

   In science class, we tested the effects of force on objects. I learned that when a force is applied, an equal but opposite force is created. The coach let us borrow materials, and we completed the experiment in the gym. The other team won when they crossed the line. Our team fell down to the ground. Learning about forces was fun!

---

&#9398; Pulling a rope

&#9399; Pushing against a wall

&#9400; Partners pushing their hands against each other

&#9401; Throwing a ball against the wall

**14** A marble is rolled in a straight line inside a box. When the marble gets to the end of the box, it changes direction and rolls the other way.

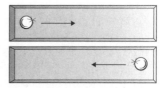

Which statement best describes why this happens?  **5.2(D)**

&#9403; The marble had nowhere else to go, so it moved in the opposite direction.

&#9404; The force of gravity on the box pushed the marble in the opposite direction.

&#9405; The force of the marble hitting the box produced an opposite force, pushing the marble in the opposite direction.

&#9406; The marble stopped by the wall, and then magnetic force pushed it in the opposite direction.

### Roller Coaster

The principals of force, gravity, motion, and acceleration are used to create roller coasters.

- In groups, use the knowledge you have about forces and gravity to design a new roller coaster for an amusement park. In the space below, draw a model of the roller coaster.
- Develop a list of materials you would use to create the roller coaster.
- Create the roller coaster. Test your coaster, and improve your design as needed.
- Set up a class amusement park, and take turns presenting the models to your class.

**Roller Coaster Design**

### Formative Assessment

Describe the steps that must be included when designing and conducting an experiment or investigation.

_____

_____

_____

_____

_____

_____

_____

**Science Journal**

Write a story telling what it would be like to spend a day without gravity or a day without friction.

_____

_____

_____

_____

_____

_____

_____

_____

_____

_____

_____

_____

_____

_____

_____

_____

_____

_____

_____

_____

_____

_____

_____

_____

_____

_____

         motivation**science**™ LEVEL 5

**Science Vocabulary Builder**

Use the letters to create sentences and examples which describe forces.

**F** _____
_____

**O** _____
_____

**R** _____
_____

**C** _____
_____

**E** _____

**Unit 9** Homework

Supporting Standard 5.6(D)

**Testing Forces at Home**

At school, you designed an experiment to test the effect of force on an object.

What other questions do you have about force and motion?

_____

_____

What investigations could you plan to test force on objects? How would you carry out the investigation?

_____

_____

Develop an experiment to test force with objects found at your home. Illustrate the experiment below. Then, write a brief summary of the experiment and the outcome.

Summary

_____

_____

_____

_____

_____

✂ - - - - - - - - - - - - - - - - - - - - - - - - - - - - - - - - - - - - - - - - - - - - - - - - - - - -

**Parent Activities**

1. Help your child complete the investigation above to test the effect of force on an object.

2. Look for opportunities to discuss how forces impact our daily lives. For example, discuss the importance of driving slower on a rainy day due to reduced friction.

3. Take a trip to a nearby amusement or water park. As you enjoy the rides, discuss the forces of gravity and friction. On a roller coaster, where is the highest hill located? Why?

motivation**science**™LEVEL 5

**Motivation Station: Molly's Cool Science Fact**

The pulley, a simple machine made of a rope or chain and a grooved wheel, has been around since ancient times. Although the origin of the single pulley is unknown, a mathematician named Archimedes is believed to be the inventor of the compound pulley.

**After this lesson I will be able to:**

- **Demonstrate** and **observe** how position and motion can be changed by pushing and pulling objects to show work being done, such as swings, balls, pulleys, and wagons.

## Experimental Investigations

### Activity 1: Pendulums

1. Measure and cut two pieces of string the following lengths:

   - 8 centimeters
   - 15 centimeters

2. Tie a washer to one end of each string. Make a loop at the other end of the string.

3. Tape a pencil to the table so it extends over the edge. Place the loop of one string over the pencil.

4. Raise the washer so it is even with the table. Release the pendulum (washer), and count the number of swings it makes in one minute.

5. Conduct 3 trials for each length of string. Record your results in the data table.

| Length of String | Trial 1 | Trial 2 | Trial 3 |
|---|---|---|---|
| 8 centimeters | | | |
| 15 centimeters | | | |

6. What was the variable in the investigation?

_____

_____

7. What can you conclude from your results?

_____

_____

_____

## Activity 2: Bounce Height

### Question

Which type of ball will bounce the highest?

### Hypothesis

I believe the _____ ball will bounce the highest.

### Procedure

- Have one group member hold the meter stick vertically, as shown.
- Drop each ball from a height of 1 meter.
- Watch to see how high each ball bounces. Record the results.
- Conduct 3 trials for each type of ball.

### Results

Create a data table to show your results.

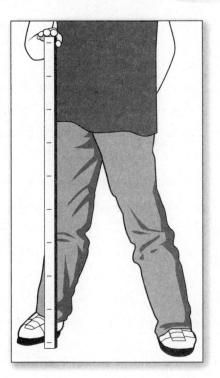

Use the results in the data table to complete the graph.

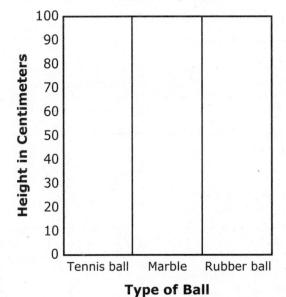

### Conclusion

_____

_____

_____

**Use the table below and your knowledge of science to answer questions 1–3.**

A cotton ball is catapulted from two different sized paper clips. The table below shows the distances the cotton ball travels.

| Paper Clips | Trial 1 | Trial 2 | Trial 3 |
| --- | --- | --- | --- |
| Large paper clip | 10 cm | 14 cm | 19 cm |
| Small paper clip | 8 cm | 5 cm | 8 cm |

**1** Which conclusion is best supported by the results shown in the table? **5.2(D)**

Ⓐ A cotton ball travels farther when launched from a small paper clip.

Ⓑ Using a large paper clip allows the cotton ball to travel farther.

Ⓒ A cotton ball does not travel as far when launched from a large paper clip.

Ⓓ Using a smaller cotton ball allows it to travel even farther.

**2** What is the significance of conducting three trial runs for the experiment above? **5.2(E)**

Ⓕ Conducting three trials shows the differences in the way the experiment was done.

Ⓖ The results of two of the trial runs are incorrect and need to be redone.

Ⓗ Repeating the investigation increases the validity of the results.

Ⓙ It is fun to repeat the investigation and observe the cotton ball traveling through the air.

**3** What variable is tested in the experiment above? **5.2(A)**

Ⓐ Size of the cotton ball

Ⓑ Size of the paper clip

Ⓒ Distance the cotton ball traveled

Ⓓ Type of catapult

**4** Flagpoles have pulleys which allow the flag to be raised or lowered. How does a pulley transfer motion in the raising and lowering of a flag?

Ⓕ Pulling down on one side of the rope causes the opposite side of the rope to go up.

Ⓖ Pushing up on one side of the rope causes the opposite side of the rope to go up.

Ⓗ The pushing force alone causes the motion of the rope to move up or down.

Ⓙ There is no need for a transfer of motion when raising and lowering a flag.

**5** Students design an experiment to see if it is easier for girls or boys to pull a wagon loaded with textbooks to the top of a hill.

| Students | Time it Takes to Pull a Wagon |
| --- | --- |
| Boys | 10 minutes 20 seconds |
| Girls | 8 minutes 12 seconds |

Which conclusion is best supported by the results shown in the table? **5.2(D)**

Ⓐ It is easier for boys to pull the wagon.

Ⓑ It is easier for girls to pull the wagon.

Ⓒ It is more difficult to pull a wagon than to push one.

Ⓓ It is more difficult to pull a full wagon than an empty one.

**6** A kickball is rolled toward home plate and kicked by a player. Which statement best describes the movement of the ball?

Ⓕ The ball is pushed by both the pitcher and the kicker.

Ⓖ The ball is pushed by the pitcher and pulled by the kicker.

Ⓗ The ball is pulled by the pitcher and pushed by the kicker.

Ⓙ The ball is pulled by both the pitcher and the kicker.

**Unit 10** Check for Understanding

**1** Which of the following is true of force?

Ⓐ Force can cause an object to change its speed.

Ⓑ Force can change the direction of an object.

Ⓒ The motion of an object changes when a force is applied to it.

Ⓓ All of the above

**2** Students are given objects and are told to measure the amount of force required to push each object.

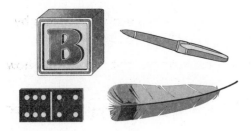

Which item requires the least amount of force to push across a table?

Ⓕ Block     Ⓗ Pen

Ⓖ Domino    Ⓙ Feather

**3** In which position would a person need to be standing to cause the swing to be in the position pictured below?

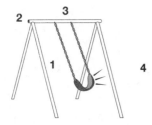

Ⓐ Position 1     Ⓒ Position 3

Ⓑ Position 2     Ⓓ Position 4

**4** Swing A is shorter in length than Swing B.

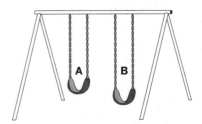

What effect will this have on swinging?

Ⓕ When pushed, Swing B will move back and forth slower than Swing A.

Ⓖ When pushed, Swing A will move back and forth slower than Swing B.

Ⓗ When pushed, both swings will move back and forth at the same pace.

Ⓙ When pushed, both swings will move back and forth at a faster pace.

**5** A group of students observes pushing and pulling of objects. Which of the following would **NOT** be an example of work being done by changing the position and motion of an object?

Ⓐ Opening the front door using the door handle

Ⓑ Playing a game of baseball

Ⓒ Trying unsuccessfully to move a large boulder across the playground

Ⓓ Moving a shopping cart down the aisle at the grocery store

**6** In order for work to be done —

Ⓕ an object must move

Ⓖ an object can stay in the same location

Ⓗ two forces must be applied to an object

Ⓙ objects must remain in stationary positions

motivation**science**™LEVEL 5

## Scientific Investigation and Reasoning Skills: Questions 7–14

**7** A pulley is a rope wrapped around a wheel. Precautions must be taken to avoid getting loose clothing or hair caught in a pulley. It is also important to be very cautious when lifting heavy objects with a pulley.

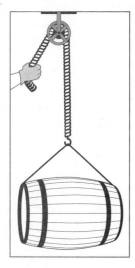

Which of the following is the best safety rule to follow when working with pulleys? **5.1(A)**

Ⓐ Always wear an apron

Ⓑ Listen to the teacher

Ⓒ Wear safety goggles

Ⓓ Keep a fire extinguisher nearby

**8** The picture shows a man pulling a heavy box toward him with a rope.

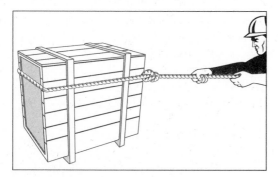

In order for the box to move, the man must apply — **5.2(D)**

Ⓕ gravity      Ⓗ friction

Ⓖ magnetism      Ⓙ force

**9** A teacher places groups of students around the classroom to investigate force. She places 3 balls of different sizes and masses at one station. A starting point is marked with masking tape on the floor. Students are asked to observe the position and motion of each ball while another student gives the ball a push, causing it to roll across the floor. Students measure the distance with a meter stick and record the results on a data table in their notebooks. What is one of the principles students learn during this investigation? **5.2(C)**

Ⓐ Ask a well-defined question, and form a hypothesis

Ⓑ Collect and record information by observation and measuring

Ⓒ Draw a model that represents how something works

Ⓓ Create a graph to display collected results

**10** Students collect information on objects which change position due to a push or a pull. What is the best unit of measurement to use when recording an object's change of position? **5.2(C)**

Ⓕ Gram

Ⓖ Milliliter

Ⓗ Centimeter

Ⓙ Inch

**11** The graph shows how far each object rolled after being pushed.

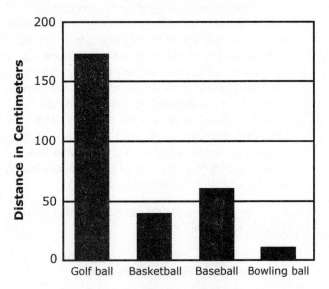

**Distance Rolled**

Based on the graph, which object requires the greatest force to put it in motion? **5.2(G)**

Ⓐ Golf ball

Ⓑ Basketball

Ⓒ Baseball

Ⓓ Bowling ball

**12** Students notice that an object changes position and motion when it is pushed or pulled. The students are making — **5.2(C)**

Ⓕ a hypothesis

Ⓖ a conclusion

Ⓗ a prediction

Ⓙ an observation

**13** Students investigate how position and motion can be changed by pulling objects. For the investigation, they pull three identical wagons up a steep hill behind the school. Each wagon is loaded with objects of different masses. The students decide the conclusion will be based on the amount of time needed to pull each loaded wagon up the hill. What important part of the investigation do the objects of different masses represent? **5.2(A)**

Ⓐ Valid conclusion

Ⓑ Variable

Ⓒ Reasonable explanation

Ⓓ Selecting appropriate equipment

**14** A large load of fish needs to be brought onto a dock from a fishing boat. Which tool is best used for doing the work of pulling weight upward? **5.2(B)**

Ⓕ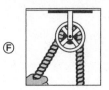

Ⓖ

Ⓗ

Ⓙ

motivation**science**™ LEVEL 5

## Pushing and Pulling Skit

In groups, create and perform a skit to demonstrate how pushing and pulling can be used to move objects. Describe the characters below.

Student 1: _____

Student 2: _____

Student 3: _____

Describe each group member's part in the skit using the boxes below.

> **Student 1**

> **Student 2**

> **Student 3**

## Formative Assessment

Describe how position and motion can be changed by pushing and pulling when playing your favorite game.

_____

_____

_____

_____

_____

**Science Journal**

Pushing and pulling can change the position and motion of an object. Create a toy that can be used to help other students understand force by pushing and pulling. Describe the toy, what it does, and how it looks.

## Science Vocabulary Builder

Complete the graphic organizer below for the terms *work* and *force*.

|  | Work | Force |
|---|---|---|
| **Illustration** |  |  |
| **Definition** |  |  |
| **Examples** |  |  |
| **Non-examples** |  |  |
| **Sentence** |  |  |
| **Tool used to measure** |  |  |
| **Unit of measurement** |  |  |

## Unit 10 Homework

Supporting Standard 3.6(B)

**Push or Pull Hunt**

1. Go on a scavenger hunt for objects that require a push or a pull to show work being done. An example would be a door that needs to be pushed to be opened or a plastic container with a top that needs to be pulled to be opened.

2. Draw the object, and describe how its position or motion changes.

### Push or Pull Hunt

| Object | Push | Pull |
|---|---|---|
| 1. | | |
| 2. | | |
| 3. | | |
| 4. | | |
| 5. | | |

3. Explain why a push or a pull is needed for work to be done.

_____

_____

_____

✂ - - - - - - - - - - - - - - - - - - - - - - - - - - - - - - - - - - - - - - - - - - - - -

**Parent Activities**

1. While riding in the car, look around town for examples of pulleys. Discuss how pulleys make work easier.

2. Experiment with a wagon to learn how position and motion are changed by pushing and pulling.

3. Visit a park with your child, and discuss the forces at work. Compare the movement of a swing to other playground equipment, such as a merry-go-round.

motivation**science**™ LEVEL 5

**1** A portable game player stops working because the batteries are dead. What type of energy does the game player need to begin working again?

Ⓐ Mechanical energy

Ⓑ Thermal energy

Ⓒ Sound energy

Ⓓ None of the above

**2** In an activity, students are given a circuit diagram.

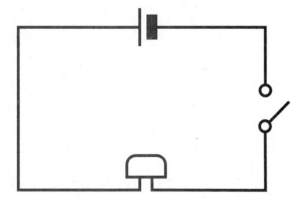

Which statement explains why the buzzer will **NOT** sound when the switch is open?

Ⓕ Sound energy from the buzzer cannot travel through the open switch.

Ⓖ Electrical energy produced by the switch cannot travel through the opening to produce sound energy.

Ⓗ Sound energy from the battery cannot travel to the buzzer through the open switch.

Ⓙ Electrical energy from the battery cannot travel through the open switch to produce sound energy.

**3** What do all the objects below have in common?

Ⓐ They all refract light.

Ⓑ They all reflect light.

Ⓒ They are all conductors.

Ⓓ They all make objects appear **smaller.**

**4** Students use a spring scale to **measure the** differences in force when a block **is moved** across smooth and rough surfaces. **What** unit of measurement should **the students** use when recording the data?

Ⓕ Centimeter

Ⓖ Celsius

Ⓗ Newton

Ⓙ Gram

**Use the information below and your knowledge of science to answer questions 5 and 6.**

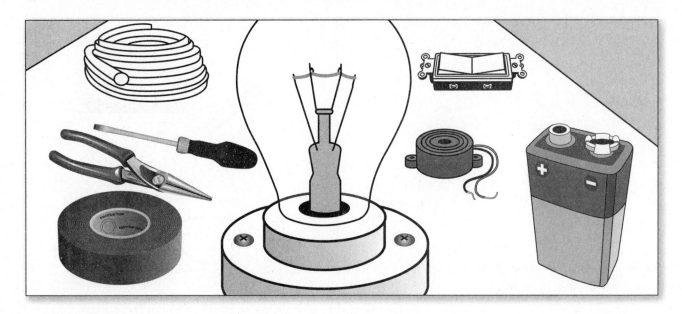

Students design an experiment to demonstrate the flow of electricity in circuits. Some of the available materials are a battery, battery holder, lightbulb, lightbulb holder, copper wires, and a switch. After testing objects that conduct electricity to prove that an electric current passes through, the students notice the lightbulb is not shining as brightly. They decide to dispose of the battery and replace it with a new one.

**5** Which of the following is a wise choice for disposal of the battery? **5.1(B)**

 Ⓐ Place the battery in an incinerator

 Ⓑ Dispose of the battery in the trash

 Ⓒ Place the battery in the recycling bin

 Ⓓ All of the above

**6** Electricity can seriously harm people. Adults and students should be aware of electrical safety advice to avoid such things as electric shock. Which of the following is considered the most vital piece of advice to follow when exploring electrical circuits? **5.1(A)**

 Ⓕ Always follow the teacher's directions

 Ⓖ Always use new wire when building circuits

 Ⓗ Always put materials away after building circuits

 Ⓙ Always take the advice of your group members

**7** A boy pushes a cart across the floor.

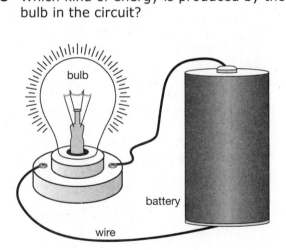

What is the push most likely to change?

Ⓐ The mass of the cart

Ⓑ The shape of the cart

Ⓒ The position of the cart

Ⓓ All of the above

**8** Which kind of energy is produced by the bulb in the circuit?

Ⓕ Electrical

Ⓖ Mechanical

Ⓗ Light

Ⓙ Sound

**9** Students are asked to construct a graphic organizer to assist with organizing data on a study of light.

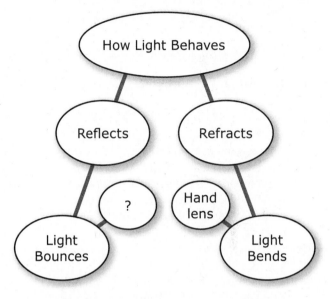

Which of the following is needed to complete the graphic organizer?   **5.2(G)**

Ⓐ Wooden boat

Ⓑ Camera

Ⓒ Shoebox

Ⓓ Mirror

**10** Which motion causes a flag to be raised or lowered from a flagpole?

Ⓕ Back and forth motion

Ⓖ Push or pull force

Ⓗ Magnetic attraction

Ⓙ Rubbing together of surfaces

**11** Which of the following produces mechanical energy?

Ⓐ An outlet plug

Ⓑ A flashlight

Ⓒ A burning campfire

Ⓓ Riding a skateboard

**12** After an investigation demonstrating that a circuit requires a complete path so a current can pass, four students draw a diagram representing the experiment. Which student designs an accurate diagram of a closed circuit?

Ⓕ Student A

Ⓖ Student B

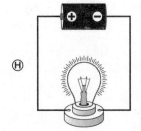

Ⓗ Student C

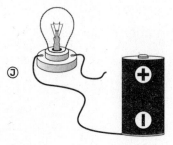

Ⓙ Student D

**13** In science class students learn that to calculate force, they need to multiply mass times acceleration. If the mass of an object is 7 g and the acceleration of an object is 20 km/s, what is the force?

Record your answer and fill in the bubbles below.

| ⓪ | ⓪ | ⓪ | • |
|---|---|---|---|
| ① | ① | ① | |
| ② | ② | ② | |
| ③ | ③ | ③ | |
| ④ | ④ | ④ | |
| ⑤ | ⑤ | ⑤ | |
| ⑥ | ⑥ | ⑥ | |
| ⑦ | ⑦ | ⑦ | |
| ⑧ | ⑧ | ⑧ | |
| ⑨ | ⑨ | ⑨ | |

**14** Which project will best test this statement? **5.2(A)**

> Objects pushed with the same force will slow down when moving across surfaces with more friction.

Ⓕ Build ramps and cover with materials like wax paper, foil, sandpaper, and carpet. Roll a ball down each ramp using the same amount of force.

Ⓖ Cover flat surfaces with different materials like carpet, silk, cotton, and wool. Roll a ball across each surface using different amounts of force.

Ⓗ Build ramps and cover with carpet or sandpaper. Roll a ball down each ramp using different amounts of force.

Ⓙ Cover a flat surface with silk and a ramp with cotton. Roll a ball across each using the same amount of force.

**15** Based on the advertisement, what can be inferred about the expansion of this mirror company? **5.3(B)**

> # Magic Mirror
>
> is one of the fastest growing providers of standard and custom automotive mirrors in the world.
>
> ## Yes, the world!
>
>
>
> **Yes, we are coming up fast... faster than the competition ever expected!**
>
> Eight international locations and eleven U.S. distribution centers provide our customers access to the widest range of high quality commercial mirrors.
>
> For ordering information, contact us by phone, or visit our website.

Ⓐ Mirrors can be customized to fit any automobile.

Ⓑ Magic Mirror is quickly becoming a top competitor.

Ⓒ Magic Mirror provides mirror products only in the U.S.

Ⓓ The company may be contacted by telephone only.

**16** What is shown in the image below?

Ⓕ The force needed to use a pulley

Ⓖ The path light takes when it is refracted

Ⓗ The flow of an electrical current

Ⓙ The path light takes when it is reflected

**17** After studying uses of energy, a student makes the following conclusion.

> Thermal energy is heat energy.

Is the statement accurate? **5.2(F)**

Ⓐ Yes, thermal energy is also known as heat energy.

Ⓑ No, thermal energy involves sound.

Ⓒ No, thermal energy is energy converted from electricity.

Ⓓ Yes, thermal energy is converted into heat energy.

**18** A student pushes against a brick wall with a force of 25 Newtons, but the brick wall does not move. Does work take place?

Ⓕ Yes, because the student pushes with a force of 25 Newtons.

Ⓖ No, because the wall does not move.

Ⓗ Yes, because for every action there is an equal and opposite reaction.

Ⓙ No, because the student does not use force.

**Use the information in the story below and your knowledge of science to answer questions 19 and 20.**

## Newton's Laws of Motion

   Isaac Newton was one of the world's most influential scientists. It is said that Isaac Newton began his discoveries about gravity after observing an apple fall from a tree. Whether this story is a myth or fact is unknown, but we do know Isaac Newton experimented with gravity and wrote the Laws of Motion. Newton's three laws are:

- First Law of Motion–An object at rest remains at rest, and an object in motion remains in motion unless acted upon by a force.

- Second Law of Motion–The acceleration of an object depends on its mass and the amount of force applied.

- Third Law of Motion–For every action, there is an equal and opposite reaction.

---

**19** Two marbles collide, sending each marble into opposite directions. Which of Newton's Laws best explains this event?   **5.3(D)**

Ⓐ  The acceleration of an object depends on its mass and the amount of force applied.

Ⓑ  An object at rest remains at rest, and an object in motion remains in motion unless acted upon by a force.

Ⓒ  For every action, there is an equal and opposite reaction.

Ⓓ  Gravity is a force that pulls objects toward each other.

**20** The teacher places a stack of books on a chair with wheels. The teacher pushes the chair across the floor, but then stops the chair abruptly. The pile of books continues to move, flying forward and spilling onto the floor. Which of Newton's Laws of Motion does the teacher demonstrate?   **5.3(D)**

Ⓕ  Newton's First Law of Motion

Ⓖ  Newton's Second Law of Motion

Ⓗ  Newton's Third Law of Motion

Ⓙ  Not here

# Chart Your Success

**Color Mike or Molly *green* if your answer was correct or *red* if your answer was incorrect.**

### Energy

| Total Correct | Total Possible |
|---|---|
| | **4** |

### Electric Circuits

| Total Correct | Total Possible |
|---|---|
| | **4** |

### Light Energy

| Total Correct | Total Possible |
|---|---|
| | **4** |

### Forces

| Total Correct | Total Possible |
|---|---|
| | **4** |

### Motion

| Total Correct | Total Possible |
|---|---|
| | **4** |

motivation**science**™ LEVEL 5

# Notes

 motivation**science**™LEVEL 5

**Motivation Station: Mike's Cool Science Fact**

Coal has a nickname: Buried Sunshine. Millions of years ago, the plants which later became coal used energy from the Sun to grow. When coal is burned, the energy produced can be traced back to the Sun as its original source of energy.

## After this lesson I will be able to:

- **Explore** the processes that led to the formation of sedimentary rocks and fossil fuels.

## Comparative Investigations

**Activity 1:** Formation of Sedimentary Rock

Record your hypothesis about the formation of sedimentary rock in the table. Then, create a model to represent the formation of sedimentary rocks. Shave a crayon with scissors or crayon sharpener onto a piece of wax paper. Cover shavings with another piece of wax paper, and press down. You can also use a book or other object to help press the shavings. During the experiment, fill in the observation section of the table. When the experiment is finished, write a conclusion.

| Hypothesis | Observations | Conclusion |
|------------|--------------|------------|
|            |              |            |

Which part of the model represented sediment?

_____

_____

Which parts of the model represented rock?

_____

_____

_____

What can be concluded about the formation of sedimentary rocks?

_____

_____

**Unit 11** Introduction

**Activity 2:** Fossil Fuel Research

Use books and websites to learn about the formation of fossil fuels. Fill in the table, and record information about each of the three fossil fuels: coal, oil, and natural gas.

| Fossil Fuel | Where is it found? | How does it form? |
| --- | --- | --- |
| Coal | | |
| Oil | | |
| Natural Gas | | |

What did you learn about the formation of fossil fuels?

_____

_____

Are fossil fuels found everywhere? Are certain conditions necessary for fossil fuels to form?

_____

_____

_____

How long does it take for fossil fuels to form?_____

Are there any fossil fuels found near your school or town? Where?

_____

Fill out the recipe card to explain the ingredients necessary for the formation of fossil fuels.

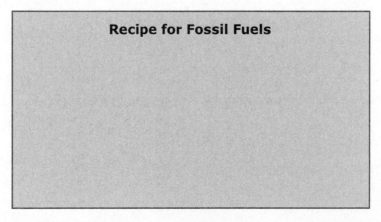

**Recipe for Fossil Fuels**

**1** The rock in Grand Canyon National Park is formed from layers of sand, minerals, and shells. Which type of rock is present at Grand Canyon National Park?

Ⓐ Igneous  Ⓒ Metamorphic

Ⓑ Sedimentary  Ⓓ Lava

**2** The most important factor in forming the sedimentary rock layers below is —

Ⓕ volcanic eruptions

Ⓖ scorching Sun

Ⓗ moving water

Ⓙ earthquakes

**3** Sedimentary rocks are formed from sediments of weathered material that have been eroded and then deposited in layers. This process requires —

Ⓐ temperature and time

Ⓑ deposition and melting

Ⓒ collection and transportation

Ⓓ time and pressure

**4** Students are learning about the formation of fossil fuels. They decide to construct a representation of how pressure and time cause organisms to turn into oil. The physical representation the students constructed is called a — **5.3(C)**

Ⓕ model  Ⓗ design

Ⓖ clone  Ⓙ structure

**5** A group of students explores the steps required for sedimentation of rocks. They record the results of the process in the table below.

**Sedimentary Rock Formation**

| Steps | Process |
|-------|---------|
| 1 | Weathering |
| 2 | Erosion |
| 3 | Deposition |
| 4 | ? |

Which of these best completes the table? **5.2(G)**

Ⓐ Layering  Ⓒ Compacting

Ⓑ Transporting  Ⓓ Fragmenting

**6** The research of geologists B. W. Murck and B. J. Skinner claims that rock formations like these of the beautiful Bryce Canyon in Utah provide information about past climates and life forms that inhabited Earth. These rock formations are made up largely of sandstone, limestone, and shale.

Which Earth process is evident in this canyon? **5.3(D)**

Ⓕ Formation of sedimentary rock

Ⓖ Erosion of shorelines

Ⓗ Weathering of hilltops

Ⓙ Supporting plant growth

**1** Coal, petroleum, and natural gas are all fossil fuels. Fossil fuels originated from —

Ⓐ buried, dead organisms changed by heat and pressure

Ⓑ heat preserved within Earth's crust

Ⓒ decayed rocks from within Earth's crust

Ⓓ plants that survived Earth's changes

**2** Look at the diagram below.

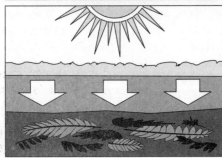

Which of the following is formed in the process shown in the diagram?

Ⓕ Coal       Ⓗ Gold

Ⓖ Glass      Ⓙ Water

**3** A river deposits layers of minerals and other rocks at its mouth. Over time, what kind of rock is formed by the deposits?

Ⓐ Igneous

Ⓑ Metamorphic

Ⓒ Sedimentary

Ⓓ Not here

**4** Which processes are required for the formation of sedimentary rock?

Ⓕ Boiling and pressure

Ⓖ Deposition and compaction

Ⓗ Weathering and melting

Ⓙ Pressure and cooling

**5** Which is **NOT** a factor in the formation of fossil fuels?

Ⓐ Time

Ⓑ Heat

Ⓒ Melting

Ⓓ Pressure

**6** All of these are examples of fossil fuels **EXCEPT** —

Ⓕ coal

Ⓖ petroleum

Ⓗ corn oil

Ⓙ natural gas

Scientific Investigation and Reasoning Skills: Questions 7–14

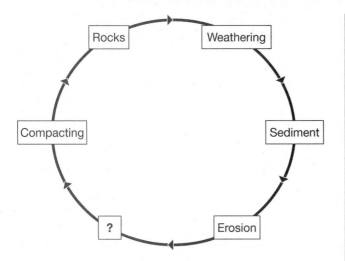

**7** Which of the following best completes the process shown in the flow chart? **5.2(D)**

Ⓐ Layers

Ⓑ Deposition

Ⓒ Cementing

Ⓓ Transporting

**8** A teacher conducts an experiment to help students learn about the formation of sedimentary rocks. The teacher uses a chocolate chip cookie to show how small pieces of rock and other sediment are compressed together under heavy pressure. What tool would be most beneficial in examining the sedimentary rock "cookie"? **5.4(A)**

Ⓕ Camera

Ⓖ Hand lens

Ⓗ Microscope

Ⓙ Metric ruler

**9** Students prepare an activity to **determine** what led to the formation of **fossil fuels.** Before the experiment, students **record** ideas about what would happen **in a science** notebook. What important part **of the** investigation are students recording **in the** notebook? **5.2(B)**

Ⓐ Conclusion

Ⓑ Hypothesis

Ⓒ Observation

Ⓓ Inference

**10** What do the processes of the **formation of** sedimentary rocks and fossil **fuels have in** common? **5.2(F)**

Ⓕ Sedimentary rocks are the **only type** of rock where fossils are **found that** produce energy.

Ⓖ Sedimentary rocks and fossil **fuels are** mixed with fossils to provide **energy.**

Ⓗ Fossil fuels and sedimentary **rocks are** burned to release energy.

Ⓙ Sedimentary rocks and fossil **fuels are** both formed over a long **period of time** with high pressure.

11 Fossil fuels such as coal, natural gas, and oil are considered nonrenewable resources because they were formed from the buried remains of plants and animals. The process that led to this formation takes a very long time, which means fossil fuels cannot be replaced in our lifetime. The pie chart below displays the energy sources used to make electricity in the U.S.

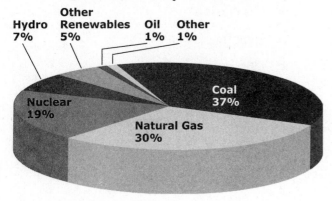

**U. S. Electricity Generation**

Which statement can be inferred from the chart? **5.2(D)**

Ⓐ About two-thirds of the electricity produced comes from the conversion of fossil fuels.

Ⓑ Electricity is used to do many jobs for people on a daily basis.

Ⓒ Coal is the only fossil fuel used to generate electricity.

Ⓓ Burning fossil fuels is harmful to the environment and causes air pollution.

12 Students have been studying fossil fuels. What is an example of conservation by using less fossil fuel resources? **5.1(B)**

Ⓕ Riding a bike instead of driving a car

Ⓖ Burning coal for heat

Ⓗ Taking a taxi to work

Ⓙ Flying in an airplane

13 A student creates a model to show how sedimentary rock is formed by placing rocks, pebbles, and soil in a jar. The student adds water to the jar, puts on the lid, and shakes the mixture. After settling, the sediment in the jar forms layers. Which describes why the layers form in the student's model? **5.3(C)**

Ⓐ The sediment particles settle with the largest at the top and the least dense at the bottom.

Ⓑ The densest particles of sediment settle at the bottom, and the smallest particles of sediment settle at the top.

Ⓒ The least dense particles settle on top, and pebbles float in the water.

Ⓓ Shaking creates a solution in which all parts are evenly mixed.

14 Some oil, a type of fossil fuel, is formed from organic matter in the ocean. The diagrams below display the process that leads to the formation of this type of fossil fuel.

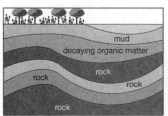
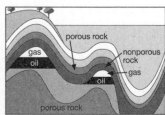

**A**       **C**

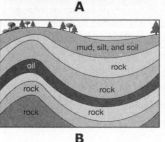
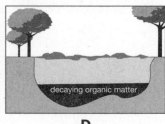

**B**       **D**

Which of the following depicts the correct order of this process? **5.2(D)**

Ⓕ D, B, A, C     Ⓗ D, A, B, C

Ⓖ B, D, A, C     Ⓙ C, B, A, D

Synthesis · Create

## A Day in the Life of a Drop

Pretend you are a drop of oil. Write a story describing your life as a drop of oil. Include details about how oil is formed, and follow the oil drop through its life until it is finally consumed by humans.

_____

_____

_____

_____

_____

_____

_____

_____

Draw pictures for a photo album showing important events in your life as an oil drop.

## Formative Assessment

How is the formation of fossil fuels similar to and different from the formation of sedimentary rocks?

_____

_____

_____

_____

_____

_____

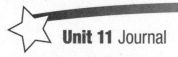

**Science Journal**

Write a letter urging someone to conserve energy by using less fossil fuels. Give reasons to support your argument.

_____

_____

_____

_____

_____

_____

_____

_____

_____

_____

_____

_____

_____

_____

_____

_____

_____

_____

_____

_____

_____

_____

_____

 motivation**science**™LEVEL 5 ©2011–2014 mentoring**minds**.com

## Science Vocabulary Builder

Describe each vocabulary word by completing the boxes below.

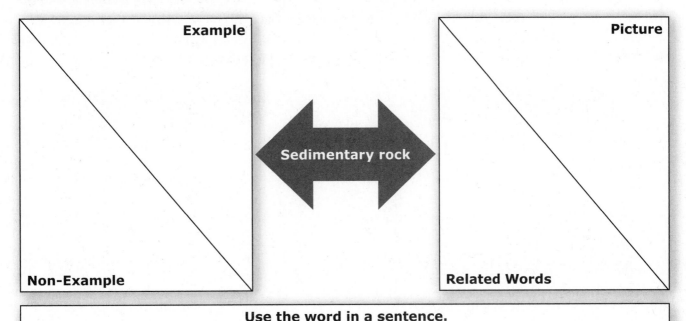

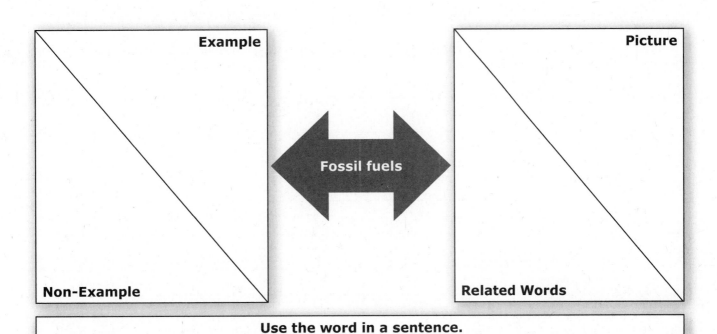

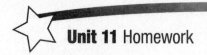

**Unit 11** Homework

### Sedimentation

Collect rocks, sand, pebbles, and soil at home. Place the rock, sand, pebble, and soil mixture in a jar, filling $\frac{1}{3}$ of the jar. Observe the jar and draw what you see in the jar below.

Add water to the jar until the container is $\frac{3}{4}$ full. Replace the lid, and carefully shake the jar. Leave the jar undisturbed for one hour. Observe the jar again, and draw what you see in the jar below.

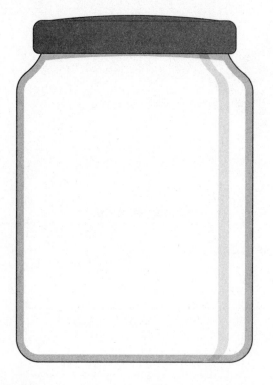

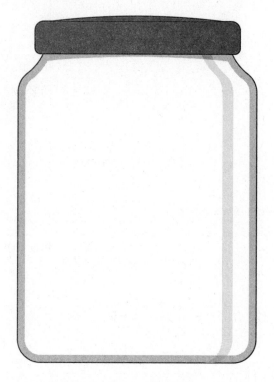

What did you discover from your investigation? Allow the jar to sit overnight. Observe again the next morning. Did any other changes occur?

_____

_____

_____

_____

_____

### Parent Activities

1. Begin a family rock collection by gathering rocks and fossils from around your neighborhood. Observe the rocks and notice their physical characteristics. Then describe their features such as texture, color, and size. Keep a record showing where the rocks were found and how they may have been formed.

2. Use research materials to identify the rocks in your collection.

**Motivation Station: Molly's Cool Science Fact**

Earth is not the only place with sand dunes.
Titan, one of Saturn's moons, has sand dunes.
So do Mars and Venus.

## After this lesson I will be able to:

- **Recognize** how landforms such as deltas, canyons, and sand dunes are the result of changes to Earth's surface by wind, water, and ice.

## Comparative Investigations

**Activity 1:** Canyon Model

1. Cut a 20-ounce foam cup in half vertically. Make a small hole near the bottom of the cup using the tip of a pencil.

2. Near the open end of the cup, create a mound with a slightly damp sand and soil mixture. Keep the mixture near the top half of the cup.

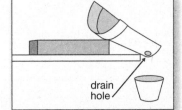

drain hole

3. Place the cup on a box with the sand mound at the top of the slope. Allow the hole near the bottom of the cup to hang over the edge of the table. Have one member of the group hold a cup beneath the hole to catch any water that drains.

4. Slowly pour 200 mL of water down the slope. Observe what happens, and record results.

5. Rebuild your mound, and conduct a second test. This time, quickly pour 200 mL of water down the slope. Observe what happens, and record results.

6. Draw and explain what happened with each investigation.

| Water poured slowly | Water poured quickly |
|---|---|
|  |  |

**Unit 12** Introduction

## Activity 2: Delta Model

1. Again, pile the sand and soil mixture at the top of the cup. If the soil is too wet, use paper towels to remove some of the excess water.

2. Add 4 drops of blue food coloring to 200 mL of water.

3. Pour the water slowly down the slope. Observe the path the water takes, and notice where the sediment deposits.

4. Draw and describe the path of the water and the location of the deposited sediment in the space below. Label the parts of the model that represent the land, river, delta, and ocean.

## Activity 3: Sand Dune Model

1. Research the five basic types of sand dunes: crescentic, linear, star, dome, and parabolic.

2. Follow the recipe below to make salt dough. Use the salt dough to create a model of one of the types of sand dunes. Place your model on a paper plate.

3. Display the models in the classroom, classifying them by type.

> **Salt Dough Recipe**
>
> 1 cup flour
> 1 cup salt
> $\frac{1}{2}$ cup water
>
> In a bowl, mix the dry ingredients. Pour in water, and mix with your hands, kneading the dough. Add more water if the dough is too dry.

4. What did you learn from creating your salt dough model? How is your model similar to a real sand dune? How is it different?

_____

_____

_____

**1** Which of the following contributes to changes on Earth's surface, creating a delta?

Ⓐ Volcanic eruptions

Ⓑ Fast moving rivers

Ⓒ Wind erosion

Ⓓ Shifting from an earthquake

**2** Which method would be the most effective to show moving water as the most important factor in forming canyons? **5.3(C)**

Ⓕ Construct a model

Ⓖ Ask questions

Ⓗ Construct a graph

Ⓙ Recycle materials

**3** All of the following questions are testable in a scientific exploration about changes to Earth's surface **EXCEPT** — **5.2(B)**

Ⓐ How can the effects of wind and water erosion be measured?

Ⓑ How does water erosion and deposition result in the construction of a delta?

Ⓒ Why does the Sun appear to move across the sky?

Ⓓ What constructive forces result in changes to Earth's surface?

**4** A student visits a beach and wants to explore how landforms, such as sand dunes, are the result of changes caused by wind. What is the best tool to use while observing these changes? **5.4(A)**

Ⓕ Graduated cylinder

Ⓖ Hand lens

Ⓗ Camera

Ⓙ Microscope

**5** Earth's surface is constantly changing. As a result of these changes, landforms such as deltas, cliffs, canyons, and sand dunes are formed. The development of these landforms is caused by all the following agents of erosion **EXCEPT** —

Ⓐ weathering

Ⓑ wind

Ⓒ water

Ⓓ waves

**6** Observe the pictures below. These pictures show a change over time.

**Before**          **After**

What agent of erosion influenced this change over time?

Ⓕ Waves          Ⓗ Water

Ⓖ Wind          Ⓙ Ice

**Unit 12** Check for Understanding

**1** Which of the following describes deposition?

Ⓐ A process by which wind or water drops sediment in a new location

Ⓑ The wearing away and breaking down of rocks caused by wind, water, and ice

Ⓒ The process in which the weight of sediment squeezes particles together and pushes out the water

Ⓓ The downward movement of water through soil and rocks as a result of gravity

**Use the image below and your knowledge of science to answer questions 2 and 3.**

**2** What landform is shown in the image?

Ⓕ Delta

Ⓖ Sand dune

Ⓗ Canyon

Ⓙ Mountain

**3** Which condition would likely be the cause of change in the landform?

Ⓐ Rain

Ⓑ Ice

Ⓒ Wind

Ⓓ Snow

**4** In an activity, students place an amount of sand in an aquarium and blow on the sand in one direction.

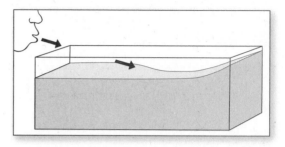

Which type of landform is being made in the activity?

Ⓕ Mountain     Ⓗ Delta

Ⓖ Dune     Ⓙ Canyon

**5** The Mississippi River deposits silt, a material made of soil and rock, at the mouth of the river. Each year the silt deposits enlarge a land mass at the mouth of the river. Which type of landform is being made by the silt deposits?

Ⓐ Canyon     Ⓒ Mountain

Ⓑ Dune     Ⓓ None of the above

**6** A class tours a cavern and sees formations like the ones shown in the picture.

Which process most likely caused these structures to form?

Ⓕ Decrease in temperature

Ⓖ Weathering by wind

Ⓗ Erosion by fast moving water

Ⓙ Deposition of minerals

## Scientific Investigation and Reasoning Skills: Questions 7–14

**7** Students take a field trip to the nearest beach to explore the formation of sand dunes. What is the best tool to use to measure the height of a sand dune? **5.4(A)**

Ⓐ
metric ruler

Ⓑ
stopwatch

Ⓒ cm 10 20 30 40 50 60 70 80 90
meter stick

Ⓓ
calculator

**8** A group of students explores the effects of wind erosion on sand dunes. The teacher instructs students to demonstrate safe practices during the experiment by — **5.4(B)**

Ⓕ using a fire extinguisher

Ⓖ using safety goggles

Ⓗ wearing open-toed shoes

Ⓙ wearing a face cover

**9** All of the statements below describe physical changes made to Earth's surface **EXCEPT** — **5.2(F)**

Ⓐ water eroding rocks on a mountainside

Ⓑ lava flowing from a volcanic explosion

Ⓒ release of carbon dioxide in the atmosphere

Ⓓ glacial ice melting due to the heat of the Sun

**10** The picture shows a river flowing through a canyon.

The change in the canyon's shape is a result of — **5.2(D)**

Ⓕ glacial erosion

Ⓖ fast moving water

Ⓗ volcanic activity

Ⓙ earthquakes

**Use your knowledge of science and the table below to answer questions 11 and 12.**

**Causes of Change**

| Landforms | ? |
|-----------|------|
| Sand dune | Wind |
| Valley | Water |
| Delta | Water |
| Canyon | Water |
| Glacier | Ice |

11  What would be the best title for the column heading marked with a question mark? **5.2(G)**

   Ⓐ  Physical Changes

   Ⓑ  Agents of Erosion

   Ⓒ  States of Matter

   Ⓓ  Evidence of Nature

12  What conclusion can be made based on the information given in the table above? **5.2(F)**

   Ⓕ  Wind, water, and ice are forces that change Earth's surface.

   Ⓖ  Landforms are the result of the temperature change of water on Earth's surface.

   Ⓗ  Physical changes to Earth's surface take a long time.

   Ⓙ  Earth's surface is no longer changing because of wind, water, and ice.

13  Models are used to help students understand observations and to visualize processes that cannot easily be seen. One limitation of using a model of a delta is — **5.3(C)**

   Ⓐ  a model helps to better understand the formation process

   Ⓑ  the effects of erosion can be seen using a model

   Ⓒ  a model helps to visualize how a delta is formed

   Ⓓ  a model only partially represents something much larger

14  A group of scientists researches a glacier. Which of these statements made by the researchers is **NOT** empirical evidence? **5.3(A)**

   Ⓕ  The glacier is retreating at a rate of 5 cm per year.

   Ⓖ  The glacier feels cold.

   Ⓗ  The glacier measures 54 km long.

   Ⓙ  The glacial ice measures 0°C.

### Field Trip–Glacier National Park

Take an electronic field trip to Glacier National Park by visiting the websites below:

- *http://www.nationalparkreservations.com/info/glacier/photogallery.php*

- *http://www.nationalparkreservations.com/info/glacier/*

After visiting the websites, create a postcard to send to a friend. Illustrate the front of the postcard to represent Glacier National Park. On the back of the card, write a letter describing Glacier National Park and comparing landforms there to others you have seen.

To _____

From _____

_____

_____

_____

_____

_____

_____

### Formative Assessment

Stalactites, stalagmites, flowstones, soda straws, and columns are cave formations. Explain the processes that result in the creation of cave formations.

_____

_____

_____

_____

_____

_____

Name _____

**Science Journal**

What would you do if you were lost in a canyon? Create a story about getting lost on a canyon adventure. Include a description of features in the canyon.

_____

_____

_____

_____

_____

_____

_____

_____

_____

_____

_____

_____

_____

_____

_____

_____

_____

_____

_____

_____

_____

 motivation**science**™LEVEL 5

**Science Vocabulary Builder**

Create a drawing of the landforms. Then, describe the landforms, and list examples of each.

## Landforms

| Illustration | Description | Examples |
|---|---|---|
| Sand dune | | |
| Delta | | |
| Canyon | | |

## Unit 12 Homework

### Landforms

Create a list of the different landforms in and around the area in which you live. What is the most common landform found in your area? What is the largest landform known in your area? Which landform is the smallest?

Design a map showing the landforms in your area and where they are located. Include a compass rose on your map. Create map symbols to represent landforms. Color and label the parts of the map. Give the map a title.

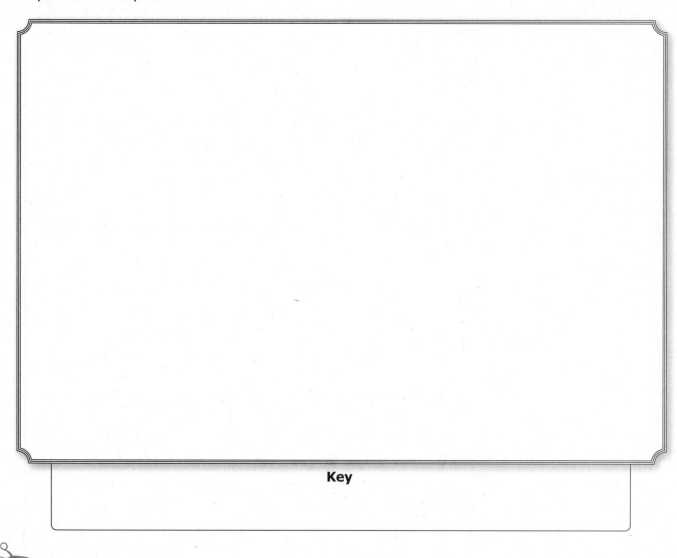

**Key**

---

### Parent Activities

1. Help your child brainstorm the landforms around your area.

2. Talk about the landforms, and discuss how they look, where they are located, and how they may have been formed.

3. Visit a landform for a close-up view of how it looks. If unable to visit a landform, research landforms on the Internet, and browse pictures and information.

 motivation**science**™ LEVEL 5

**After this lesson I will be able to:**

- **Identify** alternative energy resources, such as wind, solar, hydroelectric, geothermal, and biofuels.

## Experimental and Descriptive Investigations

**Activity:** The Power of Energy

Travel to each station, read the station directions, and complete each activity to collect data and investigate the power of energy.

**Station 1:** Solar Power

1. Fill a black cooking pan with 2 cm of water. Take the temperature of the water and record below.

2. Place the pan in a sunny place so that the Sun is directly over the container. Record the temperature of the water every 10 minutes.

3. Calculate and record the changes in temperature. Be sure to use the Celsius scale.

| | |
|---|---|
| **Beginning temperature of water** | |
| **Temperature after 10 minutes** | |
| **Temperature after 20 minutes** | |
| **Temperature after 30 minutes** | |

4. Look at the data. What did you learn about collecting solar energy?

_____

_____

_____

_____

**Station 2:** Wind/Hydroelectric Power

Read and discuss the books and printed material on wind power and hydroelectric energy at your station, and answer the questions below. Report your findings to your group.

1. Where does the wind get its energy?_____

2. Why is hydropower considered renewable?_____

_____

3. What are the advantages and disadvantages of using wind energy?

_____

_____

4. What are the advantages and disadvantages of using hydroelectric energy?

_____

_____

**Station 3:** Biofuel Power

1. Empty one packet of yeast in the plastic bottle. Add 50 mL of corn syrup (corn syrup is made from the sugars inside corn). Add warm water to the bottle so it is half full. Twist on the lid. Shake the bottle to mix. Take off the lid, quickly replacing it with a balloon. Observe changes, and measure the size of the balloon using yarn. Record your measurement in centimeters.

2. Draw a picture of your observation.

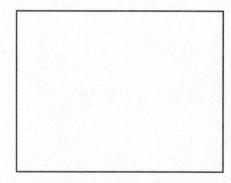

**Station 4:** Geothermal Power

Read and discuss the books and printed information on geothermal energy, and answer the questions below. Report your findings to your group.

1. Why is geothermal energy considered to be clean energy?

_____

_____

2. What are the advantages and disadvantages of this alternative source?

_____

_____

**1** Hydroelectric, geothermal, and biofuel energy are all renewable sources of energy. They are called renewable because they —

Ⓐ can be converted directly into heat and electricity

Ⓑ are clean and cost effective

Ⓒ do not produce air pollutants

Ⓓ can be replenished in a short period of time

**2** Which energy source is considered nonrenewable?

Ⓕ Biofuel

Ⓗ Solar

Ⓖ Natural gas

Ⓙ Hydropower

**3** The diagram below shows a dam and power plant.

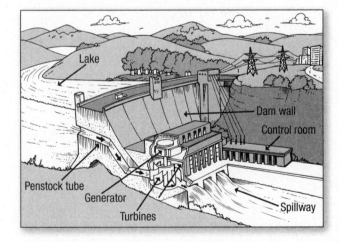

What is one positive impact of this electric power plant on the environment?

Ⓐ Obstructs the migration of fish

Ⓑ Produces electricity without polluting the air

Ⓒ Changes the natural water temperatures

Ⓓ Causes the relocation of animals and people

**4** What is an advantage of using wind to produce electricity?   **5.1(B)**

Ⓕ Pollutants are emitted into the atmosphere.

Ⓖ It is cost effective over time.

Ⓗ Oil spills may occur.

Ⓙ The local ecosystem may be disrupted.

**5** What is one disadvantage of using wind energy rather than burning coal to produce electricity?   **5.1(B)**

Ⓐ The power it produces is economical.

Ⓑ Wind energy can be converted directly into electricity.

Ⓒ The turbines are too large.

Ⓓ It does not cause pollution.

**6** Geothermal energy is considered a renewable resource because it —

Ⓕ is heated water

Ⓖ is used to heat buildings

Ⓗ is made of natural gas

Ⓙ is continually produced inside Earth

motivation**science**™LEVEL 5 **145**

**Unit 13** Check for Understanding

1  Biofuel is an energy resource that is advantageous because it causes less pollution. Biofuels come from —

Ⓐ  rocks that have been changed by heat and pressure

Ⓑ  plants and animals

Ⓒ  geothermal energy

Ⓓ  hydroelectric energy

2  Which of the following is **NOT** an example of an alternative energy resource?

Ⓕ  Biofuel

Ⓖ  Wind

Ⓗ  Petroleum

Ⓙ  Solar

3  Energy derived from the Sun is called —

Ⓐ  hydroelectric energy

Ⓑ  geothermal energy

Ⓒ  solar energy

Ⓓ  biofuel energy

4  Which of the following describes hydroelectric power?

Ⓕ  Energy created by moving water

Ⓖ  Fuel formed by biological materials

Ⓗ  Energy that uses the Sun's rays to produce power

Ⓙ  Energy produced by moving air

5  Which of the following best explains the energy created from a geyser?

Ⓐ  It is hydroelectric energy created by water power.

Ⓑ  It is a biofuel formed from biological raw materials.

Ⓒ  It is energy from the Sun.

Ⓓ  It is geothermal energy powered from heat within Earth.

6  An option used for powering cars as an alternative to fossil fuels is —

Ⓕ  geothermal energy

Ⓖ  hydroelectric energy

Ⓗ  petroleum

Ⓙ  biofuel

 motivation**science**™LEVEL 5

## Scientific Investigation and Reasoning Skills: Questions 7–14

**Use the diagram below and your knowledge of science to answer questions 7 and 8.**

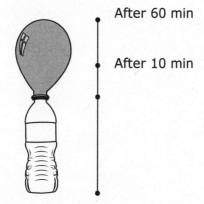

After 60 min

After 10 min

Key: 1 cm = 10 cm

Students explore ethanol as a type of biofuel made from plants to see how much energy can be produced. They construct a model using active yeast, warm water, and corn syrup. They record the height of the balloon after 10 minutes and after 60 minutes.

**7** What is the difference in the height of the balloon after 10 minutes and the height of the balloon after 60 minutes? **5.2(C)**

  Ⓐ  5 cm

  Ⓑ  10 cm

  Ⓒ  25 cm

  Ⓓ  15 cm

**8** How can students test the reliability of the biofuel experiment? **5.2(E)**

  Ⓕ  Use flour instead of corn syrup

  Ⓖ  Wear safety goggles

  Ⓗ  Wait for the teacher's instructions

  Ⓙ  Repeat the investigation

**9** The choices we make about how we use energy — **5.1(B)**

  Ⓐ  cause fossil fuels to be replenished

  Ⓑ  affect only those who use the energy

  Ⓒ  impact our environment and our lives

  Ⓓ  result in higher gas prices

**10** What science tools are necessary to explore solar energy production? **5.4(A)**

  Ⓕ  Goggles, science journal, collecting net

  Ⓖ  Ruler, thermometer, sound recorder

  Ⓗ  Timer, thermometer, science journal

  Ⓙ  Goggles, timer, magnet

**Unit 13** Check for Understanding

**11** Which two sources complete the table below? **5.2(D)**

### Resources

| Renewable | Nonrenewable |
|---|---|
| Geothermal | Coal |
| Hydroelectric | Natural gas |
| ? | ? |
| Biofuel | Fossil fuel |

Ⓐ Water, Minerals

Ⓑ Oil, Solar

Ⓒ Aluminum, Minerals

Ⓓ Soil, Geothermal

**12** Which action below would **NOT** be considered an act of energy conservation? **5.1(B)**

Ⓕ Turning the lights off when not in use

Ⓖ Using petroleum oil for gasoline in cars

Ⓗ Recycling aluminum cans

Ⓙ Turning machines off when not in use

**13** Thomas Edison is most famous for creating a longer lasting lightbulb. Edison also built the first power plant. What type of energy did the power plant generate? **5.3(D)**

Ⓐ Light

Ⓑ Heat

Ⓒ Electricity

Ⓓ None of the above

**14** According to the advertisement below, what can we infer is the primary advantage of using solar energy? **5.3(B)**

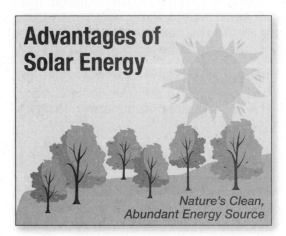

Ⓕ It is plentiful.

Ⓖ It is manmade.

Ⓗ It produces air pollutants.

Ⓙ It cannot be replenished.

 motivation**science**™LEVEL 5

## Which Form of Energy is Best?

Explore the advantages and disadvantages of alternative energy resources. Research the areas of hydroelectric, geothermal, wind, solar, and biofuels, and analyze the pros and cons of each. Present your campaign in a power point presentation.

• Identify your chosen alternative energy source.

• Describe the advantages and disadvantages of your chosen source.

• Participate in a debate to present your case.

• Judge each presentation, and take a class vote to decide which group was most persuasive.

Use the space below to plan your argument and to design your power point presentation.

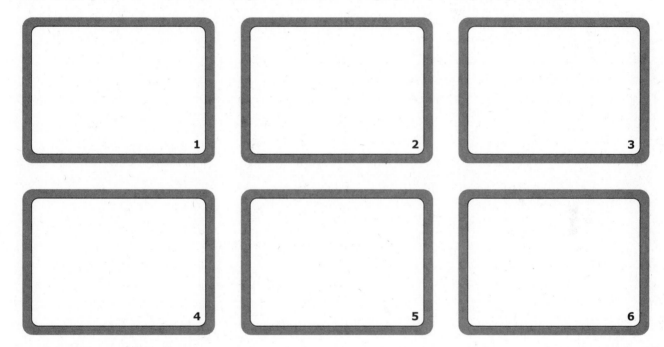

## Formative Assessment

Complete the following statement. Explain why you feel it is the most important point to remember.

*The most important point to remember about alternative energy is —*

_____

_____

_____

_____

**Science Journal**

Write a letter to someone explaining why it is important to use alternative energy resources. Be sure to explain the advantages of using alternative energy.

_____

_____

_____

_____

_____

_____

_____

_____

_____

_____

_____

_____

_____

_____

_____

_____

_____

_____

_____

_____

_____

_____

_____

_____

## Science Vocabulary Builder

Using the vocabulary words write a word in the first section. Next, write the definition of the word. In the third column, write a sentence using the vocabulary word. In the final column, draw a picture that represents the word.

| wind | solar | hydroelectric | geothermal | biofuels |
|------|-------|---------------|------------|----------|

| Word | Definition | Sentence | Picture |
|------|------------|----------|---------|
|      |            |          |         |
|      |            |          |         |
|      |            |          |         |
|      |            |          |         |
|      |            |          |         |

**Resource Use**

We use energy every day. Make a list of the types of energy you used today. Put each energy type in the appropriate category: nonrenewable resources, alternative energy resources, or not sure.

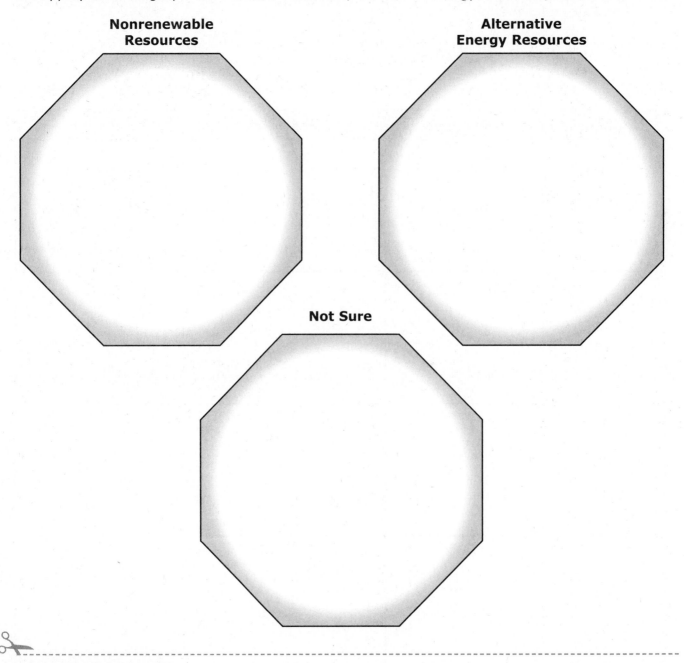

**Nonrenewable Resources**

**Alternative Energy Resources**

**Not Sure**

✂ - - - - - - - - - - - - - - - - - - - - - - - - - - - - - - - - - - - - - - - - - - - - - - - - - - - - - - - - - -

**Parent Activities**

1. Talk with your child about the importance of saving energy.

2. Create new ideas to save energy at home, such as turning off lights when not in use, opening the windows instead of using the air conditioner, or using sunlight during the day as an alternative to lights.

3. Discuss ways to use alternative energy resources at home.

**Motivation Station: Molly's Cool Science Fact**

The fossil of a bone does not have any bone in it.
A fossilized object has the same shape as
the original object, but the organic matter
has been replaced with minerals.

**After this lesson I will be able to:**

- **Identify** fossils as evidence of past living organisms and the nature of the environments at the time using models.

## Comparative Investigations

### Activity 1: Finding Fossils

Paleontologists are scientists who study fossils. In order to recover fossils, they use special tools to clear dust, dirt, and other particles. Use the tools provided to find fossils in the containers of sand. Record the findings on the chart.

**Fossil Identification Chart**

| Fossil | Special Characteristics | How could the organism have looked before fossilization? | Possible Environment |
|--------|------------------------|----------------------------------------------------------|----------------------|
| 1. | | | |
| 2. | | | |
| 3. | | | |
| 4. | | | |
| 5. | | | |

## **Activity 2:** Make a Fossil

1. Use scissors to cut the top off a milk carton.

2. Put one cup plaster of paris into the carton. Add one-fourth cup water and stir with a craft stick to mix.

3. Pick a shell or other object to use for your fossil. Coat the object with a light layer of petroleum jelly.

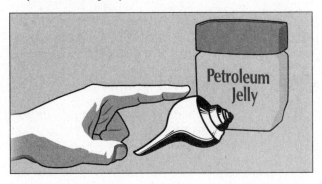

4. Place the shell on top of the plaster mixture. Press down gently to set the shell in the plaster. Allow the plaster to set, then remove the shell and observe.

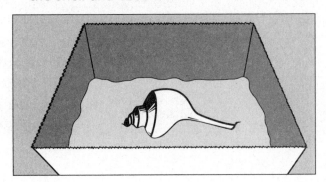

## **Answer the questions below.**

What is a fossil?_____

_____

What can we learn about the past from studying fossils?_____

_____

_____

How is the model you created similar and different from real fossils?_____

_____

_____

Is your model fossil a mold or cast fossil? Explain. _____

_____

_____

**1** During a museum field trip, students observe the fossil remains of a woolly mammoth. The sign next to the fossil remains is below:

---
**Woolly Mammoth**
(lived 1.65 million years to 10,000 years ago)

- Hairy coat, 3 feet long in places
- Thick layer of wool next to the skin
- Up to 4 inches of fat beneath the skin
- Small ears and a short tail
---

Based on the information on the sign, in which type of environment did the woolly mammoth live?

Ⓐ Very hot and dry

Ⓑ Wet and humid

Ⓒ Warm and sunny

Ⓓ Cold and snowy

**2** In 1970, fossil remains of a Tyrannosaurus Rex were found in Big Bend National Park. The Tyrannosaurus Rex fossils included part of an upper jaw and some very sharp teeth. Which conclusion is best supported by the discovery of these fossils?

Ⓕ The Tyrannosaurus Rex fossils were carried to Big Bend by a river.

Ⓖ The Tyrannosaurus Rex became extinct because Big Bend was uninhabitable.

Ⓗ The Tyrannosaurus Rex ate animals that were living in Big Bend.

Ⓙ The Tyrannosaurus Rex ate plants that were native to Big Bend.

**3** Which of the following would be the best to use when gathering information to identify fossils as evidence of past living organisms? **5.4(A)**

Ⓐ Terrarium      Ⓒ Computer

Ⓑ Microscope     Ⓓ Collecting net

**4** Marine geologists conduct field investigations to collect samples of fossils such as those pictured below.

Based on the information in the pictures, what conclusion can be made about marine fossils and their environment? **5.3(D)**

Ⓕ They were animals that lived in caves.

Ⓖ They were plants that lived in caves.

Ⓗ They were plants that lived in the sea.

Ⓙ They were animals that lived in the sea.

**5** Students compare the fossils shown in layer A with those in layer C.

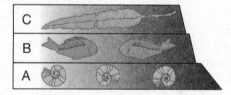

What conclusion can be made by comparing the fossils in these two layers?

Ⓐ Fossils in layer A are younger than those in layer C.

Ⓑ Fossils in layers A and C are the same age.

Ⓒ Fossils in layer A are older than those in layer C.

Ⓓ Fossils in layers A and C are younger than those in layer B.

**6** Fossils are found in which of the following?

Ⓕ Seashells

Ⓖ Sedimentary rocks

Ⓗ Igneous rocks

Ⓙ Metamorphic rocks

**Unit 14** Check for Understanding

**1** All of the following are very helpful when identifying evidence of past living plants **EXCEPT** —

Ⓐ a fossil of a plant from long ago which has now changed to stone

Ⓑ an impression left by a plant that lived a very long time ago

Ⓒ the remains of the plant replaced with minerals

Ⓓ a rock from the mantle, located deep underneath Earth's surface

**Use the information below and your knowledge of science to answer questions 2 and 3.**

> **Mineral Fossilization**
>
> When an organism dies and becomes buried in sediment, mineral fossilization may occur. Soft parts of the organism decay quickly, while hard parts, such as bones, take more time. As water seeps through the sediment and bone, minerals in the water begin to replace the cells in the bone. It eventually turns into stone.

**2** What type of conditions must be present for mineral fossilization to occur?

Ⓕ Wet climate     Ⓗ Dry climate

Ⓖ Windy climate     Ⓙ Hot climate

**3** Can mineral fossilization occur without the presence of water?

Ⓐ Yes, because as long as the organism is buried, it can become fossilized.

Ⓑ Yes, because the water will eventually evaporate.

Ⓒ No, because the water replaces cells in the bone and is a factor in mineral fossilization.

Ⓓ No, because water is the only factor needed in order for an organism to become fossilized.

**4** Students are creating models of fossils during science class. Which explains why scientists study fossils?

Ⓕ Fossils help predict climate changes.

Ⓖ Fossils help keep species from becoming extinct.

Ⓗ Fossils help understand about past organisms and their environments.

Ⓙ Fossils help understand what to expect in the future.

**5** An ancient fossil of a fish is found in a dry area. What does this suggest about how this area used to look?

Ⓐ The land was a dense forest.

Ⓑ The land was a dry desert.

Ⓒ There was once water in the area.

Ⓓ The fossil was moved because there could not have been water there in the past.

**6** When examining sedimentary rock layers to better understand the nature of a fossil's environment, which layer is considered to have evidence of the oldest past living organisms?

Ⓕ The top layer of rock

Ⓖ The middle layer of rock

Ⓗ The bottom layer of rock

Ⓙ All of the above

## Scientific Investigation and Reasoning Skills: Questions 7–14

**7** Which of the following would be best to use when identifying various fossils? **5.2(B)**

Ⓐ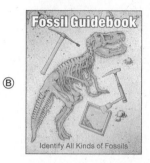

Ⓑ
Fossil Guidebook
Identify All Kinds of Fossils

Ⓒ

Ⓓ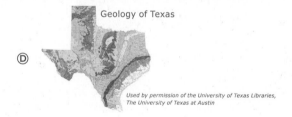
Geology of Texas

Used by permission of the University of Texas Libraries, The University of Texas at Austin

**8** After studying about fossils, a student said, "I want to be a paleontologist when I grow up." Which describes the work of a paleontologist? **5.3(D)**

Ⓕ A paleontologist studies the remains of organisms that have been fossilized.

Ⓖ A paleontologist studies cultures of the past.

Ⓗ A paleontologist is a park ranger.

Ⓙ A paleontologist is a scientist who studies living things.

**9** Students record data to determine if the objects they collect are fossils. They create a table to organize their data. They place an X in the correct column to show whether each item is a fossil.

| Object | Fossil | Not a Fossil |
|---|---|---|
| Seashell found on beach | | |
| Petrified wood | | |
| Imprint of leaf in mud | | |
| Dog's footprint | | |
| Bone turned to stone | | |

Which two items can be marked with an X under the column labeled "Fossil"? **5.2(G)**

Ⓐ Seashell found on beach and bone turned to stone

Ⓑ Petrified wood and bone turned to stone

Ⓒ Imprint of leaf in mud and dog's footprint

Ⓓ Petrified wood and seashell found on beach

**10** After studying fossils, a student makes the following conclusion, "Fossils help us understand past environments." Is the student's conclusion valid? **5.2(F)**

Ⓕ Yes, because fossils are remains of plants and animals of the past.

Ⓖ Yes, because fossils can no longer be formed.

Ⓗ No, because fossils do not give us a clue about past environments.

Ⓙ No, because fossils can no longer be found.

**11** "Most living things that die become fossils." This hypothesis was formulated before learning about fossils. Is it accurate?  **5.3(A)**

Ⓐ Yes, because many fossils have been found.

Ⓑ Yes, because fossils can be easily formed.

Ⓒ No, because certain conditions need to be present in order for fossils to form.

Ⓓ No, because no living things that die become fossils.

**12** Fossil remains of the Stegosaurus have been found in:

- Utah, Wyoming, and Colorado
- Southern India
- Western Europe
- China
- Southern Africa

Which conclusion can be made based on the locations of these fossils?  **5.2(F)**

Ⓕ The locations of these fossil findings once had very similar climates.

Ⓖ The Stegosaurus did not have a long life span.

Ⓗ The Stegosaurus was a plant-eating dinosaur.

Ⓙ The locations of these fossil findings once were under water.

**13** The Permian Basin in West Texas has a dry and hot climate. Fusulinid fossils, like the one pictured, have been found in the Permian Basin. Fusulinids were small saltwater organisms.

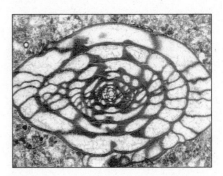

Which conclusion can best be made from the discovery of the Fusulinid fossils?  **5.2(F)**

Ⓐ Fusulinids used to live in dry, desert-like areas.

Ⓑ The Permian Basin used to be covered by water.

Ⓒ Fusulinids used to live in the ground.

Ⓓ The Permian Basin has always been dry and hot.

**14** Students are given instructions to identify and compare fossils. They are also given the data collected by the previous class. The teacher asks the students to check the accuracy of the data collected by the previous class. How can the students check the accuracy of the data collected by the previous class?  **5.2(E)**

Ⓕ Graph the data previously collected

Ⓖ Repeat the investigation using the same instructions, and compare the data

Ⓗ Change the instructions, and start a new investigation

Ⓙ Formulate a new hypothesis

## Geologic Timeline

Research each geologic era to learn the organisms that lived at the time. Create a pictorial timeline by drawing pictures of organisms for each geological period. Use the completed timeline when identifying pictures of fossils or real fossils to learn when the organism lived and what the environment was like at the time.

| Millions of Years Ago | Era | Period | Organisms |
|---|---|---|---|
| 1.8 | Cenozoic | Quaternary | |
| 50 | Cenozoic | Tertiary | |
| 100 | Mesozoic | Cretaceous | |
| 150 | Mesozoic | Jurassic | |
| 200 | Mesozoic | Triassic | |
| 250 | Paleozoic | Permian | |
| 300 | Paleozoic | Carboniferous | |
| 350 | Paleozoic | Devonian | |
| 400 | Paleozoic | Silurian | |
| 450 | Paleozoic | Ordovician | |
| 500 | Paleozoic | Cambrian | |

## Formative Assessment

Give examples of fossil clues that can be used as evidence to determine the nature of an organism's environment.

_____

_____

_____

_____

_____

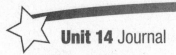

**Science Journal**

Imagine you are a paleontologist who recently discovered an unknown fossil. Create illustrations of the fossil and how the organism looked when it was alive. Name the organism, and identify the geological period in which the creature lived.

**Fossil**

**Organism**

_____

_____

_____

_____

_____

_____

_____

_____

_____

_____

_____

_____

_____

## Science Vocabulary Builder

Research the following words, describe their meanings, and give examples of each.

| Fossilization | |
|---|---|
| Definition | Examples |
|  |  |

| Fossil | |
|---|---|
| Definition | Examples |
|  |  |

| Evidence | |
|---|---|
| Definition | Examples |
|  |  |

| Paleontologist | |
|---|---|
| Definition | Examples |
|  |  |

| Model | |
|---|---|
| Definition | Examples |
|  |  |

| Environment | |
|---|---|
| Definition | Examples |
|  |  |

## Unit 14 Homework

### Fossil Fun

Look at the fossil shown below. Use your imagination to create a story of how the fossil was formed. Include the age of the fossil, the type of organism, and what life was like when the creature was alive.

_____

_____

_____

_____

_____

_____

_____

_____

✂ - - - - - - - - - - - - - - - - - - - - - - - - - - - - - - - - - - - - - - - - - -

### Parent Activities

1. Go on a hunt for fossils around your neighborhood, a park, or any other place which may have fossils from long ago.

2. Discuss the fossils found and decide where they came from, how they were created, and how old they are. If no fossils are found, talk about why there may not be any fossils found around your area.

3. Discuss how fossils can help us understand the past environment.

4. Visit a museum to view fossils from long ago.

    motivation**science**™ LEVEL 5    ©2011–2014 mentoring**minds**.com

**Motivation Station: Mike's Cool Science Fact**

The coldest temperature ever recorded in Texas was February 8, 1933, in Seminole, when temperatures dropped to –30.6°C (–23°F). The highest temperature recorded was August 12, 1936, in Seymour. The temperature was 48.9°C (120°F).

**After this lesson I will be able to:**

- **Differentiate** between weather and climate.

## Comparative Investigations

**Activity 1:** Weather

Idioms are expressions that mean something completely different than the actual meanings of the words. For example, when someone says "It's raining cats and dogs," it is not really raining cats and dogs, but raining heavily.

Illustrate the weather-related idioms in the table below.

| Idiom | Meaning of Expression | Illustration |
|---|---|---|
| You are a ray of sunshine! | | |
| Don't try to steal my thunder! | | |
| That test was a breeze! | | |
| Don't rain on my parade! | | |
| As fast as lightning! | | |

## Activity 2: Climate

Research the climate for each of the continents. Use the table to record climates for each continent. On the map, label each continent and color each area to represent the climate type. Create a key for the map showing what each color represents. Include a compass rose on the map.

| Location | Description of Climate |
|---|---|
| North America | |
| South America | |
| Europe | |
| Asia | |
| Australia | |
| Africa | |
| Antarctica | |

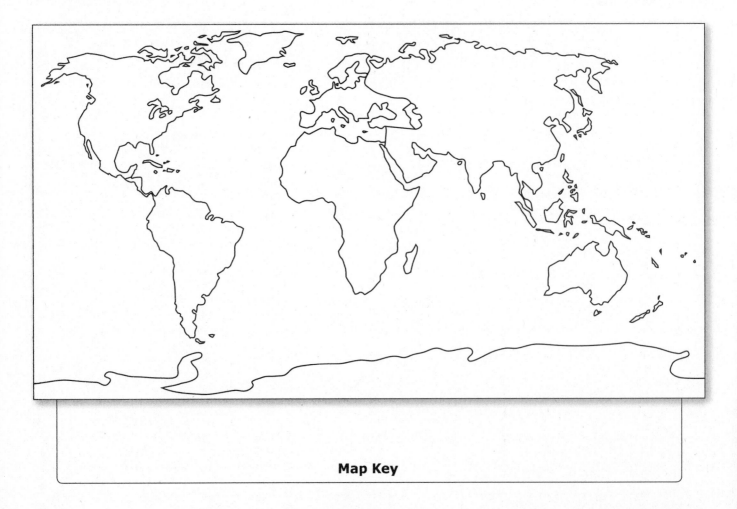

**Map Key**

**1** A sudden change in temperature can affect current weather conditions in a specific area, whereas changes in average weather conditions over a long period of time result in the area's —

Ⓐ precipitation  Ⓒ air mass

Ⓑ climate  Ⓓ global warming

**2** One vital piece of weather information scientists collect, record, and analyze is the amount of precipitation an area receives over an extended period of time. This information is used to determine long-term climate patterns within specific biomes. The tool most likely used to measure precipitation is a — **5.4(A)**

Ⓕ thermometer

Ⓖ triple beam balance

Ⓗ rain gauge

Ⓙ calculator

**3** Students observe that there are recognizable patterns in the natural world. To better understand this concept, one group observes and records information on their area's current weather conditions, while another group researches the climate of the region in which they live. Which of the following questions can best be answered from the contributions of both groups' investigations? **5.2(B)**

Ⓐ What conclusion can be made when comparing the climate of two different regions?

Ⓑ What tools and methods should be used to conduct this investigation?

Ⓒ What is the difference between climate and weather?

Ⓓ How valid is the information collected on weather and climate?

**4** Meteorologists are scientists who study patterns of change in temperature, precipitation, humidity, and air pressure. Time is spent collecting and recording data to analyze long-term patterns as well as to make predictions of future conditions of the local area. Which of the following are meteorologists investigating to determine average patterns, such as those mentioned above, over a long period of time? **5.3(D)**

Ⓕ Climate

Ⓖ Temperature changes

Ⓗ Weather

Ⓙ Hurricanes

**5** A student examines the temperature and precipitation on a given day using a thermometer and a rain gauge. The student is measuring —

Ⓐ temperature only

Ⓑ climate only

Ⓒ wind speed only

Ⓓ specific weather conditions

**6** One fall day, students discuss the decrease in the temperature and how it affects the school's decision of allowing recess. As the discussion of the outside conditions continues, students voice dissatisfaction for the long winter months they will experience in their region. Through the discussion, it can be concluded that —

Ⓕ students will have recess every day this winter

Ⓖ students can differentiate between climate and weather

Ⓗ students are satisfied with the "no recess" rule

Ⓙ students know complaining about not getting recess will change the school policy

**1** The average monthly rainfall in the Sahara Desert is 1 cm, and the average monthly temperature is 35°C. Which statement correctly describes the Sahara Desert?

Ⓐ The Sahara Desert has a cold, dry climate.

Ⓑ The Sahara Desert has a hot, dry climate.

Ⓒ The Sahara Desert has hot, dry weather every day.

Ⓓ The Sahara Desert has cold, dry weather every day.

**2** Which pair of states is most likely to have a similar climate?

Ⓕ Oregon and Arizona

Ⓖ Virginia and North Dakota

Ⓗ Ohio and Florida

Ⓙ Kansas and Missouri

**3** Which statement is related to climate?

Ⓐ The temperature has never dropped below 0°C in April.

Ⓑ The barometric pressure is high today.

Ⓒ The sky is dark and cloudy.

Ⓓ There is a severe thunderstorm warning for the Dallas area.

**4** In an activity, students look at different climatic regions of the United States to determine what types of plants will grow in certain regions. One group chooses to look at a region with heavy annual rainfall and an average annual temperature of 18°C. Which plant could best be grown in that climatic region?

Ⓕ A plant that needs constant sunlight and no watering

Ⓖ A plant that needs constant sunlight and heat

Ⓗ A plant that needs partial shade and little watering

Ⓙ A plant that needs lots of rain and mild air temperatures

**5** Which statement below best describes weather?

Ⓐ Weather is the average temperature of an area over several years.

Ⓑ Weather is recorded yearly.

Ⓒ Weather changes and is recorded daily.

Ⓓ Weather cannot be predicted.

**6** What is the difference between weather and climate?

Ⓕ Weather is measured over a period of years, and climate changes daily.

Ⓖ Weather changes daily and can be predicted, but climate cannot ever be predicted.

Ⓗ Weather cannot be predicted, but climate is certain.

Ⓙ Weather conditions describe how the air feels outside daily; climate is the average weather of an area measured over several years.

motivation**science**™LEVEL 5

Name _____

Supporting Standard 5.8(A)

## Scientific Investigation and Reasoning Skills: Questions 7–14

**Use the graph below and your knowledge of science to answer questions 7 and 8.**

**August Rainfall Over a Five-Year Period**

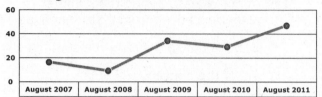

**7** The graph above represents the relationship of data collected and recorded over a 5-year period in the month of August. What does the amount of rainfall in August 2011 represent? **5.2(G)**

Ⓐ A specific weather condition for August 2011

Ⓑ The daily climate in August 2011

Ⓒ The amount of humidity for August 2011

Ⓓ A decrease in precipitation for August 2011

**8** How did the amount of rainfall compare in August 2007 and August 2011? **5.2(G)**

Ⓕ The rainfall in 2007 was greater than in 2011.

Ⓖ More precipitation fell in 2011 than in 2007.

Ⓗ Rainfall totals in both years were the same.

Ⓙ An increase in precipitation can be expected in 2012.

**9** Meteorologists are scientists who study weather conditions and climate patterns so they can prepare people for upcoming changes in the weather. The meteorologist's ability to forecast changes in the weather is the same as — **5.3(D)**

Ⓐ stating a fact

Ⓑ conducting an investigation

Ⓒ making predictions

Ⓓ explaining safety precautions

**10** Students explore the uses of different tools for measuring different types of weather, such as air pressure and precipitation. Which tool pictured below is used to measure the outside temperature? **5.4(A)**

Ⓕ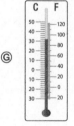

Ⓖ

Ⓗ

Ⓙ

**Unit 15** Check for Understanding

**Use your knowledge of science and the map below to answer the following question.**

**11** The process of the water cycle causes water to evaporate from Earth's lakes, condense, and then fall back to Earth as precipitation. Because of this process, water from Lake Ontario and Lake Erie may one day fall back to Earth as rain in Pennsylvania and New York. Rain falling to Earth after a clear, sunny morning is an example of — **5.2(G)**

Ⓐ a wind speed

Ⓑ a climate pattern

Ⓒ a change in weather

Ⓓ a warming trend

**12** Which of the following maps is best for analyzing changes in climatic patterns of diverse ecosystems? **5.2(D)**

Ⓕ A map that shows the climate zones for the continental United States

Ⓖ A map that shows the climate zones for different regions around the world

Ⓗ A map that shows the local weather information of a specific area

Ⓙ A map that shows the locations of mountains and oceans

**13** A student makes the observation, "The temperature is always hotter during the summer." What can you conclude from this statement? **5.2(F)**

Ⓐ The weather is always the same during the summer.

Ⓑ A hot climate during the summer is experienced where the student lives.

Ⓒ It does not rain during the summer.

Ⓓ All of the above

**14** Based on the information in the table, which month will most likely have the best weather conditions to plan a picnic at the park? **5.2(D)**

**Average Weather Conditions**

| Weather | March | May | June | November |
|---|---|---|---|---|
| Days with precipitation | 13 | 8 | 4 | 10 |
| Days without precipitation | 18 | 23 | 26 | 20 |

Ⓕ March

Ⓖ May

Ⓗ June

Ⓙ November

 motivation**science**™ LEVEL 5

## Classifying Events

In the chart, classify events that occur over days, months, years, and decades.
An example is done for you.

| Days | Months | Years | Decades |
|---|---|---|---|
| Sun rises and sets | Moon phases | Earth revolves around the Sun | A tree grows |

Where would weather changes fit in this table? Why?

_____

_____

_____

Where would you place climate changes? Why?

_____

_____

_____

## Formative Assessment

How do people use weather predictions and climate patterns to make decisions?

_____

_____

_____

_____

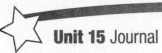

**Science Journal**

What are the differences between weather and climate? How are they similar?
Give examples of each.

_____

_____

_____

_____

_____

_____

_____

_____

_____

_____

_____

_____

_____

_____

_____

_____

_____

_____

_____

_____

_____

_____

 motivation**science**™LEVEL 5

**Science Vocabulary Builder**

Create riddles to describe each weather condition. Take turns reading the riddles with a partner and guessing the weather vocabulary terms.

**Riddles**

Wind

Atmosphere

Precipitation

Weather

Climate

Troposphere

## What's the Difference?

What is typical weather for the current season? Predict the weather for five days. Use your knowledge of the climate to make the predictions.

| Day of Week | Monday | Tuesday | Wednesday | Thursday | Friday |
|---|---|---|---|---|---|
| Temperature | | | | | |
| Weather conditions | | | | | |

Record the weather for five days. Include weather conditions such as precipitation, temperature, wind conditions, humidity, and cloud cover.

| Day | Weather |
|---|---|
| Monday | |
| Tuesday | |
| Wednesday | |
| Thursday | |
| Friday | |

In what season was the weather recorded?

_____

Were your predictions correct?

_____

Do meteorologists always predict the weather correctly? Explain your answer.

_____

✂- - - - - - - - - - - - - - - - - - - - - - - - - - - - - - - - - - - - - - - - - - - - - - - - - - - - - - -

## Parent Activities

1. Research the weather forecast with your child, and discuss why predictions are not always accurate.
2. Discuss the importance of tracking the weather and how meteorologists can help keep us safe.

**Motivation Station: Molly's Cool Science Fact**

99% of the available water on Earth is unavailable to humans for daily use. About 97% of Earth's water supply is found in oceans. Another 2% is frozen in icecaps and glaciers. That leaves only 1% fresh ground water for people and animals to drink.

**After this lesson I will be able to:**

- **Explain** how the Sun and the ocean interact in the water cycle.

## Descriptive Investigations

**Activity 1:** Water Cycle Model

In groups, research the water cycle to gather information. Create a model of the water cycle. Be sure to include the roles of the Sun and the ocean in the water cycle. Present the model to the class.

Use the spaces below to record information about each stage of the water cycle.

| **Evaporation** | **Condensation** |
|---|---|
|  |  |

| **Collection** | **Precipitation** |
|---|---|
|  |  |

## Activity 2: Leading Roles

In groups, design a short play to model the stages of the water cycle. Explain the role of the Sun, oceans, evaporation, condensation, precipitation, and collection. Perform the play in class. Vote on a best actor and best actress after viewing each group's performance.

The space below can be used to write dialogue and brainstorm ideas for the play.

**Title of Play**

_____

| **Dialogue** | **Ideas for Play** |
|---|---|
| Sun – _____ <br> _____ <br> Water – _____ <br> _____ <br> Oceans – _____ <br> _____ <br> Evaporation – _____ <br> _____ <br> Precipitation – _____ <br> _____ <br> Collection – _____ <br> _____ | _____ <br> _____ <br> _____ <br> _____ <br> _____ <br> _____ <br> _____ <br> _____ <br> _____ <br> _____ <br> _____ <br> _____ |

**Answer the questions.**

What is the role of the Sun in the water cycle?

_____

_____

_____


What role does the ocean play in the water cycle?

_____

_____

_____

1 A teacher asks a group of students to explain how the Sun interacts with the ocean. The students describe how the Sun heats the ocean waters, causing the water to evaporate. Water vapor rises into the atmosphere where it condenses, creating clouds. Then, the water returns back to Earth in the form of precipitation. The process the students describe is known as the —

Ⓐ Sun and ocean cycle

Ⓑ water recycle

Ⓒ carbon cycle

Ⓓ water cycle

2 Students conduct an outdoor field investigation to learn what causes water to evaporate. What is a safety precaution the students must follow during the outdoor investigation? **5.1(A)**

Ⓕ Wear goggles

Ⓖ Wear aprons

Ⓗ Do not look directly at the Sun

Ⓙ None of the above

3 Which of the following best describes one way the Sun interacts with the ocean in the water cycle?

Ⓐ The Sun reflects off the ocean, causing the development of waves.

Ⓑ The ocean absorbs the heat from the Sun, which influences marine life.

Ⓒ The Sun heats the water in the ocean, creating tides.

Ⓓ The Sun heats the water in the ocean, causing the water to evaporate.

4 Students learn that several factors, such as gravity and temperature, play important roles in the continuous process of the water cycle. The students form a hypothesis stating that the most vital part of the water cycle process is the interaction between the Sun and the ocean. To find out if their hypothesis is correct, the students will most likely want to — **5.2(A)**

Ⓕ take a field trip to the beach to observe the Sun and the ocean water

Ⓖ draw a picture of how the water cycle works

Ⓗ plan and implement a simple, experimental investigation testing only this factor

Ⓙ create a graph from collected data

5 Which of these best describes how the ocean waters respond to the Sun's heat?

Ⓐ Ocean waters dissolve.

Ⓑ Ocean water temperatures decrease.

Ⓒ Ocean waters release oxygen.

Ⓓ Ocean waters evaporate.

6 In the water cycle, which of these best describes the Sun's role in relation to the ocean?

Ⓕ Powers the water in a continuous cycle

Ⓖ Energizes the water to provide life for marine plants

Ⓗ Provides heat to keep the water temperatures very warm

Ⓙ Forms clouds from excess overflow along the shoreline

**1** During an experiment on a sunny day, students pour water on the sidewalk. Every 30 minutes, they check the water to record any changes. After 1 hour, they observe that all the water is gone. What happens to the water?

Ⓐ The water turns into precipitation.

Ⓑ The water condenses and forms clouds.

Ⓒ The water becomes water vapor.

Ⓓ The water sinks into the ground to form groundwater.

**2** In an activity, students pour a cup of saltwater into a pan to model the ocean. If the students place the pan in the Sun for several hours, which statement best describes what happens to the ocean model?

Ⓕ The saltwater solution becomes water vapor.

Ⓖ The salt evaporates, leaving the water in the pan.

Ⓗ The water becomes water vapor, leaving the salt in the pan.

Ⓙ The solution increases in volume, spilling over the pan to form runoff.

**3** What happens to the water that does **NOT** fall into oceans or other water sources when it rains?

Ⓐ The water instantly evaporates.

Ⓑ The water sinks into the ground to form groundwater.

Ⓒ The water stays in puddles forever.

Ⓓ All water falls in lakes, rivers, and ponds.

**4** Which of these best describes the relationship between the Sun and the ocean?

Ⓕ The Sun's heat causes the ocean waters to flow into rivers.

Ⓖ The Sun's heat causes the ocean waters to condense.

Ⓗ The Sun's heat causes the ocean waters to dissolve.

Ⓙ The Sun's heat causes the ocean waters to evaporate.

**5** What is the Sun's role in the water cycle?

Ⓐ To provide light energy for the cycle

Ⓑ To provide the energy to drive the cycle

Ⓒ To produce precipitation during the cycle

Ⓓ To cause water to condense in the cycle

**6** Which step in the diagram represents condensation?

Ⓕ Step A     Ⓗ Step C

Ⓖ Step B     Ⓙ Step D

## Scientific Investigation and Reasoning Skills: Questions 7–14

**7** A student is writing a research paper on the water cycle. The student focuses on three processes which allow water to cycle continuously. Which diagram correctly displays these processes? **5.2(G)**

Ⓐ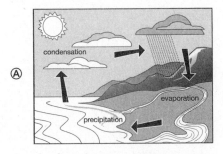

Ⓑ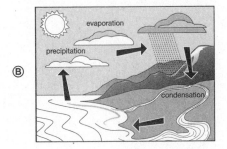

Ⓒ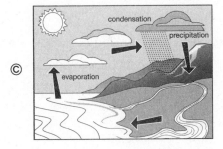

Ⓓ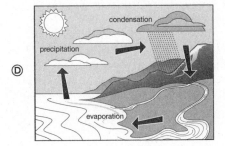

**8** Which of the following is most appropriate to use when collecting and recording temperature data about the Sun's interaction with oceans in the water cycle? **5.4(A)**

Ⓕ Thermometer

Ⓖ Hand lens

Ⓗ Anemometer

Ⓙ Wind Sock

**9** Students are exploring how water changes state in the water cycle through evaporation, condensation, and precipitation. They notice that the Sun heats the ocean water, and it evaporates from the ocean, changing into a gas. It then enters the atmosphere where the temperature decreases, and it changes back into a liquid. Based on the information given, the students are making — **5.2(C)**

Ⓐ a hypothesis

Ⓑ a prediction

Ⓒ an observation

Ⓓ a data table

**10** Hydrologists are scientists who study the flow of water in the water cycle. Which of the following is another name for the water cycle? **5.3(D)**

Ⓕ Life cycle

Ⓖ Lunar cycle

Ⓗ Carbon-dioxide cycle

Ⓙ Hydrologic cycle

**Use the picture below and your knowledge of science to answer questions 11–13.**

The picture shows how students design an experiment to demonstrate how water is cycled through evaporation, condensation, and precipitation.

**11** The teacher instructs students to take precautions during the investigation by using — **5.4(B)**

Ⓐ goggles and insulated gloves

Ⓑ a science notebook and a thermometer

Ⓒ goggles and a science notebook

Ⓓ insulated gloves and a thermometer

**12** Which part of the investigation models the Sun heating the ocean water? **5.3(C)**

Ⓕ Boiling water

Ⓖ Glass plate

Ⓗ Hot plate

Ⓙ Metal pot

**13** What can students do to validate the results of the experimental investigation? **5.2(E)**

Ⓐ Draw a diagram

Ⓑ Repeat the investigation

Ⓒ Develop another model

Ⓓ Use thin disposable gloves

**14** Earth is sometimes called the "Blue Planet" because $\frac{3}{4}$ of Earth is covered with water. Why is water conservation important when such a large portion of our planet contains water? **5.1(B)**

Ⓕ Much of the available water on Earth's surface is contained in the ocean and is lost to evaporation.

Ⓖ Clouds in the atmosphere hold the majority of Earth's water.

Ⓗ Only 1% of Earth's water is fresh water.

Ⓙ The polar ice caps are melting.

 motivation**science**™LEVEL 5

## Water Cycle Questions

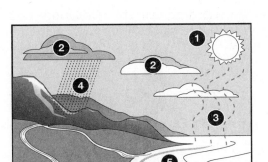

Study the diagram of the water cycle. Create 4 multiple choice questions about the water cycle. Write the questions below. Trade pages with a partner, and answer each other's questions.

## Formative Assessment

Approximately 70% of Earth's surface is covered with water. What do you think would happen if only 25% of Earth's surface was covered with water?

_____

_____

_____

_____

**Science Journal**

Compose a passage about the life of a drop of water. Describe the stages of the water cycle the droplet of water experiences. What happens to the drop of water? Where is it now?

_____

_____

_____

_____

_____

_____

_____

_____

_____

_____

_____

_____

_____

_____

_____

_____

_____

_____

_____

_____

_____

_____

_____

_____

_____

_____

_____

ILLEGAL TO COPY motivation**science** LEVEL 5 ©2011–2014 mentoring**minds**.com

## Science Vocabulary Builder

Describe the importance of each step of the water cycle. Then, draw an image to support the description.

**Ocean**
Description

_____

_____

Image

**Condensation**
Description

_____

_____

Image

**Sun**
Description

_____

_____

Image

**Precipitation**
Description

_____

_____

Image

**Evaporation**
Description

_____

_____

Image

**Collection**
Description

_____

_____

Image

**Water Cycle**

Draw a diagram of the water cycle. Label the parts. Include evaporation, condensation, precipitation, and collection. Make sure your diagram includes the ocean and the Sun.

Explain how the Sun and ocean interact in the water cycle. _____

_____

_____

How would the water cycle change if the Sun was removed from the diagram?_____

_____

_____

How would the water cycle change if Earth had no oceans?_____

_____

_____

_____

✂ - - - - - - - - - - - - - - - - - - - - - - - - - - - - - - - - - - - - - - - - - - - - - - - - - - - - - - - - -

**Parent Activities**

1. Discuss the diagram above. When was the last time the precipitation stage of the water cycle occurred at your home?

2. Pour water on concrete on a sunny day. Check the water every 2 minutes, and describe the changes that occur. What happened to the water?

**Motivation Station: Mike's Cool Science Fact**

Earth actually takes 23 hours, 56 minutes, and 4 seconds to make one complete rotation. While Earth is rotating, it is also revolving around the Sun. It takes an extra 4 minutes for Earth to rotate to the same spot it was the day before while it is also revolving. This makes a day 24 hours long.

**After this lesson I will be able to:**

• **Demonstrate** that Earth rotates on its axis once approximately every 24 hours causing the day/night cycle and the apparent movement of the Sun across the sky.

## Descriptive Investigations

**Activity 1:** Rotation

Watch as your teacher presents a demonstration of Earth's rotation.

What did the orange represent?

_____

What did the flashlight represent during the experiment?

_____

What happened during the demonstration?

_____

_____

_____

Illustrate the demonstration by drawing the position of the light hitting Earth during the demonstration.

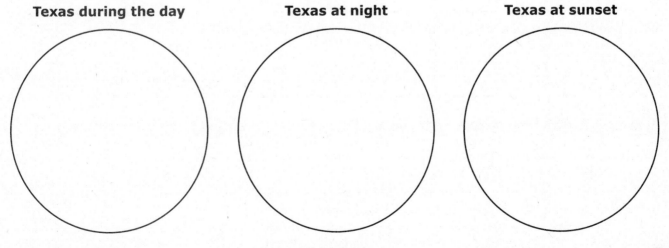

| **Texas during the day** | **Texas at night** | **Texas at sunset** |

## Activity 2: Apparent Movement

**Never look directly at the Sun.**

On the table, record the position of the Sun in the sky throughout the day. Face south when you make your observations. This activity begins at school and is completed at home.

| Time | Position |
|------|----------|
| 8:00 A.M. | Description |
| 10:00 A.M. | Description |
| 12:00 P.M. | Description |
| 2:00 P.M. | Description |
| 4:00 P.M. | Description |
| 6:00 P.M. | Description |

Illustrate the position of the Sun throughout the day. Face south for each observation. Be sure to include the time of day the Sun appeared in each position, and include drawings of nearby landmarks.

Why does the Sun appear to change its position throughout the day?

_____

_____

How does Earth's rotation cause day and night? What would happen if Earth did not rotate?

_____

_____

_____

Name _____

**The picture below represents a June day. Use the picture below and your knowledge of science to answer questions 1 and 2.**

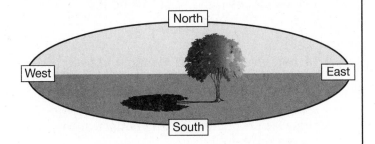

**1** The Sun appears to change position or move across the sky during daylight hours. Which of the following causes the shadow to form in the picture above?

Ⓐ Earth's rotation

Ⓑ Earth's revolution

Ⓒ Sun's revolution

Ⓓ Earth's orbit

**2** Approximately what time of day is it in the picture above? **5.2(D)**

Ⓕ 12:00 P.M.

Ⓖ 8:00 A.M.

Ⓗ 6:00 P.M.

Ⓙ 12:00 A.M.

**3** Earth rotates on its axis approximately once every 24 hours, causing the day/night cycle and —

Ⓐ the Moon phases

Ⓑ the orbiting of Earth around the Sun

Ⓒ the Sun's apparent movement across the sky

Ⓓ the four seasons

**4** Which of the following would be the best example to explain Earth's rotation?

Ⓕ Merry-go-round

Ⓖ Funnel

Ⓗ Doorknob

Ⓙ Swing

**5** In what direction does the Sun appear to move across the sky?

Ⓐ West to east

Ⓑ North to south

Ⓒ East to west

Ⓓ South to north

**6** Many cultures have different methods of telling what time of day it is. Which of the following is an ancient tool invented to determine the time of day? **5.3(D)**

Ⓕ Watch

Ⓖ Clock

Ⓗ Sundial

Ⓙ Compass

**Unit 17** Check for Understanding

**1** Which of these does **NOT** demonstrate how Earth rotates on its axis to cause day and night?

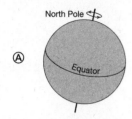

Ⓐ

North Pole

Equator

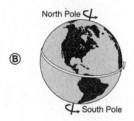

Ⓑ

North Pole

South Pole

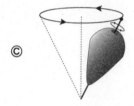

Ⓒ

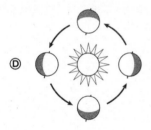

Ⓓ

**2** Earth's rotation causes the day and night cycle. It also causes —

Ⓕ the Sun to appear to move

Ⓖ the Sun to remain in orbit

Ⓗ the Sun to orbit Earth

Ⓙ all of the above

**3** Earth rotates on its axis once every —

Ⓐ month

Ⓑ 24 hours

Ⓒ year

Ⓓ 12 hours

**4** A person standing in Alabama notices the Sun is rising. At the same moment, a person in Japan sees that the Sun has just set. Which statement correctly describes how it can be sunrise and sunset at the same moment?

Ⓕ The Sun's rotation around Earth enables part of Earth to have sunlight while the other part is in darkness.

Ⓖ The Sun has moved from one location to the other during the course of a day.

Ⓗ Earth's rotation on its axis enables part of Earth to have sunlight while the other part is in darkness.

Ⓙ Earth has circled around the Sun during the course of a day.

**5** Which statement correctly describes the Sun's apparent movement across the sky?

Ⓐ As Earth spins on its axis, it makes the Sun appear to move across the sky.

Ⓑ As the Sun spins around Earth, it moves across the sky.

Ⓒ Earth rotates around the Sun every 24 hours, making the Sun appear to move across the sky.

Ⓓ The Sun rotates around Earth every 12 hours, making the Sun appear to move across the sky.

**6** A student looks outside and observes the Sun in the western sky. Which of the following times could it be?

Ⓕ Sunrise

Ⓖ Sunset

Ⓗ Noon

Ⓙ Midnight

motivation**science**™ LEVEL 5

## Scientific Investigation and Reasoning Skills: Questions 7–14

**7** Which picture was taken at 9:00 A.M.?
**5.2(D)**

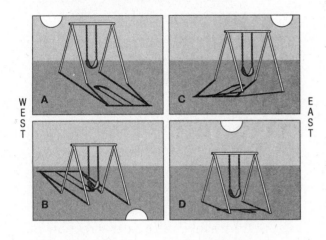

Ⓐ Diagram A     Ⓒ Diagram C

Ⓑ Diagram B     Ⓓ Diagram D

**8** Models are not perfect, but models have been used for many years by scientists to help explain ideas. Scientists use models to make predictions about the future as well as understand the vast world in which we live. Why would a physical model demonstrating Earth's rotation be considered less than perfect? **5.3(C)**

Ⓕ Models are an exact copy of the object or idea they represent.

Ⓖ Models have limitations in representing the object or idea.

Ⓗ Models are identical to the object or idea they represent.

Ⓙ Models match the object or idea they represent exactly.

**9** Astronomers are scientists who study the universe. To an astronomer, the word "rotate" means — **5.3(D)**

Ⓐ orbit around another object

Ⓑ move in opposite directions

Ⓒ spin around an axis

Ⓓ revolve around another object

**10** A science teacher evaluates students' understanding of the causes of day and night. Students are asked to draw a diagram to show the process. Which of the following student diagrams correctly shows the process that causes the day/night cycle? **5.3(A)**

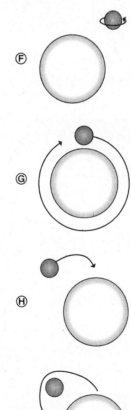

**11** Many cultures believed the Sun traveled around Earth. In the 1500s, a man named Copernicus proposed that Earth traveled around the Sun. A scientist named Galileo found evidence to support Copernicus' idea. Earth revolves around the Sun, but it also makes a complete rotation. How long does it take Earth to make one complete rotation on its axis? **5.3(D)**

Ⓐ 365 days

Ⓑ 1 day

Ⓒ 1 month

Ⓓ 1 week

**12** Observe the diagram below.

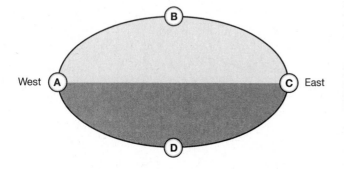

Which of the following shows where the Sun's position should be at 12:00 P.M.? **5.2(D)**

Ⓕ Position A

Ⓖ Position B

Ⓗ Position C

Ⓙ Position D

**13** The picture is a photograph of the night sky over a period of many hours.

Why does the night sky appear to move in a circular pattern as shown in the photograph? **5.2(D)**

Ⓐ Earth rotates on its axis once a day.

Ⓑ The night sky rotates over Earth.

Ⓒ Stars travel in a circular direction around Earth.

Ⓓ Earth rotates on its axis once every 12 hours.

**14** In an activity, students make a large human sundial. The sundial uses the Sun to tell the approximate time of day.

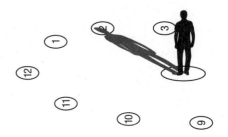

How is this possible? **5.2(D)**

Ⓕ The Sun moves across the sky each day because it spins around Earth.

Ⓖ The sundial measures the distance from Earth to the Sun as it moves across the sky.

Ⓗ Earth moves around the Sun each day, making the Sun appear to move across the sky.

Ⓙ The position of the Sun in the sky appears to change during the day because Earth rotates on its axis.

### Analyzing Rotation

Observe the picture of Earth, and draw where the Sun would be located to create the view shown.

1. Does the picture show day or night where you live? _____

2. Why does the Sun appear to move across the sky during the day?

   _____

   _____

3. How long does it take for Earth to rotate one time? _____

4. If Earth is constantly spinning, why do we not feel the movement?

   _____

   _____

   _____

   _____

   _____

5. How many times has Earth rotated since your last birthday? _____

### Formative Assessment

Describe some advantages and disadvantages of the models you used to demonstrate Earth's rotation?

_____

_____

_____

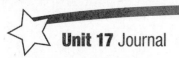
**Science Journal**

Pretend you are Earth. Write a story about a 24-hour time period from Earth's point of view.

_____

_____

_____

_____

_____

_____

_____

_____

_____

_____

_____

_____

_____

_____

_____

_____

_____

_____

_____

_____

_____

_____

_____

_____

_____

## Science Vocabulary Builder

With a partner, create a vocabulary poster describing Earth's rotation on its axis. Explain facts about the cycle of day and night, the Sun's apparent movement across the sky, and facts about Earth's rotation. Display posters around the classroom, and have a picture walk to see what classmates have created. Include these vocabulary words on your poster: day, night, rotation, axis, apparent movement, and Sun. Use the organizer below to brainstorm ideas for the poster.

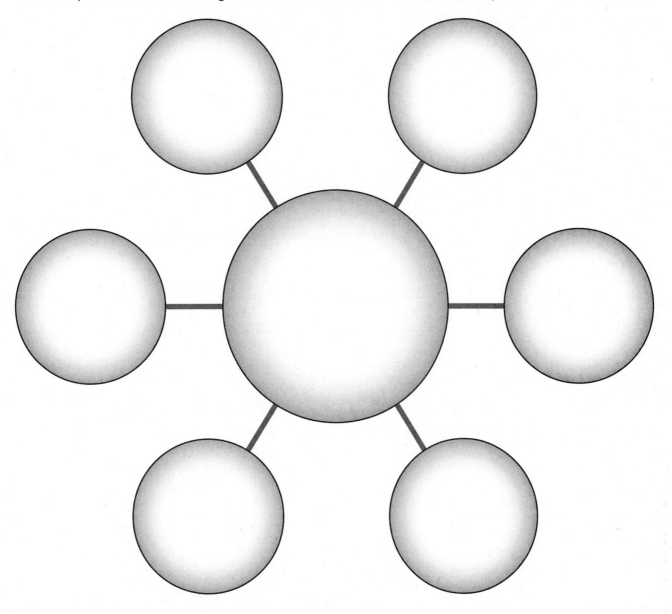

Notes

## Rotation of Earth

Create a model demonstrating Earth's rotation.

- Use materials found at home to make your model.
- Write a brief report about the model in the space below.
- Describe why you chose the materials used to make your model.
- Explain why the Sun appears to move across the sky throughout the day.

| Model Illustration | Materials Used to Create Model |
|---|---|
| | |

**Report**

_____

_____

_____

_____

_____

_____

_____

_____

_____

_____

- - - - - - - - - - - - - - - - - - - - - - - - - - - - - - - - - - - - - - - -

## Parent Activities

1. Help your child build a model of Earth's rotation.
2. Record the position of the Sun across the sky throughout the day.
3. Discuss how the rotation of Earth causes daytime and nighttime.

**Motivation Station: Molly's Cool Science Fact**

Our Sun, the center of the solar system, is one of many stars. The Milky Way Galaxy alone is estimated to have 1,000,000,000,000 stars. The next closest star is Proxima Centauri and is 4.2 light years from Earth.

**After this lesson I will be able to:**

• **Identify** and **compare** the physical characteristics of the Sun, Earth, and Moon.

## Comparative Investigations

**Activity 1:** Objects on Earth and the Moon

Describe what would happen if you used each of the objects below on Earth and on the Moon.

| Object | Earth | Moon |
|---|---|---|
| Soccer ball | | |
| Pogo stick | | |
| Sand castle | | |
| Trampoline | | |
| Compass | | |

## Activity 2: The Sun

**Part 1:** Create a papier maché model of the Sun. First, blow up a balloon. In a bowl, mix 2 cups of water and $\frac{1}{2}$ cup of flour. Dip strips of newspaper in the mixture, and place flat all over the balloon. Add additional paper to create flares, prominences, and other features. Set the sculpture to dry. After drying, paint the model. Remember to include sunspots.

**Part 2:** Research the layers of the Sun and Earth. Then, illustrate the layers of the Sun and Earth below. Label the parts of the illustration.

|  Layers of the Sun  |  Layers of Earth  |
| :---: | :---: |

| What are the layers of the Sun? | What are the layers of Earth? |
| :---: | :---: |

Compare the layers of the Sun and Earth. List the similarities and differences.

_____

_____

_____

_____

_____

**1** Studies of the surface of the Moon increased with Galileo's invention, the — **5.3(D)**

Ⓐ microscope    Ⓒ camera

Ⓑ telescope    Ⓓ computer

**2** While Earth is characterized as possessing an atmosphere with the ability to produce winds, the Moon is characterized as —

Ⓕ having only a very thin atmosphere

Ⓖ possessing large bodies of liquid water

Ⓗ lacking surface dust

Ⓙ possessing an atmosphere with large amounts of oxygen

**3** Students know there are patterns in the natural world. One of these patterns is the relationship between the Sun, Earth, and Moon. Which of the following correctly explains the relationship of the Sun, Earth, and Moon?

Ⓐ Earth revolves around the Moon as Earth revolves around the Sun.

Ⓑ The Sun revolves around Earth as the Moon revolves around Earth.

Ⓒ The Moon revolves around Earth as Earth revolves around the Sun.

Ⓓ Earth revolves around the Moon as the Sun revolves around Earth.

**4** Students were asked to think about how the Moon and Earth are different. Conclusions were recorded on a table constructed by each group.

| | Air | Oceans | Surface Landscape |
|---|---|---|---|
| Earth | Yes | Yes | ? |
| Moon | No | No | Dust, rocks |

Which of the following pairs could be classified as surface landscape for Earth but could **NOT** be classified as surface landscape for the Moon? **5.2(G)**

Ⓕ Rocks, craters

Ⓖ Trees, oceans

Ⓗ Mountains, craters

Ⓙ Craters, dust

**5** The surfaces of the Sun, Earth, and Moon are described as having different physical characteristics. How is the Sun different from Earth and the Moon?

Ⓐ The Sun has no gravity.

Ⓑ The Sun is a solid.

Ⓒ The Sun does not produce its own heat.

Ⓓ The Sun is capable of producing its own light.

**6** We know that Earth consists of different layers. The Sun also has layers, but unlike Earth, the Sun is entirely —

Ⓕ solid    Ⓗ melted rock

Ⓖ gas    Ⓙ liquid

**Unit 18** Check for Understanding

**1** Earth is like the Moon in many ways. One way the Moon is different from Earth is —

Ⓐ there is no weather on the Moon

Ⓑ there are no craters on Earth

Ⓒ there is no weather on Earth

Ⓓ there is more gravity on the Moon

**2** Which statement correctly describes the Sun and Earth?

Ⓕ The Sun and Earth both have water.

Ⓖ The Sun and Earth both have a surface called the crust.

Ⓗ The Sun and Earth both have an atmosphere.

Ⓙ The Sun and Earth both have breathable air.

**3** The Sun, like Earth, has —

Ⓐ life

Ⓑ water

Ⓒ mountains

Ⓓ layers

**4** All of the following are characteristics of both Earth and the Moon **EXCEPT** —

Ⓕ solid rocks          Ⓗ oceans

Ⓖ craters              Ⓙ gravity

**5** Which layer of the Sun shown below is also a layer of Earth?

**Layers of the Sun**

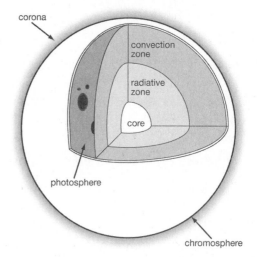

Ⓐ Corona

Ⓑ Convection zone

Ⓒ Radiative zone

Ⓓ None of the above

**6** Which statement does **NOT** correctly describe the Moon and Earth?

Ⓕ They both have craters, mountains, and plains.

Ⓖ They both have gravity.

Ⓗ They both can sustain life.

Ⓙ They both rotate and revolve.

 motivation**science**™LEVEL 5

## Scientific Investigation and Reasoning Skills: Questions 7–14

**7** Scientists who study the Sun are called astronomers. Our Sun gives us light, heat, and energy. Without the Sun, life on Earth would not exist. The Sun is a normal star, but it is much closer to us than any other star. By studying the Sun we can learn more about — **5.3(D)**

   Ⓐ  other planets

   Ⓑ  other asteroids

   Ⓒ  other stars

   Ⓓ  other satellites

**8** The Sun and Earth are both constantly changing. Students research and collect information to compare the physical characteristics by observing detailed photographs of the Sun and Earth on the Internet. Which of the following is a physical characteristic of the Sun but **NOT** of Earth? **5.2(C)**

   Ⓕ  Sunspots

   Ⓖ  Layers

   Ⓗ  Atmosphere

   Ⓙ  Spherical shape

**9** An astronomer writes several books on the effects of the Moon on Earth. He collects information by making detailed observations over an extended period of time and then records his findings in a science journal. Which is the most important reason why a scientist would record the findings of a scientific investigation? **5.2(F)**

   Ⓐ  To provide evidence to support a conclusion

   Ⓑ  To write a narrative encouraging people to visit the Moon

   Ⓒ  To provide other scientists with interesting facts

   Ⓓ  To encourage students to read about science

**10** Which of the following tools would be most useful for demonstrating and comparing characteristics of the Sun, Earth, and Moon? **5.2(B)**

   Ⓕ  Microscope

   Ⓖ  Triple beam balance

   Ⓗ  Terrarium

   Ⓙ  Model

**Unit 18** Check for Understanding

**11** Scale models are often used to compare the sizes of objects in space. Compared to the size of Earth, the Sun is about one million times bigger. Compared to Earth, the Moon is 4 times smaller.

Which combination of items should be used to make the closest scale model of the Sun and Earth? **5.3(C)**

Ⓐ Beach ball and soccer ball

Ⓑ Baseball and soccer ball

Ⓒ Basketball and pea

Ⓓ Basketball and soccer ball

**12** Groups of students write comparisons about the Sun, Earth, and Moon. Which comparison is correct? **5.2(D)**

| 1 | The Sun is made of molten metals. Earth is made of only metals. The Moon is made of only solid rock. |
|---|---|
| 2 | The Sun has an atmosphere. The Moon does not have a viable atmosphere. Earth has an atmosphere. |
| 3 | The Sun has less gravity than the Moon and Earth. The Moon has more gravity than the Sun. Earth has more gravity than the Sun and Moon. |
| 4 | The Sun is larger than Earth but smaller than the Moon. The Moon is smaller than Earth. Earth is larger than the Moon and Sun. |

Ⓕ Comparison 1     Ⓗ Comparison 3

Ⓖ Comparison 2     Ⓙ Comparison 4

**13** Students design an experiment to investigate how craters were formed on the Moon. The students put flour in a pan and cover the flour with a layer of cocoa powder. Then, students drop the same size marbles from heights of 5 centimeters, 10 centimeters, and 20 centimeters. They measure the depth and width of each crater and record the data on a table. What is the variable in the investigation? **5.2(A)**

Ⓐ The amount of flour

Ⓑ The cocoa powder

Ⓒ The size of marble

Ⓓ The height from which the marbles were dropped

**14** According to the advertisement below, Moon Rocks — **5.3(B)**

Quality Moon Rocks are available now in a limited supply!

Act fast to receive a genuine handcrafted Moon Rock sure to please any budding astronomer!

Each Moon Rock purchased comes with a certificate and a six-week warranty.

Ⓕ come in a variety of colors

Ⓖ are replicas of rocks found on the Moon

Ⓗ are rocks taken from the surface of the Moon

Ⓙ come with a lifetime guarantee

motivation**science**™ LEVEL 5

## Comparing the Sun, Earth, and Moon

Research the characteristics of the Sun, Earth, and Moon. Compare and contrast each using the Venn diagram below. After filling in the diagram, color each to represent the Sun, Earth, and Moon. Share your diagram with a partner and add any new information.

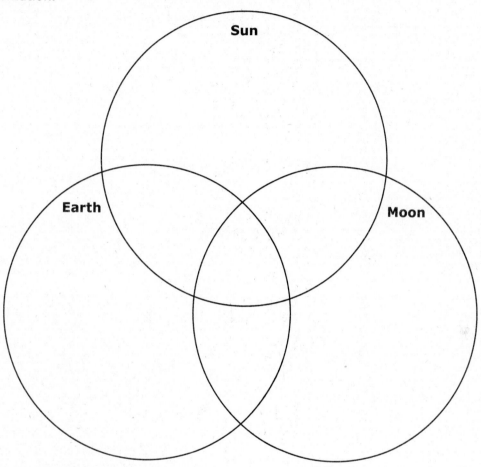

## Formative Assessment

Provide evidence to support the following claim.

> *The Moon does not create light of its own. It reflects light from the Sun.*

_____

_____

_____

_____

_____

## Science Journal

If you could visit any place on Earth or visit the Moon, which would you choose? Explain your decision and what you would do when you reached your destination.

_____

_____

_____

_____

_____

_____

_____

_____

_____

_____

_____

_____

_____

_____

_____

_____

_____

_____

_____

_____

_____

_____

_____

_____

_____

**Science Vocabulary Builder**

Write the words which describe the physical characteristics of the Sun, Moon, or Earth. The first one has been done for you.

| Words | Physical Characteristics |
|---|---|
| 1. C r a t e r s | 1. Large holes formed by meteorites, found on the Moon and Earth |
| 2. H _ _ _ | 2. A high area of land, often round, but not as high as a mountain, found on the Moon and Earth |
| 3. A _ _ | 3. Natural resource people breathe, found only on Earth |
| 4. R _ _ _ _ _ | 4. The motion the Sun, Earth, and Moon make when they turn on their axis |
| 5. A _ _ _ _ _ _ _ _ _ | 5. The layer of air that surrounds Earth |
| 6. C _ _ _ _ _ | 6. Group of water droplets or ice crystals floating in the air, found on Earth but not the Sun or Moon |
| 7. T _ _ _ _ | 7. A plant that has leaves, branches, and wood, only found on Earth |
| 8. E _ _ _ _ _ _ _ _ | 8. All living and nonliving things in a certain environment, only found on Earth |
| 9. R _ _ _ _ | 9. A hard, nonliving thing made of minerals, found on the Moon and Earth |
| 10. I _ _ | 10. The solid form of water, found on both Earth and the Moon |
| 11. S _ _ _ _ _ _ _ | 11. Cooler, dark spots on the Sun's surface |
| 12. T _ _ _ _ | 12. The regular rise and fall of ocean levels on Earth caused by the pull of gravity from the Moon and Sun |
| 13. I _ _ _ _ _ | 13. A land area completely surrounded by water, found only on Earth |
| 14. C _ _ _ | 14. The innermost layer of Earth and the Sun |
| 15. S _ _ _ | 15. A form of precipitation, found only on Earth |

**Unit 18** Homework

## Earth Model

Common everyday household items can be used to represent a model of Earth's layers.
An example is an avocado.

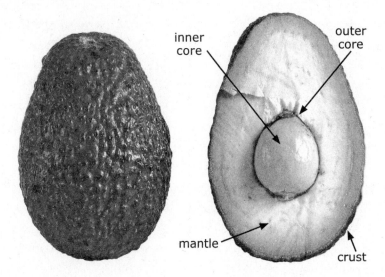

Find an object at home that represents the layers of Earth. Illustrate and label the model.

What object did you find to represent the layers of Earth? What limitations are there with the model?

_____

_____

_____

✂ - - - - - - - - - - - - - - - - - - - - - - - - - - - - - - - - - - - - - - - - - - - - - - -

## Parent Activities

1. Help your child find an object at home that models the layers of Earth.
   Assist with any cutting of objects.

2. Create a list of other objects that could be used to represent the layers of
   Earth. Discuss the differences between the model representation and Earth.

**Motivation Station: Mike's Cool Science Fact**

There are many different types of soil. Scientists in the United States have discovered over 70,000 varieties of soil.

**After this lesson I will be able to:**

- **Examine** properties of soils, including color and texture, capacity to retain water, and ability to support the growth of plants.

## Comparative and Experimental Investigations

**Activity 1:** Properties of Soils

In this investigation, the properties of soils are examined. The following are the properties to be tested:

- Color and texture
- Capacity to retain water
- Ability to support the growth of plants

Find a sample of soil in an outdoor location. Examine the properties of the soil sample, and answer the questions below.

1. Does the soil feel dry, moist, or soaked? Describe the texture.

_____

_____

2. What color is the soil? Is it the same color as other soils found in the same area?

_____

_____

3. Are there any places where the soil appears extremely dry or extremely wet?

_____

_____

4. What plants grow well in the soil? What plants are currently growing in the soil sample?

_____

_____

## Activity 2: Soil Tests

Perform three experiments to test the properties of soils. Record the findings in the table.

### Soil Test 1
Observe the soils. Touch the soils to examine the textures. Describe the colors and textures of the soils in the table.

### Soil Test 2
Place each container of soil over a 250 mL beaker. The containers have several holes in the bottom to allow water to drain. Slowly pour 150 mL water into each container of soil and observe. Measure the amount of water drained from each soil. Determine the amount of water retained by each soil, and record the information for each soil type.

### Soil Test 3
This test takes several weeks to complete. In each container of soil, plant a seed provided by the teacher. Give each plant the same amount of water each time you water. Every day, check the soil, and record any changes on the homework page. After 4 weeks, rate each soil according to its ability to support the growth of plants, with 1 being the best and 4 being the worst.

| Soil (Illustrate Below) | Color/Texture | Capacity to Retain Water | | Ability to Support Growth of Plants |
|---|---|---|---|---|
| Soil 1: Potting Soil | Color | Amount of Water Drained from the Soil | Amount of Water Retained by the Soil | |
| | Texture | | | |
| Soil 2: Gravel | Color | Amount of Water Drained from the Soil | Amount of Water Retained by the Soil | |
| | Texture | | | |
| Soil 3: Clay | Color | Amount of Water Drained from the Soil | Amount of Water Retained by the Soil | |
| | Texture | | | |
| Soil 4: Sand | Color | Amount of Water Drained from the Soil | Amount of Water Retained by the Soil | |
| | Texture | | | |

 motivation**science**™LEVEL 5 ©2011–2014 mentoring**minds**.com

**1** Students investigate properties of soil. They pick up the soil and rub it back and forth between their fingers. They notice the soil is made of many different sized particles and feels smooth.

Which property of soil are the students examining?

Ⓐ Color

Ⓒ Fragrance

Ⓑ Mass

Ⓓ Texture

**2** Soil in one location is different than soil in another location. To better understand soil and how it is different, geologists observe and measure the soil's — **5.2(C)**

Ⓕ length

Ⓖ mass

Ⓗ properties

Ⓙ none of the above

**3** Geologists can tell a lot about soil from its color. Nutrient rich soil is generally —

Ⓐ darker in color

Ⓑ gray in color

Ⓒ red in color

Ⓓ colorless

**4** Students conduct an investigation to study the effects of soil on a tomato plant. They place plants in four different types of soil to determine which type would best support plant growth. They place the plants by a window and water each with equal amounts of water every day for two weeks. What is the variable in this simple experimental investigation? **5.2(A)**

Ⓕ Soil

Ⓗ Water

Ⓖ Tomato plant

Ⓙ Sunlight

**5** Which of the following has the greatest effect on soil's capacity to retain water?

Ⓐ Soil color

Ⓑ Soil particle size

Ⓒ Soil texture

Ⓓ Soil fragrance

**6** In an activity, students measure how much water is held by different soil types. Each pot has 100 milliliters of water poured into it.

| Material | Water Drained Out (mL) |
|---|---|
| Clay | 30 |
| Gravel | 90 |
| Sand | 40 |
| Potting soil | 25 |

According to the table, which material absorbs the most water?

Ⓕ Clay

Ⓗ Sand

Ⓖ Gravel

Ⓙ Potting soil

**1** Which type of soil would be least likely to support the growth of a rose bush?

Ⓐ Potting soil    Ⓒ Topsoil

Ⓑ Loamy soil    Ⓓ Clay soil

**2** Students select soil to use in a group project requiring the planting of a bean seed. They want to select a soil that is rich in nutrients. Which of the following properties would help students determine which type of soil to use for their plant project?

Ⓕ Texture    Ⓗ Particle size

Ⓖ Color    Ⓙ Density

**3** A clear plastic box is divided into four sections and holes are drilled in each so water can drain. Each section is filled with a different type of soil.

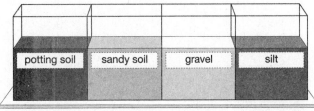
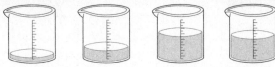

If a plant that requires constant moisture is placed in each section, which would have the healthiest plant?

Ⓐ Potting soil    Ⓒ Gravel

Ⓑ Sandy soil    Ⓓ Silt

**4** The table shows soil content and its associated color. The Red River on the Oklahoma-Texas border is named for the colored sedimentary rocks that make up the riverbed.

| Content | Color |
|---------|-------|
| Calcite | White |
| Carbon | Black |
| Glauconite | Green |
| Iron | Red |

According to the table, which mineral is most likely contained in the riverbed?

Ⓕ Carbon

Ⓖ Calcite

Ⓗ Iron

Ⓙ Glauconite

**5** Soil with humus helps support the growth of plants. Which of the soil types below would most likely contain the greatest amount of humus?

Ⓐ Sand    Ⓒ Loam

Ⓑ Gravel    Ⓓ Clay

**6** Which of the following soils has the roughest texture?

Ⓕ Potting soil

Ⓖ Silt

Ⓗ Clay

Ⓙ Sand

## Scientific Investigation and Reasoning Skills: Questions 7–14

### Soil Comparison

| Soil Type | ??? |
|-----------|-----|
| Clay | red, fine texture, small particles |
| Sand | tan, large particles, course texture |
| Potting soil | black, medium coarse texture, medium particles |

**7** Based on the information provided in the table above, what would be the most appropriate title for the second column? **5.2(D)**

Ⓐ Soil Color

Ⓑ Soil Behavior

Ⓒ Soil Properties

Ⓓ Soil Texture

**8** Which tool would be useful in measuring the amount of water that drained from a pot of soil? **5.4(A)**

Ⓕ Beaker

Ⓖ Collecting net

Ⓗ Pan balance

Ⓙ Ruler

**9** What is the first step in designing an investigation examining properties of soil? **5.2(B)**

Ⓐ Repeat the investigation to find the properties

Ⓑ Ask a well-defined question about the properties of soil

Ⓒ Formulate a hypothesis about the properties of soil

Ⓓ Identify the solution for soil erosion

**10** Students decide to create a terrarium as a model of a miniature ecosystem. Each type of soil covering the floor of the terrarium serves a specific purpose. The first layer is made of gravel or small pebbles. The primary layer of soil is made from a potting soil. Moss is used to separate the potting soil from the gravel.

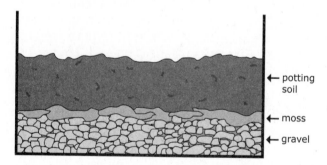

What is the purpose in using the gravel? **5.2(D)**

Ⓕ To assist with drainage

Ⓖ To retain moisture

Ⓗ To eliminate odors

Ⓙ To support plant growth

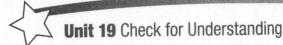

**11** Environmental scientists focus on studying soil for all of the following reasons **EXCEPT —** **5.3(D)**

Ⓐ to focus on environmental quality as it relates to soil

Ⓑ to investigate issues like soil contamination

Ⓒ to analyze how human use impacts local soil

Ⓓ to study how soil can be used destructively and ineffectively

**13** Upon completion of a soil investigation, students conclude that the soil's ability to retain water was an important factor in sustaining plant growth. Which of the following questions would be appropriate when testing this hypothesis? **5.2(B)**

Ⓐ Do plants grow better by adding water to the soil?

Ⓑ How does water change the texture of the soil?

Ⓒ Which type of soil has the capacity to hold in the most water?

Ⓓ How much water is needed to test soil retention?

**12** Students extend a soil investigation over a four-week period in order to conduct two more trial runs before reporting their final conclusions. What is the purpose in repeating the investigation? **5.2(E)**

Ⓕ To make accurate measurements

Ⓖ To collect detailed information

Ⓗ To increase reliability of results

Ⓙ To form a testable hypothesis

**14** Students examine properties of soil, such as a soil's ability to support the growth of diverse plants. Which would be most effective to use for an extended period of time when observing plant growth in soil? **5.4(A)**

Ⓕ Beaker

Ⓖ Planetarium

Ⓗ Terrarium

Ⓙ Stadium

### Soil Museum

Work with your group to collect 14 different types of soil from home and around school. Place each soil sample in a different compartment in an ice cube tray, saving additional soil for the Museum Art activity. Number each soil sample, and use an index card to provide the following information for each soil sample.

> Soil sample # _____
>
> Type of soil– _____
>
> Location where soil was found– _____
>
> Color– _____
>
> Texture– _____
>
> Particle size– _____
>
> Other observations– _____
>
> _____

Complete the diagram below. Color each compartment to match the soil collected by your group.

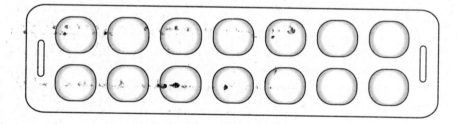

**Museum Art**

Use your multi-colored soil samples to create a work of art for your Soil Museum. Sketch a picture on paper. Cover each section lightly with glue, and sprinkle soil of different colors and textures to fill in the design. Display your masterpiece along with your 14 soil samples.

### Formative Assessment

Explain the importance of understanding soil properties in the scenarios shown in the table below.

| Planning a Garden | Building a House |
|---|---|
|  |  |

**Science Journal**

Write a composition explaining why soil is a useful and important natural resource.

_____

_____

_____

_____

_____

_____

_____

_____

_____

_____

_____

_____

_____

_____

_____

_____

_____

_____

_____

_____

_____

_____

_____

_____

Name

Name _____

## Science Vocabulary Builder

Create filmstrips to explain each concept.

| Soil Formation | Soil Properties | Capacity to Retain Water |
|:---:|:---:|:---:|

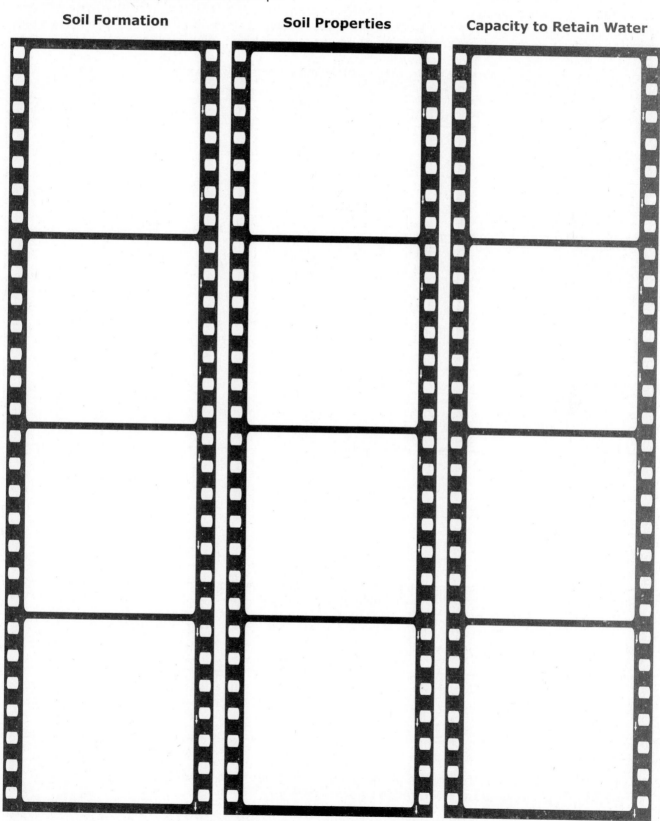

**Unit 19** Homework

Supporting Standard 4.7(A)

## Soil Test 3 Data Log

Take home the bean seeds planted in four different types of soil and place in a sunny location. Every few days, water each container using the same amount of water. Record the growth of each plant and other observations every week in the table below. At the end of 4 weeks, bring your data to class, and rank each soil according to its ability to support the growth of plants.

| Soil | Potting Soil | | Gravel | | Clay | | Sand | |
|---|---|---|---|---|---|---|---|---|
| Week | Height | Observations | Height | Observations | Height | Observations | Height | Observations |
| 1 | | | | | | | | |
| 2 | | | | | | | | |
| 3 | | | | | | | | |
| 4 | | | | | | | | |

0 1 2 3 4 5 6 7 8 9 10 11 12 13 14 15 16 17
cm

✂ - - - - - - - - - - - - - - - - - - - - - - - - - - - - - - - - - - - - - - -

## Parent Activities

1. Help your child record the growth of the plants every week. At the end of the fourth week, send the information back to school.

2. Plant a different type of seed in different soils. Are the results the same?

 motivation**science**™ LEVEL 5

**After this lesson I will be able to:**

- **Identify** and **classify** Earth's renewable resources, including air, plants, water, animals; and nonrenewable resources, including coal, oil, and natural gas; and the importance of conservation.

## Comparative Investigations

**Activity 1:** Conserving Resources

Follow the teacher's directions to demonstrate graham cracker conservation. Answer the questions below.

1. What did the graham cracker represent?

_____

2. How did the graham cracker demonstration model the idea of scarcity?

_____

_____

3. How did you feel during this investigation? Did you feel you were treated fairly?

_____

_____

_____

4. What is the best way to share a limited number of resources?

_____

_____

_____

5. Why is conservation important?

_____

_____

_____

**Activity 2:** Unlimited vs. Limited Consumption

Use the data tables and graphs below to record data collected during Activity 2.

## Unlimited Consumption

| Time in Seconds | Number of Students Finished |
|---|---|
| 20 | |
| 40 | |
| 60 | |
| 80 | |
| 100 | |
| 120 | |
| 140 | |
| 160 | |
| 180 | |
| 200 | |

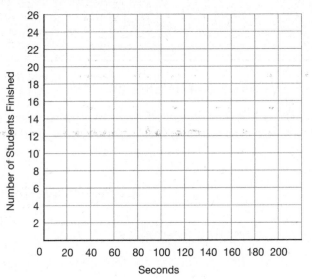

## Limited Consumption

| Time in Seconds | Number of Students Finished |
|---|---|
| 20 | |
| 40 | |
| 60 | |
| 80 | |
| 100 | |
| 120 | |
| 140 | |
| 160 | |
| 180 | |
| 200 | |

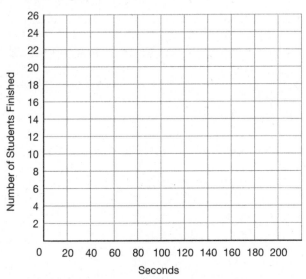

Compare the information collected from each trial. How are the results different?

_____

_____

How can we apply the knowledge learned from the investigation to the use of renewable and nonrenewable resources?

_____

_____

**1** Students classify renewable and nonrenewable resources. They create a table to organize their data.

| Renewable Resources | Nonrenewable Resources |
|---|---|
| Plants | Coal |
| Animals | Natural gas |
| Water | ? |

Which resource below best completes the table? **5.2(G)**

Ⓐ Air

Ⓒ Oil

Ⓑ Solar

Ⓓ Soil

**2** Many of our daily routines rely on the use of nonrenewable resources. Because there is only a limited supply available, conserving these resources is very important. What is another important reason to conserve these limited supplies? **5.1(B)**

Ⓕ To learn how to function when the supplies run out

Ⓖ To create more nonrenewable resources

Ⓗ To harm the environment and cause drastic changes

Ⓙ To increase the cost of resources

**3** All of the following are advantages for using renewable resources **EXCEPT** —

Ⓐ they can be replenished in a short period of time

Ⓑ they can be used repeatedly without decreasing the supply

Ⓒ they reduce the demand of fossil fuels

Ⓓ they have a positive impact on our environment and our lives

**4** Why are coal, oil, and natural gas considered nonrenewable resources?

Ⓕ There is a limited supply, and they can be replaced in a short period of time.

Ⓖ There is not a limited supply, and they cannot be replenished in a short period of time.

Ⓗ There is a limited supply, and they cannot be replenished in a short period of time.

Ⓙ There is not a limited supply, and they can be replaced in a short period of time.

**5** Scientists are looking for ways to produce energy from natural materials, such as plants, without depleting limited natural resources. Plants are considered a good alternative because they are —

Ⓐ nonrenewable

Ⓒ reusable

Ⓑ renewable

Ⓓ not here

**6** All the pictures below identify conserving renewable and nonrenewable resources **EXCEPT** —

**A**

**C**

**B**

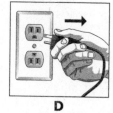

**D**

Ⓕ picture A

Ⓗ picture C

Ⓖ picture B

Ⓙ picture D

**1** Fossil fuels were formed from organic matter buried more than a hundred thousand years ago. This matter changed over a long period of time into coal, oil, and natural gas. Fossil fuels formed from plants and animals are —

Ⓐ renewable

Ⓑ nonrenewable

Ⓒ unusable

Ⓓ all of the above

**2** Which of the following is **NOT** identified as a renewable resource?

Ⓕ Fish population

Ⓖ Natural vegetation

Ⓗ Mineral deposits

Ⓙ Corn crop

**3** Which item in the picture is an example of a nonrenewable resource?

Ⓐ Animal

Ⓑ Cactus

Ⓒ Wind

Ⓓ Oil

**4** Which statement best describes a way to conserve energy?

Ⓕ Leave the lights on when you leave a room

Ⓖ Run the faucet while you are brushing your teeth

Ⓗ Walk or ride a bike to school instead of riding in a car

Ⓙ Take long showers with hot water

**5** Fossil fuels are used to produce about 80% of the energy we use on Earth. Which statement best describes how fossil fuels affect the environment?

Ⓐ Fossil fuels produce carbon dioxide and pollution.

Ⓑ Fossil fuels are used faster than they can be replaced.

Ⓒ Fossil fuels are used to make energy for engines.

Ⓓ Fossil fuels produce oxygen which plants turn into carbon dioxide.

**6** Which best explains why air is classified as a renewable resource?

Ⓕ It is formed by the remains of plants and animals.

Ⓖ It is recycled in the water cycle.

Ⓗ It is formed over time by heat and pressure.

Ⓙ It is recycled in the carbon dioxide-oxygen cycle.

## Scientific Investigation and Reasoning Skills: Questions 7–14

**7** According to the advertisement, how much water can be saved by taking a bath in a full tub of water rather than taking a 10-minute shower? **5.3(B)**

LESS is MORE...

...any time of the year!

| Shower | 26 liters/minute |
|---|---|
| Bathtub | 132 liters/fill |
| Clothes washer | 125 liters/load |
| Dishwasher | 57 liters/load |
| Bathroom faucet | 19 liters/minute |

Record your answer and fill in the bubbles below. Be sure to use the correct place value.

**8** Scientists are working very hard to develop new ways to use clean energy sources, which come from renewable resources. Which of the following is an example of a renewable resource? **5.3(D)**

  Ⓕ  Natural gas    Ⓗ  Water

  Ⓖ  Petroleum    Ⓙ  Coal

**9** All of the following are wise choices of conserving nonrenewable resources **EXCEPT** — **5.1(B)**

  Ⓐ  cutting back what is used

  Ⓑ  reusing materials

  Ⓒ  reprocessing used materials

  Ⓓ  using as many materials as possible

**10** The chart classifies renewable and nonrenewable resources.

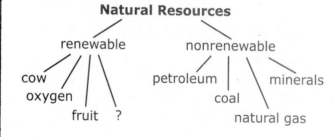

**Natural Resources**

renewable      nonrenewable

cow   oxygen   fruit   ?      petroleum   coal   natural gas   minerals

Which best completes the chart? **5.2(D)**

  Ⓕ  Oil    Ⓗ  Fossils

  Ⓖ  Timber    Ⓙ  Fossil fuels

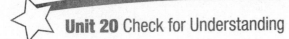

**Unit 20** Check for Understanding

**11** Which picture below shows a wise choice for disposal of resources? **5.1(B)**

Ⓐ

Ⓑ

Ⓒ

Ⓓ

**12** A group of students plans to conduct an activity to determine which natural resources are renewable and nonrenewable. Before starting the activity, the students write down which materials they think are renewable and which they guess are nonrenewable. What information do the students record before the activity begins? **5.2(B)**

Ⓕ An observation

Ⓖ A hypothesis

Ⓗ An inference

Ⓙ A conclusion

**13** Conserving any resource always makes sense. Which of the following is **NOT** a good reason to conserve renewable and nonrenewable resources? **5.1(B)**

Ⓐ To produce pollutants

Ⓑ To reduce waste

Ⓒ To care for future generations

Ⓓ To preserve the environment

**14** The table shows the approximate number of animals remaining for certain species on the endangered species list.

| Animal Name | Number Remaining |
|---|---|
| Tiger | 3200 |
| Mountain gorilla | 786 |
| Giant panda | 2500 |
| Black rhinoceros | 3725 |
| Hawksbill turtle | 8000 |
| Blue whale | 4000 |
| Amur leopard | 50 |
| Bactrian camel | 1000 |

Based on the information in the table, which animal has the greatest chance of becoming extinct? **5.2(G)**

Ⓕ Hawksbill turtle

Ⓖ Blue whale

Ⓗ Amur leopard

Ⓙ Mountain gorilla

motivation**science**™LEVEL 5

## Identifying Renewable and Nonrenewable Resources

Describe renewable and nonrenewable resources in the spaces below. Give three examples of each, and explain your thinking.

| What are renewable resources? | | |
|---|---|---|
| 1. | 2. | 3. |

| What are nonrenewable resources? | | |
|---|---|---|
| 1. | 2. | 3. |

## Formative Assessment

Complete the following statement.

*Something new I learned about natural resources is —*

_____

_____

_____

## Science Journal

What renewable and nonrenewable resources do you use every day? Design a plan to conserve resources at home. Explain how you will apply the plan and what changes can be made to everyday routines in order to conserve resources.

_____

_____

_____

_____

_____

_____

_____

_____

_____

_____

_____

_____

_____

_____

_____

_____

_____

_____

_____

_____

_____

_____

_____

_____

_____

**Science Vocabulary Builder**

Stop and think when you use natural resources. In the signs below, classify each word in the box as nonrenewable or renewable.

| livestock | oxygen | water | coal | carbon dioxide | crops |
| electricity | fossil fuels | natural gas | tuna | oil | wheat | petroleum |

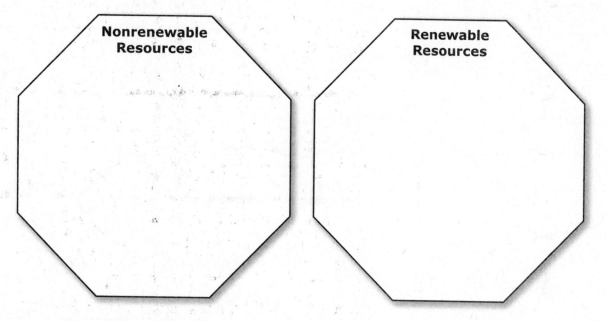

**Nonrenewable Resources**

**Renewable Resources**

Choose a resource from above that you use often. Explain how the resource is used. List ways the resource could be conserved.

Draw a visual representation for the words renewable and nonrenewable in the boxes below.

**Renewable**

**Nonrenewable**

# Unit 20 Homework

## Importance of Conservation

Animals are one of our most valuable renewable resources. Although they are classified as renewable, poaching and destruction of habitats have caused many animal populations to decrease. Thousands of animal species are classified as being threatened or endangered. The table below shows the approximate numbers for some endangered animals.

| Animal Name | Tiger | Mountain gorilla | Giant panda | Black rhinoceros | Hawksbill turtle | Blue whale | Amur leopard | Bactrian camel |
|---|---|---|---|---|---|---|---|---|
| Number Remaining | 3200 | 786 | 2500 | 3725 | 8000 | 4000 | 50 | 1000 |

Design a T-shirt about one of these magnificent animals. Try to persuade others to take measures to protect these important renewable resources.

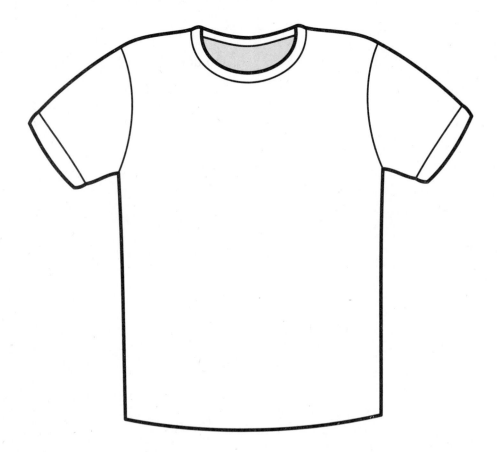

## Parent Activities

1. Discuss the types of resources used in daily life. Which resources could be used less at home?

2. Talk about the importance of conserving natural resources.

3. Visit a local zoo. Discuss which animals are endangered and threatened. Why are zoos important?

 motivation**science**™LEVEL 5

**After this lesson I will be able to:**

- **Measure** and **record** changes in weather and make predictions using weather maps, weather symbols, and a map key.

## Descriptive and Comparative Investigations

**Activity 1:** Weather Symbols

Knowing the meaning of weather symbols enables us to understand weather maps. Study the weather map symbols.

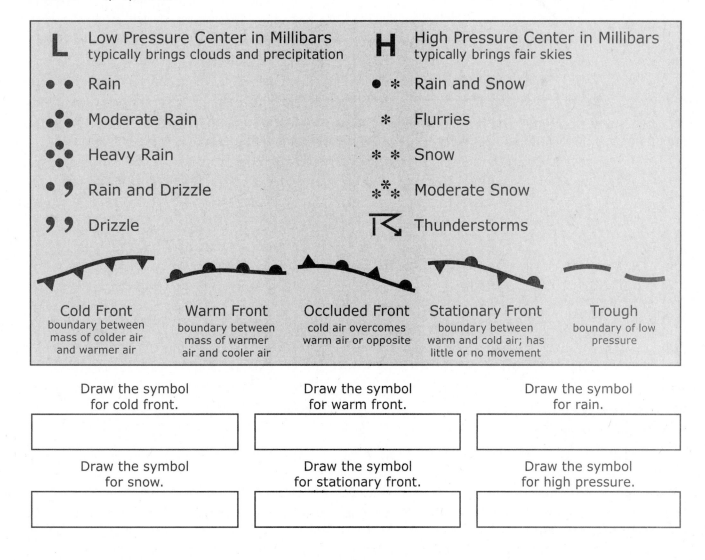

| Draw the symbol for cold front. | Draw the symbol for warm front. | Draw the symbol for rain. |
|---|---|---|
| | | |

| Draw the symbol for snow. | Draw the symbol for stationary front. | Draw the symbol for high pressure. |
|---|---|---|
| | | |

## Activity 2: Weather Predictions

Meteorologists are scientists who predict weather. Research the work of meteorologists by watching several forecasts. Record the weather for the next five days in the table. Be sure to include the predicted temperature, cloud cover, and weather conditions such as rain, snow, high winds, etc. In the last column, record the actual weather conditions for each day.

| Day of the Week | Weather Prediction | Weather Conditions |
|---|---|---|
| | | |
| | | |
| | | |
| | | |
| | | |

Create a weather report and a weather map to show the weather conditions for your area. Include a map of the United States to show fronts or other weather conditions. Display a key for the map.

**Map**

**Weather Report**

_____

_____

_____

_____

_____

_____

_____

_____

_____

_____

_____

**1** Students measure changes in weather temperature. Which tool is used when measuring this type of weather condition? **5.4(A)**

Ⓐ Triple beam balance

Ⓑ Graduated cylinder

Ⓒ Celsius thermometer

Ⓓ All of the above

**2** Pictured below is a weather map of the United States.

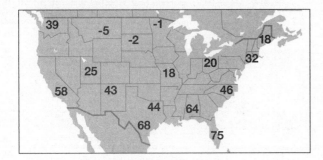

What do the numbers represent on the map?

Ⓕ Precipitation      Ⓗ Wind speed

Ⓖ Temperature      Ⓙ Humidity

**3** Students observe the local weather forecast in the newspaper and notice there is a chance of rain expected in the area late that night. The students want to determine how much rain is received, so they use a tool in the science lab to measure the precipitation. What tool do the students use?   **5.4(A)**

Ⓐ Celsius thermometer

Ⓑ Meter stick

Ⓒ Rain gauge

Ⓓ Metric ruler

**4** A group of students cuts out the weather map from the newspaper. The weather forecast predicts a cold front will move through the area. Students mark the map with the appropriate weather symbol. Which symbol below represents a cold front?

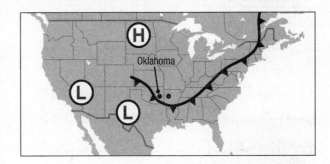

**Use the weather map below to answer questions 5 and 6.**

**5** Look at the areas that have the capital "L" symbol. What type of weather is usually associated with this symbol?

Ⓐ Fair weather

Ⓑ Good weather with sunny skies

Ⓒ Clear skies

Ⓓ Cloudy with a chance of precipitation

**6** Observe the weather map above. What type of activity would be most appropriate for people living in the northern part of Oklahoma?

Ⓕ Watch a movie at home

Ⓖ Picnic at the park

Ⓗ Visit to the local zoo

Ⓙ Swim at the lake

Name _____

**1** All of the following weather changes can be measured **EXCEPT** —

&#9398; precipitation    &#9400; humidity

&#9399; thermometer    &#9401; air pressure

**2** According to the map key below, which weather conditions are measured in millibars?

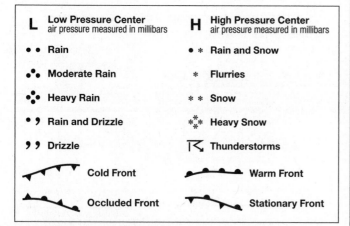

| **L** | Low Pressure Center<br>air pressure measured in millibars | **H** | High Pressure Center<br>air pressure measured in millibars |
|---|---|---|---|

&#9402; Cold and warm fronts

&#9404; Thunderstorms and tornadoes

&#9405; High and low pressure centers

&#9406; Freezing rain and heavy fog

**3** The most influential factors affecting weather change in the atmosphere are —

&#9398; clouds and the Moon

&#9399; air pressure and the Sun

&#9400; snow and rainfall

&#9401; day and night

**4** A weather map may display all of the following information **EXCEPT** —

&#9403; precipitation

&#9404; low pressure

&#9405; weather fronts

&#9406; seasonal forecast

**5** A meteorologist predicts that a warm front will arrive tomorrow. Which weather symbol would be used to indicate the warm front on a map?

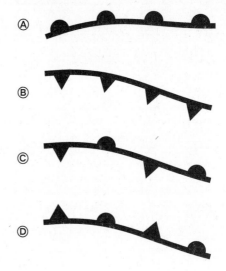

**6** Which is used to make forecasts of the weather?

&#9403; Weather map

&#9404; Line graph

&#9405; Pie chart

&#9406; Diagram

motivation**science**™ LEVEL 5

## Scientific Investigation and Reasoning Skills: Questions 7–14

**7** A website records the average temperatures for June in Austin, Texas.

| Year | Average High (°C) | Average Low (°C) |
|------|-------------------|------------------|
| 5 | 37.2 | 21.6 |
| 4 | 33.3 | 20.5 |
| 3 | 32.7 | 22.2 |
| 2 | 32.7 | 21.6 |
| 1 | 33.8 | 22.2 |

Based on the information in the table, which is the best prediction for the June temperatures in year 6?   **5.2(D)**

Ⓐ The temperatures will range between 15.5 and 26.6 degrees.

Ⓑ The temperatures will range between 18.3 and 32.2 degrees.

Ⓒ The temperatures will range between 21.1 and 32.2 degrees.

Ⓓ The temperatures will range between 23.8 and 40.1 degrees.

**8** The ancient Greeks observed the clouds, wind, and rain to understand how they were connected. Weather patterns, however, are very difficult to project. The term used by meteorologists for predicting the weather is —   **5.3(D)**

Ⓕ hypothesis

Ⓖ foreshadowing

Ⓗ educated guess

Ⓙ forecast

**9** Which of the following units of measurement is used when recording temperature?   **5.2(C)**

Ⓐ Grams

Ⓑ Centimeters

Ⓒ Celsius

Ⓓ Meters

**10** The map below shows weather conditions for the United States.

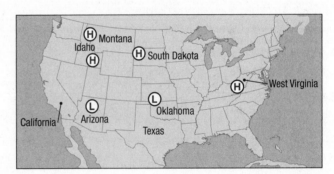

According to the weather map, which states are most likely experiencing sunny skies with little chance of precipitation?   **5.2(G)**

Ⓕ Oklahoma and Texas

Ⓖ Idaho and Montana

Ⓗ California and Arizona

Ⓙ West Virginia and Oklahoma

**Use the weather log and your knowledge of science to answer questions 11–13.**

Students measure the temperatures and record the changes over a 5-day period in science notebooks.

### Weather Forecast for April

|  | Mon | Tue | Wed | Thu | Fri |
|---|---|---|---|---|---|
| High Temp | 74 | 69 | 65 | 63 | 58 |
| Low Temp | 57 | 49 | 44 | 38 |  |

**11** Based on the information in the table, what prediction can be made regarding the low temperature on Friday?  **5.2(D)**

Ⓐ The low temperature will decrease.

Ⓑ The low temperature will increase.

Ⓒ The low temperature will stay the same.

Ⓓ The low temperature will become warmer.

**12** Based on the information in the table, what hypothesis can be made about the cause of the temperature change?  **5.2(G)**

Ⓕ The change in temperature was caused by high winds.

Ⓖ The change in temperature was caused by a cold front.

Ⓗ The change in temperature was caused by heavy fog.

Ⓙ The change in temperature was caused by a warm front.

**13** What tool was most likely used to gather the data collected in the table?  **5.2(B)**

Ⓐ Barometer

Ⓑ Anemometer

Ⓒ Thermometer

Ⓓ Rain gauge

**14** The diagram below shows a mass of cold air colliding with a mass of warm air.

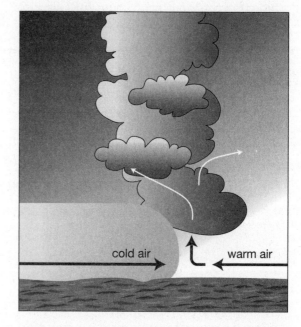

Which of the following conditions is least likely to occur when a warm front and a cold front meet?  **5.2(D)**

Ⓕ Thunderstorms

Ⓖ Clear skies

Ⓗ Tornadoes

Ⓙ Snow

motivation**science**™ LEVEL 5

## Weather Map Analysis

Use your knowledge of weather maps and symbols to complete the questions.
Justify your answers.

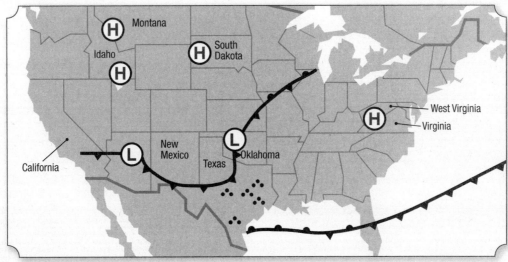

1. Which states are experiencing high pressure? Explain your answer. _____

   _____

2. What type of front is Texas experiencing? Explain your answer. _____

   _____

3. What weather condition is Texas experiencing? Explain your answer. _____

   _____

4. Which states are experiencing low pressure? Explain your answer. _____

   _____

5. Create a key to read the map. Include symbols and what they represent.

   **Map Key**

   _____



## Formative Assessment

Create a graphic organizer to name and describe tools used to measure and record weather changes.

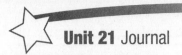

Name _____

**Science Journal**

Describe a day in which the weather took an unexpected turn. What would a meteorologist do to explain the new weather?

_____

_____

_____

_____

_____

_____

_____

_____

_____

_____

_____

_____

_____

_____

_____

_____

_____

_____

_____

_____

_____

_____

_____

     motivation**science**™LEVEL 5

## Science Vocabulary Builder

For each vocabulary word, provide a synonym, antonym, definition, and illustration.

| weather map | meteorologist | low pressure | cold front |
| forecast | warm front | high pressure | precipitation |

### Low Pressure

| Synonym | Antonym |
|---------|---------|
| **Definition** | **Illustration** |
| | |

### High Pressure

| Synonym | Antonym |
|---------|---------|
| **Definition** | **Illustration** |
| | |

### Warm Front

| Synonym | Antonym |
|---------|---------|
| **Definition** | **Illustration** |
| | |

### Cold Front

| Synonym | Antonym |
|---------|---------|
| **Definition** | **Illustration** |
| | |

### Weather Map

| Synonym | Antonym |
|---------|---------|
| **Definition** | **Illustration** |
| | |

### Forecast

| Synonym | Antonym |
|---------|---------|
| **Definition** | **Illustration** |
| | |

### Precipitation

| Synonym | Antonym |
|---------|---------|
| **Definition** | **Illustration** |
| | |

### Meteorologist

| Synonym | Antonym |
|---------|---------|
| **Definition** | **Illustration** |
| | |

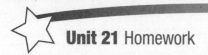
## Create a Weather Map

Create a weather map for the current weather conditions for the United States. Include weather symbols and a key.

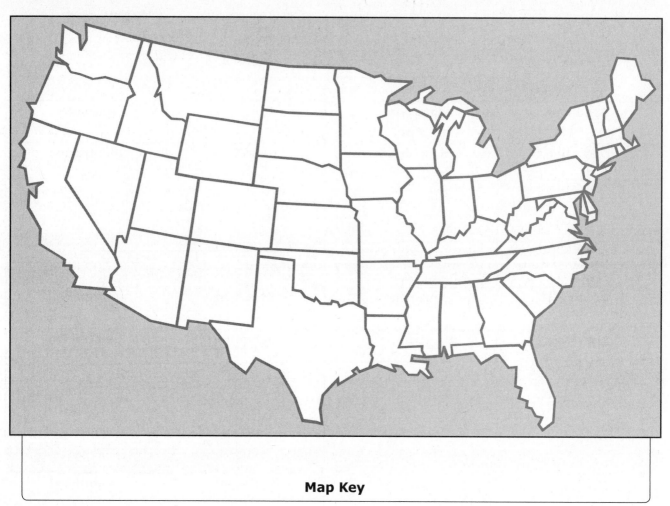

**Map Key**

Describe the above weather conditions.

_____

_____

_____

- - - - - - - - - - - - - - - - - - - - - - - - - - - - - - - - - - - - -

## Parent Activities

1. Watch the weather reports on TV, or read forecasts in the newspaper. Discuss the current and upcoming weather.

2. Track the daily weather for a month. Was any of this weather unusual for the current season?

### Motivation Station: Molly's Cool Science Fact

Water is not a mixture. It is a compound formed from two elements: hydrogen and oxygen. When two atoms of hydrogen are chemically combined with one atom of oxygen, they bond together to form $H_2O$, also known as water.

**After this lesson I will be able to:**

- **Describe** and **illustrate** the continuous movement of water above and on the surface of Earth through the water cycle and **explain** the role of the Sun as a major energy source in this process.

## Experimental Investigations

**Activity 1:** How Does the Sun Affect Water?

**Do not leave lamps on during hours when school is not in session.**

With a permanent marker, draw a line approximately halfway on the inside of two cups. Then, pour water until even with the line. Place one cup of water under a lamp and the other cup in a place away from the lamp. The experiment may need to be continued the next day. Check the cups every 2 hours for changes. Record the observations.

| Time | Observations |
|------|--------------|
| After 2 Hours | |
| After 4 Hours | |
| After 6 Hours | |
| Next Day (if necessary) | |

| When did you begin to notice changes? | What changes occurred? |
|---|---|
| **Which part of the water cycle does the lamp represent in this experiment?** | **What can be concluded from this experiment?** |

# Unit 22 Introduction

## Activity 2: Groundwater

In this activity, groundwater is explored. This investigation explains how precipitation ends up as groundwater when it does not fall into oceans, rivers, lakes, or ponds. Use the materials provided by the teacher to complete the activity.

**Directions**

Record a hypothesis before beginning the investigation. Write observations during the experiment. Create a conclusion after the investigation.

Pour the gravel mixture into the two cups. Do not fill more than halfway. Observe what happens when $\frac{1}{2}$ cup water is poured slowly into the first cup. Next, drip 3 drops of food coloring on top of the gravel in the second cup. Use a dropper to "rain" $\frac{1}{2}$ cup water on the gravel and food coloring mixture. Observe what happens.

| Test 1 | Test 2 |
|---|---|
| Hypothesis | Hypothesis |
| Observations | Observations |
| Conclusion | Conclusion |

What happened when water was poured into the first cup?

_____

_____

What did the investigation represent? Which part represented groundwater? What did the gravel mixture represent? What did the food coloring represent?

_____

_____

_____

Was your hypothesis correct?

_____

_____

 motivation**science**™ LEVEL 5 ©2011–2014 mentoring**minds**.com

**1** Which method would be most effective for students to display the continuous movement of water through the water cycle? **5.2(G)**

&#9398; Table     &#9400; Pie chart

&#9399; Graph     &#9401; Diagram

**2** Water is considered a renewable resource because of the water cycle. How does the water cycle help identify water as a renewable resource?

&#9402; Water falls into the lakes and oceans and helps plants and animals, which are renewable resources.

&#9403; Water can be used over and over again because of its continuous movement above and on the surface of Earth.

&#9404; Rivers and streams carry the water that comes from rain and melted snow into the ocean.

&#9405; Water that falls into the lakes and oceans continuously mixes and can be used for plants.

**3** Which substance is being recycled in the diagram below?

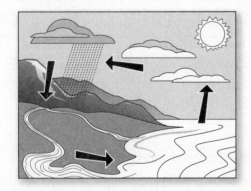

&#9398; Oxygen     &#9400; Water

&#9399; Pollution     &#9401; Carbon dioxide

**4** Students draw and label diagrams of the water cycle. Pictured below is one student's diagram of the water cycle.

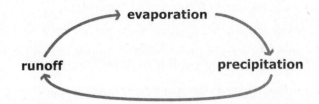

What is missing in the student's diagram?

&#9402; Erosion should be placed between runoff and evaporation.

&#9403; Deposition should be placed between precipitation and runoff.

&#9404; Condensation should be placed between evaporation and precipitation.

&#9405; Collection should be placed between evaporation and precipitation.

**5** What is the major source of energy that powers the movement of water throughout the environment?

&#9398; Wind     &#9400; Sun

&#9399; Water     &#9401; Clouds

**6** If water is constantly being cleaned and recycled through the water cycle, why do we need to conserve it? **5.1(B)**

&#9402; Water treatment plants do not have the resources to clean the water.

&#9403; Earth contains a limited amount of freshwater.

&#9404; Saving water makes it easier for it to be recycled through the environment.

&#9405; The Sun does not have the power to heat all the water on Earth.

**Unit 22** Check for Understanding

**1** The continuous movement of water above and on the surface of Earth through the water cycle means —

Ⓐ water is temporarily in motion

Ⓑ water is partially in motion

Ⓒ water movement requires no motion

Ⓓ water is constantly in motion

**2** Which of the following processes of the water cycle describes how water is continuously moving through the environment by plants releasing water from leaves?

Ⓕ Condensation

Ⓖ Transpiration

Ⓗ Respiration

Ⓙ Precipitation

**3** Water is temporarily stored in many different places such as lakes, glaciers, and even underground. Water moves from these places, returning to the oceans, by all of the following **EXCEPT** —

Ⓐ streams

Ⓑ rivers

Ⓒ animals

Ⓓ rocks

**4** Which statement correctly describes the Sun's role in the water cycle?

Ⓕ The Sun's energy causes groundwater to accumulate.

Ⓖ Gravity from the Sun causes rivers to flow into oceans.

Ⓗ The Sun's energy causes the soil to heat up, making the water boil.

Ⓙ Water is heated by the Sun's energy and turns into water vapor.

**5** A swimming pool loses 1 cm of water per day because of the Sun. What is this process called?

Ⓐ Precipitation

Ⓑ Evaporation

Ⓒ Collection

Ⓓ Condensation

**6** Cumulonimbus clouds are large and contain a significant amount of water. These towering clouds often produce thunderstorms and rain. Which part of the water cycle is represented by the rain falling from these clouds?

Ⓕ Collection

Ⓖ Evaporation

Ⓗ Condensation

Ⓙ None of the above

 motivation**science**™LEVEL 5 ©2011–2014 mentoring**minds**.com

## Scientific Investigation and Reasoning Skills: Questions 7–14

**7** In an activity, students put 100 mL of water in a clear plastic bag. They blow air into the bag, seal it, and tape it to a sunny window. After a few hours, the students notice the bag has water droplets running down the inside of the bag, and the bag appears cloudy above the water line.

Why does the inside of the bag appear cloudy? **5.2(D)**

Ⓐ Some of the water turns into water vapor.

Ⓑ The air in the bag heats up and begins to boil.

Ⓒ The ice cubes in the bag melt into liquid water.

Ⓓ Part of the water escapes the bag and condenses on the outside.

**8** Modern technologies have allowed scientists to study oceans and lakes in greater detail to better understand the hydrosphere. Most lakes contain freshwater and must have a continuous source of new water, or they will eventually dry up. What is the major source of energy that allows water to continuously move through the environment, replacing water in lakes and oceans? **5.3(D)**

Ⓕ Waves          Ⓗ Rain

Ⓖ Wind          Ⓙ Sun

**9** A group of students builds a model to better understand the water cycle. Which parts of the water cycle are necessary to include in the model? **5.3(C)**

Ⓐ Evaporation, transpiration, erosion, condensation

Ⓑ Precipitation, runoff, erosion, deposition

Ⓒ Evaporation, condensation, precipitation, collection

Ⓓ Precipitation, evaporation, accumulation, transportation

**10** How many more liters of water does the city who uses the most water utilize than the city who uses the least? **5.2(G)**

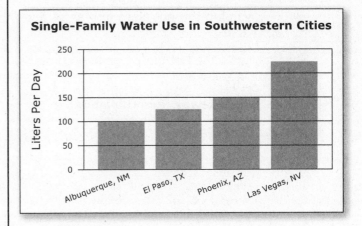

Record your answer in the box below. Be sure to use the correct place value.

Name _____

**Use the picture below and your knowledge of science to answer questions 11 and 12.**

11 Students investigate how the water cycle works using a hot plate, two pans, ice, and insulated gloves. Which safety practice is most important for students to follow during this experiment?   **5.1(A)**

Ⓐ Always listen to the teacher's directions

Ⓑ Always plug the hot plate into an outlet after use

Ⓒ Wait until the hot plate has heated up to pour in the water

Ⓓ Eat snacks away from the lab table

12 When conducting the experiment above, which safety equipment is most important? **5.4(B)**

Ⓕ Extra rolls of paper towels for spills

Ⓖ Goggles for proper eye protection

Ⓗ Latex gloves for protection against heat

Ⓙ Bucket of sand in case of chemical burn

13 Many people think Earth has an endless supply of fresh water. The water cycle teaches that water is reused, yet because of pollution, the amount of clean water on Earth has decreased. A good way to save water is to practice —   **5.1(B)**

Ⓐ conservation

Ⓑ destruction

Ⓒ neglect

Ⓓ experimentation

14 Which of the following is **NOT** a valid conclusion based on the Adjust-A-Flow advertisement?   **5.3(B)**

**Adjust-A-Flow**
The great new shower valve that allows you to adjust the flow of water for your needs.

• Easy to Install and Use   • Saves Water
• Lowers Water Bills

**This product will pay for itself!**

Ⓕ Installing Adjust-A-Flow can save water.

Ⓖ Using Adjust-A-Flow can lower water bills.

Ⓗ Adjust-A-Flow allows you to regulate the amount of water used.

Ⓙ Adjust-A-Flow costs no money to buy because it pays for itself.

 motivation**science**™LEVEL 5 ©2011–2014 mentoring**minds**.com

## Water Cycle Diagram

Describe and illustrate the parts of the water cycle with the diagram below.

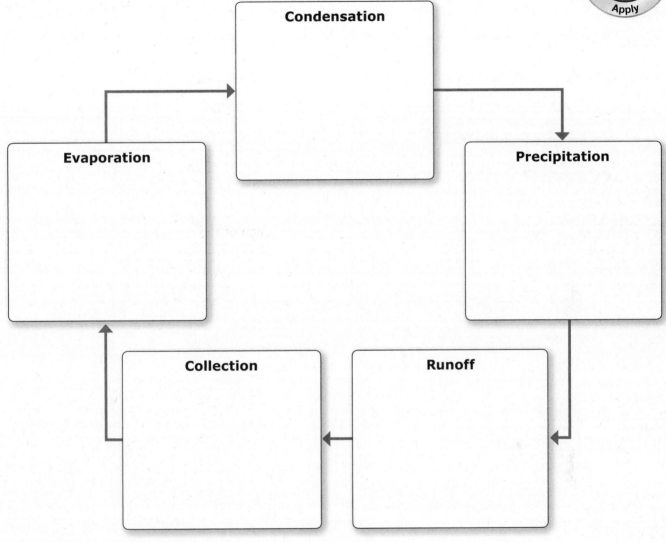

## Formative Assessment

What is the role of the Sun in the water cycle?

_____

_____

_____

_____

_____

Name _____

## Science Journal

Explain why the water cycle is a continuous cycle. Without the Sun, would the water cycle continue? Why or why not?

_____

_____

_____

_____

_____

_____

_____

_____

_____

_____

_____

_____

_____

_____

_____

_____

_____

_____

_____

_____

_____

_____

_____

_____

**Science Vocabulary Builder**

In each droplet, illustrate the vocabulary word. Then write a paragraph using all the words. Underline each vocabulary word in the paragraph.

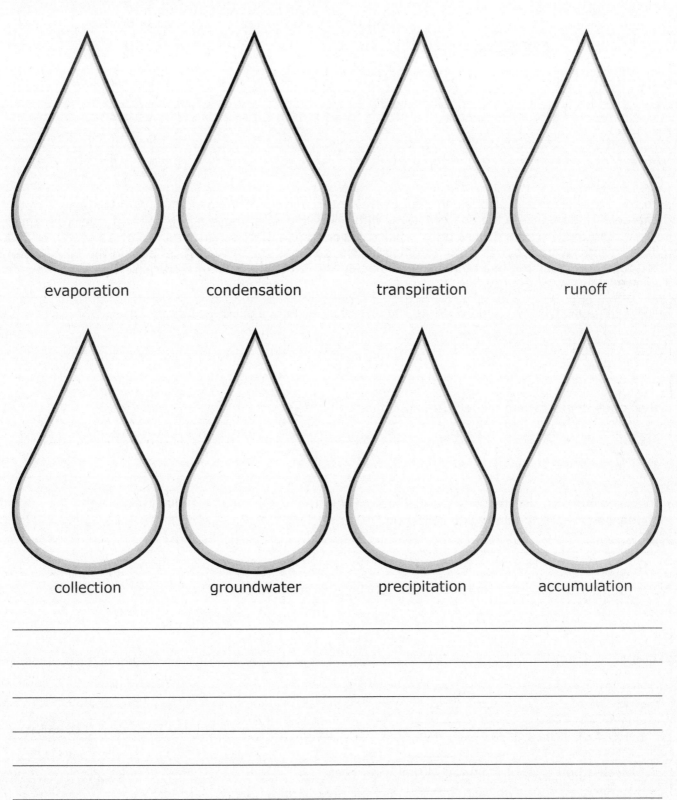

evaporation     condensation     transpiration     runoff

collection     groundwater     precipitation     accumulation

_____

_____

_____

_____

_____

Supporting Standard 4.8(B)

## Construct a Terrarium to Make a Mini-Water Cycle

A terrarium is a closed system in which plants and small animals can survive. To build a terrarium, find a container at home, such as:

jar          salad or deli container          soda bottle

To build the terrarium, place pebbles or gravel at the bottom of the container. Add some activated charcoal (optional). Top the charcoal layer with a small layer of moss. Place soil in a layer over the moss, and top with more moss (moss is also optional). Plant seeds, such as rye grass seeds, or add small plants. Water your terrarium to moisten the soil, and then cover. After adding the initial water, the terrarium does not need to be watered again. After observing your terrarium for several days, answer the following questions.

Why is it unnecessary to add water to the terrarium after the initial watering?

_____

_____

How does the terrarium model the water cycle?

_____

_____

Draw a picture of your terrarium. Label the parts of the water cycle, including evaporation, condensation, precipitation, and collection.

✂ - - - - - - - - - - - - - - - - - - - - - - - - - - - - - - - - - - - - - - - - - - - - - - - - - -

## Parent Activities

1. Discuss how a terrarium models the water cycle.
2. As different forms of weather occur, discuss precipitation and collection.

**Motivation Station: Mike's Cool Science Fact**

A Blue Moon is not really blue. It occurs when two full moons appear in the same calendar month. The second full moon is called a Blue Moon.

**After this lesson I will be able to:**

- **Collect** and **analyze** data to identify sequences and predict patterns of change in shadows, tides, seasons, and the observable appearance of the Moon over time.

## Comparative Investigations

**Activity 1:** Shadows

With a partner, record the heights and positions of your shadows throughout the day. Also record the position of the Sun.

Complete the table to compare results. Include results for each partner in the data table.

### Shadows

| Time | Height/Position Student 1 | Height/Position Student 2 | Position of the Sun |
|---|---|---|---|
|  |  |  |  |
|  |  |  |  |
|  |  |  |  |

1. What happened to the position of your shadow over time?_____

_____

_____

2. Did the height of your shadow change?_____

_____

3. Why are shadows cast differently throughout the day?_____

_____

4. What can be concluded from this experiment? _____

_____

## Unit 23 Introduction

**Activity 2:** Tides, Moon Phases, and Seasons

### Tides

Use Internet resources provided by the teacher to create a graph of predicted tides for one day. Choose the location for the tides. Write the location as a title for the table and graph. Fill in the table, and then use the information gathered to make the graph. Provide the date of the predicted tides.

| Date/Place | Time | Height |
|---|---|---|
| | High tide | High tide |
| | Low tide | Low tide |
| | High tide | High tide |
| | Low tide | Low tide |

### Moon Phases

Carefully twist the cookies in half. One half of the cookie needs to have most of the frosting. Using a plastic knife, scrape off frosting to form the phases of the Moon, as directed by the teacher. Shade in the phases of the Moon in the circles below.

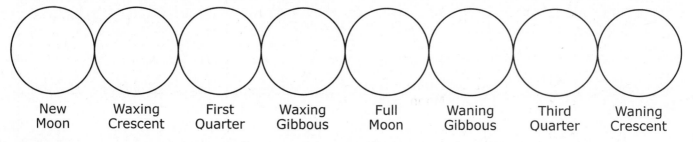

| New Moon | Waxing Crescent | First Quarter | Waxing Gibbous | Full Moon | Waning Gibbous | Third Quarter | Waning Crescent |

### Seasons

As you watch the demonstration performed by your teacher, label the correct seasons for the Northern Hemisphere in the diagram below.

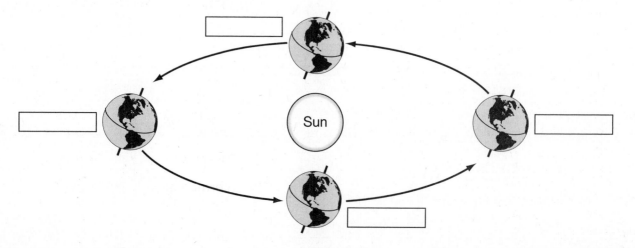

       motivation**science**™ LEVEL 5    ©2011–2014 mentoring**minds**.com

**Use this table and your knowledge of science to answer questions 1 and 2.**

The table below shows some of the characteristics of the Moon as it revolves around Earth.

**Moon Data**

| Phases | Description | Time seen during the lunar cycle |
|---|---|---|
| New Moon | Cannot be seen | 1st day |
| Waxing Crescent | Thin piece seen on right side | 3 days after New Moon |
| First Quarter | Right half seen | 7 days after New Moon |
| Waxing Gibbous | More than half seen | 10–11 days after New Moon |
| Full Moon | All of one side of Moon seen | 14 days after New Moon |
| Waning Gibbous | More than half seen | 17–18 days after New Moon |
| Last Quarter | Left half seen | 21 days after New Moon |
| Waning Crescent | Thin piece seen on left side | 25–27 days after New Moon |

**1** About how long will it take the Moon to return to the New Moon phase?  **5.2(D)**

    Ⓐ  1 day      Ⓒ  28 days

    Ⓑ  20 days      Ⓓ  2 days

**2** What causes different parts of the Moon to be lit as it orbits Earth?

    Ⓕ  Rotation around the Sun

    Ⓖ  Refraction from the Sun

    Ⓗ  Revolving around the Sun

    Ⓙ  Reflection from the Sun

**3** How would you order the pictures below to show the correct seasonal sequence?

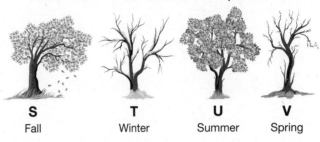

| S | T | U | V |
|---|---|---|---|
| Fall | Winter | Summer | Spring |

    Ⓐ  S, T, U, V      Ⓒ  V, S, T, U

    Ⓑ  T, V, U, S      Ⓓ  T, V, S, U

**4** Earth experiences seasonal changes because of its orbit around the Sun, which is also known as a —

    Ⓕ  revolution      Ⓗ  rotation

    Ⓖ  precipitation      Ⓙ  condensation

**5** Students notice it is fairly easy to predict the time of day from the Sun and a shadow cast on the ground since the length of a shadow changes throughout the day. The length of a shadow that is cast is comparative to the Sun's —

    Ⓐ  height and angle as it appears to move across the sky

    Ⓑ  length and height as it moves across the sky

    Ⓒ  revolution as it orbits around Earth

    Ⓓ  rotation as it appears to spin on its axis

**6** Scientists use a variety of tools and methods to conduct scientific inquiry. Which of the following tools would be helpful in studying the patterns of change in the appearance of the Moon over time?  **5.2(B)**

    Ⓕ  Telescope      Ⓗ  Microscope

    Ⓖ  Thermometer      Ⓙ  Timer

# Unit 23 Check for Understanding

**1** Every day, rising and falling of ocean water is caused by the pull of gravity from the Moon and Sun, affecting the movement of water across the ocean. Which pattern of change below is the daily rise and fall of the ocean level?

Ⓐ Tides

Ⓒ Seasons

Ⓑ Moon phases

Ⓓ Shadows

**2** The revolution of the Moon around Earth makes the Moon appear to change its shape in the sky. The changing shape of the lit part of the Moon that we see is called its —

Ⓕ crescent

Ⓗ phase

Ⓖ position

Ⓙ state

**3** The sequence below shows the amount of visible light seen during different Moon phases.

If a picture was added for the next phase, it can be predicted that the visible light seen would —

Ⓐ increase

Ⓒ expand

Ⓑ decrease

Ⓓ disappear

**4** On a bright, sunny day, which time of day can be predicted to create the shortest shadows?

Ⓕ 9:00 A.M.

Ⓗ 3:00 P.M.

Ⓖ 12:00 P.M.

Ⓙ 12:00 A.M.

**5** Which direction would the man's shadow be pointing at 3 P.M.?

10 A.M.    12 P.M.    1 P.M.    3 P.M.

Ⓐ

Ⓑ

Ⓒ

Ⓓ

**6** A student reads the following statement in a science book.

> Earth's axis is not straight up and down, but tilted. This tilt and Earth's revolution causes us to experience changes in the amount of sunlight we receive each day.

Which natural occurrence is the statement explaining?

Ⓕ Moon phases

Ⓗ Seasons

Ⓖ Tides

Ⓙ Not here

motivation**science**™ LEVEL 5

## Scientific Investigation and Reasoning Skills: Questions 7–14

**7** Based on the tide patterns seen in the table below, which time best estimates when the next low tide will occur? **5.2(G)**

| Day | Tide | Time |
|---|---|---|
| Friday | Low | 1:48 A.M. |
| Friday | High | 9:34 A.M. |
| Friday | Low | 2:35 P.M. |
| Friday | High | 4:24 P.M. |
| Saturday | Low | 2:27 A.M. |

&#9398; 6:00 A.M.      &#9400; 2:00 A.M.

&#9399; 8:00 A.M.      &#9401; 2:00 P.M.

**8** In an activity, students observe the Moon for 30 days and record what they see.

Which statement correctly gives a logical reason why the Moon appears to change shape over the 30-day period? **5.3(A)**

&#9401; Only the lit part of the Moon facing Earth can be seen as the Moon orbits Earth.

&#9415; The Moon travels between Earth and the Sun every 30 days.

&#9416; Earth's axis is tilted, making the Moon appear to change as Earth revolves.

&#9417; Only the lit part of the Moon is the part the Sun shines on each day.

**9** At high tide, the water level at the beach reaches farther up the beach than at low tide.

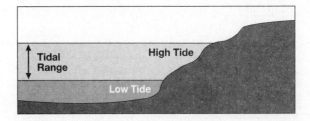

What is the cause of the water levels rising and falling during the tide cycle? **5.2(D)**

&#9398; Rotation of Earth

&#9399; Gravity from the Moon and Sun

&#9400; Evaporation of water

&#9401; Wind blowing the water

**10** What change occurs in the length of the shadow between the time shown and noon? **5.2(D)**

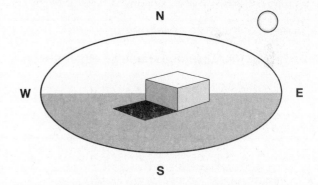

&#9401; The length of the shadow will get longer.

&#9415; The length of the shadow will remain the same.

&#9416; The length of the shadow will get shorter.

&#9417; The length of the shadow will disappear.

**Unit 23** Check for Understanding

**11** Students create a model to show how the Sun appears to move across the sky during the day. They take all the materials outside and make sure the location receives sunlight throughout the day. Each hour they record their observations and mark an X where the shadow falls. To get accurate results the model must sit in the same location and be lined up the same way hourly. The activity is repeated each month to check their markings for accuracy.

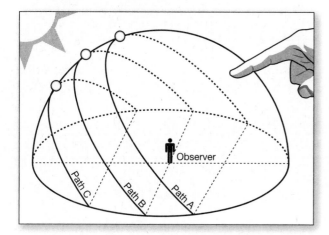

What is the purpose in repeating the activity each month?  **5.2(E)**

Ⓐ To decrease accuracy of results

Ⓑ To increase reliability of results

Ⓒ To increase questionable results

Ⓓ To decrease valid results

**12** Which observation below is **NOT** an example of empirical evidence?  **5.3(A)**

Ⓕ The shadows were 10 meters long at 4:00 P.M.

Ⓖ High tide occurred at 3:00 P.M.

Ⓗ There was a full Moon on August 13.

Ⓙ The first day of fall had very cool temperatures.

**13** Students construct a saltwater model to study ocean tides. Which tool should the students use when demonstrating how the model works?  **5.4(B)**

Ⓐ Spring scale

Ⓑ Microscope

Ⓒ Safety goggles

Ⓓ Fire extinguisher

**14** The picture below shows a beach at sunset.

What compass direction must the person face to view his shadow?  **5.4(A)**

Ⓕ North

Ⓖ South

Ⓗ East

Ⓙ West

## Cause and Effect Puppet Show

Create a puppet show to present to the class. Use your knowledge of the subjects to design the show. Choose from the following subjects. Circle your choice.

| Phases of the Moon | Tides | Seasons | Shadows |

| **Create dialogue for the puppet show here.** | **Design the puppets here.** |
|---|---|
| | |

Copy your design on another piece of paper. Glue designs for puppets to tongue depressors. Construction paper can be used to decorate the final design of the puppets.

## Formative Assessment

Patterns of change are shown in the table below. For each given pattern, record the amount of time it takes for the pattern to occur.

### Patterns of Change

| High Tide to Low Tide | Summer to Summer the Following Year | New Moon to Full Moon |
|---|---|---|
| | | |

## Science Journal

Fill in the boxes to explain the cause and effect of tides, seasons, shadows, and phases of the Moon.

**Tides**

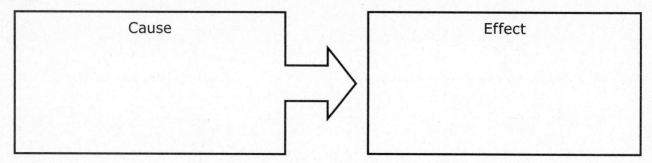

| Cause | Effect |
|-------|--------|

**Seasons**

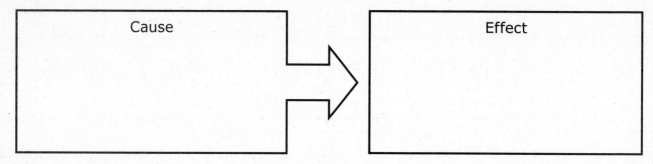

| Cause | Effect |
|-------|--------|

**Shadows**

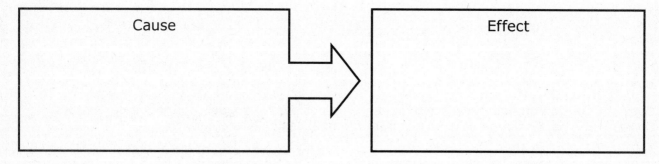

| Cause | Effect |
|-------|--------|

**Moon Phases**

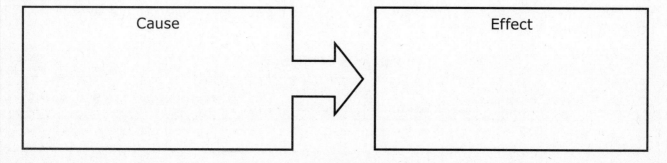

| Cause | Effect |
|-------|--------|

motivation**science**™LEVEL 5

Supporting Standard 4.8(C)

## Science Vocabulary Builder

Complete the graphic organizer below.

| Word | Definition |
|------|------------|
| **Shadow** | |
| **Picture** | **Association** This word reminds me of... |

| Word | Definition |
|------|------------|
| **Tide** | |
| **Picture** | **Association** This word reminds me of... |

| Word | Definition |
|------|------------|
| **Moon phases** | |
| **Picture** | **Association** This word reminds me of... |

| Word | Definition |
|------|------------|
| **Season** | |
| **Picture** | **Association** This word reminds me of... |

**Moon Calendar**

Create a Moon calendar to show the phases of the Moon for one month. Number the days and draw the appearance of the Moon each night.

| Sunday | Monday | Tuesday | Wednesday | Thursday | Friday | Saturday |
|--------|--------|---------|-----------|----------|--------|----------|
|        |        |         |           |          |        |          |
|        |        |         |           |          |        |          |
|        |        |         |           |          |        |          |
|        |        |         |           |          |        |          |
|        |        |         |           |          |        |          |
|        |        |         |           |          |        |          |

✂ - - - - - - - - - - - - - - - - - - - - - - - - - - - - - - - - - - - - - - - - - - - - - - - - - -

**Parent Activities**

1. Help your child conduct the above investigation. Discuss the weekly results.
2. When extreme weather conditions occur in your area, discuss the impact on local plants and animals.

**After this lesson I will be able to:**

- **Investigate** rapid changes in Earth's surface such as volcanic eruptions, earthquakes, and landslides.

## Descriptive and Comparative Investigations

**Activity 1:** Landslides

Formulate a hypothesis before beginning the experiment. Create 2–3 piles of soil in a container. Place objects on tops and sides of the hills. One at a time, pour water on the top of the hills. Observe what happens.

Hypothesis– _____

_____

1. What happened when water was poured at the top of the pile of soil?

_____

_____

2. What did this activity represent?

_____

_____

3. Did anything happen to the objects placed on the piles? Why or why not?

_____

_____

4. Was your hypothesis correct?

_____

_____

5. What may happen if a landslide occurs close to houses?

_____

_____

6. Illustrate the experiment below.

Name _____

## Activity 2: Volcano Diagram

Research the parts of volcanoes. Use the words in the box to label the volcano diagram below.

### Parts of a Volcano

| magma chamber | magma | vent | lava | crater | ash | ash cloud |

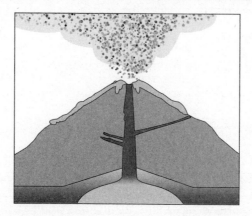

## Activity 3: Earthquakes

Observe the materials set out by the teacher. Record your observations during the experiment. Slide one half of the plate up, the other down vertically. Vertical movement occurs in a Normal Fault.

| Describe what Happens | Illustration of a Normal Fault |
|---|---|
|  |  |

Slide the plate halves creating horizontal movements. Horizontal movement is the major movement for Strike-Slip Faults.

| Describe what Happens | Illustration of a Strike-Slip Fault |
|---|---|
|  |  |

Push the plate halves toward each other until one slides above the other. This type of movement happens in Reverse Faults.

| Describe what Happens | Illustration of a Reverse Fault |
|---|---|
|  |  |

 motivation**science**™LEVEL 5

**1** Some changes occur to Earth's surface slowly while other changes occur rapidly. Which of the following changes Earth's surface rapidly?

Ⓐ Rivers          Ⓒ Weathering

Ⓑ Wind           Ⓓ Landslides

**2** A new lava flow has created a thick layer of basalt. Which unit of measure would scientists use to measure the thickness of the rock layer created as a result of volcanic activity? **5.2(C)**

Ⓕ Milliliters     Ⓗ Grams

Ⓖ Centimeters    Ⓙ Inches

**3** Earth has four major layers as seen in the diagram below. The crust makes up a thin layer on the surface of our planet. This layer is not all in one piece but is made up of many pieces, like a puzzle covering the surface of Earth. These pieces, called plates, slowly move around, sliding and bumping into each other.

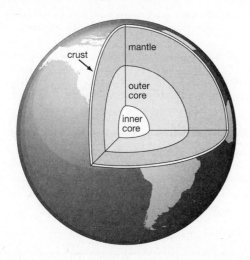

Which of the following is responsible for rapid changes to Earth's surface caused by shifting plates?

Ⓐ Rivers          Ⓒ Earthquakes

Ⓑ Erosion         Ⓓ Glaciers

**4** A teacher asks students to develop a question to research volcanoes. All of the following questions would be valid to research **EXCEPT** —     **5.2(B)**

Ⓕ How do volcanoes change Earth's surface?

Ⓖ What causes volcanoes to erupt?

Ⓗ Do scientists drive across moving lava flows?

Ⓙ Is a volcano constructive, destructive, or both?

**5** Landslides change Earth's surface rapidly when dirt, rocks, and pebbles slide down a slope together. Sometimes these landslides are small and other times they may change the entire side of a mountain.

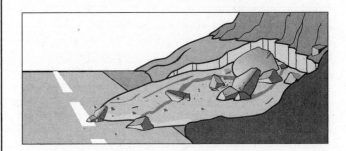

Which of the following is a cause of landslides?

Ⓐ Air pollution    Ⓒ Hailstorms

Ⓑ Condensation    Ⓓ Heavy rainfall

**6** All of the following activities negatively impact Earth **EXCEPT** —

Ⓕ volcanic eruption of gas and ash

Ⓖ delta producing fertile soil

Ⓗ landslide eroding the side of a mountain

Ⓙ crack in a field from an earthquake

**Unit 24** Check for Understanding

**1** In an activity, students rub two wood blocks together in opposite directions.

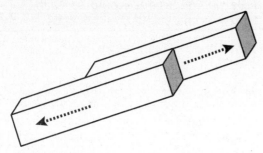

Which natural occurrence does this activity represent?

Ⓐ Earthquake

Ⓑ Volcanic eruption

Ⓒ Landslide

Ⓓ Mountain formation

**2** The Hawaiian Islands were formed and continue to grow under the ocean surface. Which natural occurrences formed the Hawaiian Islands?

Ⓕ Earthquakes

Ⓖ Landslides

Ⓗ Underwater volcanoes

Ⓙ Tectonic plate collisions

**3** A very mountainous region in California has had an extreme amount of rain over the last 2 days. People living in this area should watch out for —

Ⓐ hurricanes

Ⓑ earthquakes

Ⓒ volcanoes

Ⓓ landslides

**4** A large wave that is formed out at sea by tectonic plate movement is called a tsunami. What is the cause of a tsunami?

Ⓕ Underwater volcano

Ⓖ Underwater hurricane

Ⓗ Underwater earthquake

Ⓙ Underwater landslide

**5** How does an area benefit from volcanic activity?

Ⓐ Farmland and crops are destroyed

Ⓑ New land masses and islands are formed

Ⓒ Poisonous gases are produced

Ⓓ Roads are buried by flowing lava

**6** Which of these is least likely to cause a rapid change to Earth's surface?

Ⓕ Volcano

Ⓖ Landslide

Ⓗ Earthquake

Ⓙ Deposition

 motivation**science**™LEVEL 5

## Scientific Investigation and Reasoning Skills: Questions 7–14

**7** Which of the following most likely caused the change in the location below? **5.2(D)**

**Before**

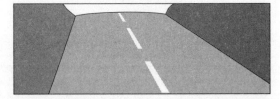

**After**

Ⓐ  Volcano
Ⓒ  Earthquake

Ⓑ  Weathering
Ⓓ  Thunderstorm

**8** Before investigating rapid changes in Earth's surface, students each developed a hypothesis about what rapid changes in Earth's surface meant. Which student's hypothesis was correct? **5.2(B)**

Ⓕ  Student 1 said rapid changes meant forms of precipitation.

Ⓖ  Student 2 guessed rapid changes were high and low temperatures.

Ⓗ  Student 3 guessed rapid changes were caused by volcanic eruptions, earthquakes, and landslides.

Ⓙ  Student 4 said rapid changes were the day and night cycle caused by Earth's rotation.

**9** Students learn through investigation that landslides travel at tremendous speeds. They research the effects of landslide speeds and report that some slides travel at speeds approaching 322 km per hour. Students decide to further investigate these reports by testing different amounts of water on three landform models all made of rock and pebbles. What is the variable in this experimental investigation? **5.2(A)**

Ⓐ  Landslide speeds

Ⓑ  Amount of water

Ⓒ  Types of soil

Ⓓ  All of the above

**10** The diagram below shows four layers of Earth identified by numbers.

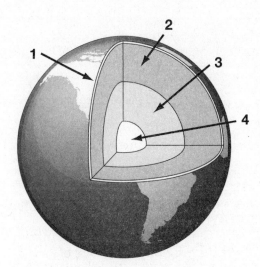

Which layer experiences changes from earthquakes? **5.2(D)**

Ⓕ  Layer 1
Ⓗ  Layer 3

Ⓖ  Layer 2
Ⓙ  Layer 4

**Use the picture below and your knowledge of science to answer questions 11 and 12.**

11  Students build volcano models for a class science project. When vinegar, baking soda, dish detergent, and food coloring are mixed, a reaction causes the volcano to look like it is erupting. In the model, what part of a volcano does the solution represent?  **5.3(C)**

Ⓐ  Vent

Ⓑ  Lava

Ⓒ  Magma chamber

Ⓓ  Ash cloud

12  When working with vinegar and baking soda, what procedure should students follow when testing the volcano model?  **5.4(B)**

Ⓕ  Stir the mixture rapidly

Ⓖ  Wear safety goggles and gloves

Ⓗ  Taste the mixture to identify the ingredients

Ⓙ  Use a fire extinguisher to stop the eruption

13  Which of the following best completes the table below?  **5.2(G)**

**Rapid Change to Earth's Surface**

| Event | Change to Land |
| --- | --- |
| Earthquake | ??? |
| Landslide | Land overlaps other land |
| Volcano | New land created |

Ⓐ  Land explodes

Ⓑ  Land melts

Ⓒ  New land forms

Ⓓ  Crust fractures

14  A seismograph is an instrument used for recording the waves caused by vibration and motion of the ground.

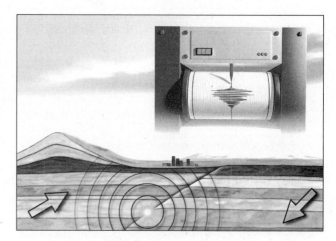

A seismograph is most useful for measuring —  **5.3(D)**

Ⓕ  tornadoes

Ⓖ  earthquakes

Ⓗ  rainfall

Ⓙ  mudslides

     motivation**science**™LEVEL 5   ©2011–2014 mentoring**minds**.com

## Earthquakes and Volcanoes

### Life Along a Fault Line

In the space below, design an earthquake safety plan for a family who is moving into a neighborhood along a fault line.

**Earthquake Safety Plan**

### Earthquakes and Volcanoes Around the World

On the map below, label the map where earthquakes and volcanic eruptions have recently occurred. Create separate symbols to represent earthquakes and volcanoes. Use a red crayon to outline the Ring of Fire.

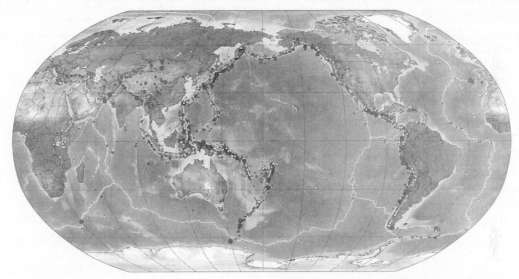

*U.S. Department of the Interior, U.S. Geological Survey*

## Formative Assessment

Complete the following statements.

• I used to think volcanic eruptions _____,

  but now I know _____.

• I used to think earthquakes _____,

  but now I know _____.

• I used to think landslides _____,

  but now I know _____.

**Science Journal**

Devise a plan of action you would take if a sudden change, such as a volcanic eruption, earthquake, or landslide, occurred close to your home. What precautions could you take to keep safe from the sudden changes in Earth's surface?

_____

_____

_____

_____

_____

_____

_____

_____

_____

_____

_____

_____

_____

_____

_____

_____

_____

_____

_____

_____

_____

_____

_____

_____

_____

**Science Vocabulary Builder**

## Sudden Changes on Earth

Classify each of the vocabulary words in the box with the correct natural disaster. Some words may be classified in more than one place.

| | | | | | | | |
|---|---|---|---|---|---|---|---|
| aftershock | ash | change | eruption | debris | fault | flood | lava |
| magma | rapid | seismograph | tectonic plates | | tsunami | | volcanic |

**Earthquake**

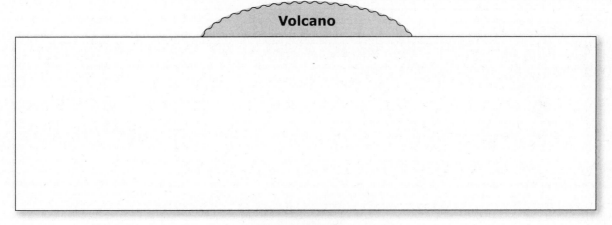

**Volcano**

**Landslide**

**Volcano Model**

Research ideas on how to make a volcano model. Create your model at home. Take your model to school ready to erupt. At school, answer the following questions in complete sentences.

1. What materials did you use to create the volcano and eruption?

_____

2. Did the volcano model erupt?

_____

3. If you could make a change to the model, what would it be?

_____

_____

4. How does the model symbolize a real volcanic eruption?

_____

_____

5. What is the difference in the way your volcano model works and the way a real volcano erupts?

_____

_____

Illustrate the model and the eruption below.

✂ - - - - - - - - - - - - - - - - - - - - - - - - - - - - - - - - - - - - -

**Parent Activities**

1. Assist your child with creating the model volcano for the above assignment.
2. If living in an area prone to earthquakes or landslides, conduct family drills to prepare for emergencies.

motivation**science**™ LEVEL 5

**Motivation Station: Mike's Cool Science Fact**

Every planet in the solar system has moons except for Mercury and Venus. Saturn and Jupiter both have over 50 moons. Ganymede, one of Jupiter's moons, is the largest in the solar system.

**After this lesson I will be able to:**

• **Identify** the planets in Earth's solar system and their positions in relation to the Sun.

## Descriptive and Comparative Investigations

**Activity 1:** Scale Model

Visit the website to create a scale model of the solar system.

*http://www.exploratorium.edu/ronh/solar_system/*

Choose an object to represent the Sun. Measure the diameter of the object. Use the diameter measurement to calculate the dimensions for the planets using the tool on the website. Then using the dimensions given, find objects to represent the planets.

Draw your model here and label the Sun and planets.

Objects used for scale model–

Sun _____    Mercury_____    Venus _____

Earth _____    Mars _____    Jupiter_____

Saturn _____    Uranus _____    Neptune _____

**Activity 2:** Your Age and Weight on Other Planets

Use the chart below to calculate your age and weight on other planets. To find your age, divide your current age (in Earth years) by the number in the *Age* column. To find your weight, multiply your weight on Earth by the number in the *Weight* column. Fill in your answers in the data tables.

| Planet | Age (divide your age by this number) | Weight (multiply your weight by this number) |
|---|---|---|
| Mercury | 0.241 | 0.38 |
| Venus | 0.615 | 0.17 |
| Earth | 1.0 | 1.0 |
| Mars | 1.88 | 0.38 |
| Jupiter | 11.9 | 2.36 |
| Saturn | 29.5 | 0.92 |
| Uranus | 84.0 | 0.89 |
| Neptune | 164.8 | 1.13 |

**Mercury**

| Age | Weight |
|---|---|
|  |  |

**Venus**

| Age | Weight |
|---|---|
|  |  |

**Earth**

| Age | Weight |
|---|---|
|  |  |

**Mars**

| Age | Weight |
|---|---|
|  |  |

**Jupiter**

| Age | Weight |
|---|---|
|  |  |

**Saturn**

| Age | Weight |
|---|---|
|  |  |

**Uranus**

| Age | Weight |
|---|---|
|  |  |

**Neptune**

| Age | Weight |
|---|---|
|  |  |

Why is your age and weight different on Earth than on other planets?

_____

_____

**1** Students research the Internet to learn who discovered the planets. To their amazement, only 3 of the 8 planets had "official" discoverers because all the other planets are easily seen with the unaided human eye. For the discovery of the 3 planets, it required a good — **5.3(D)**

Ⓐ camera

Ⓑ microscope

Ⓒ pair of binoculars

Ⓓ telescope

**2** Which force is responsible for the orbiting motion of the planets around the Sun?

Ⓕ Magnetism          Ⓗ Motion

Ⓖ Friction            Ⓙ Gravity

**3** Students construct a table to display the information collected from their research on the Sun and the eight planets. What types of data would be most helpful in displaying the relationship between the planets and the Sun? **5.2(C)**

Ⓐ Planet name, distance from the Sun, and period of revolution

Ⓑ Planet name, distance from the Sun, and period of rotation

Ⓒ Planet name, distance from the Sun, and number of moons

Ⓓ Planet name, distance from the Sun, and year of discovery

**4** Which of the following accurately compares the positions of Jupiter and Earth from the Sun?

Ⓕ Earth is positioned closer to the Sun than Jupiter.

Ⓖ Jupiter is positioned closer to the Sun than Earth.

Ⓗ Jupiter's orbit is shorter than Earth's orbit around the Sun.

Ⓙ Earth's orbit is longer than Jupiter's orbit around the Sun.

**5** The following are identified as planets in Earth's solar system **EXCEPT** —

Ⓐ Mercury          Ⓒ Sun

Ⓑ Venus            Ⓓ Saturn

**6** In an activity, students design a model of the solar system like the one shown in the picture.

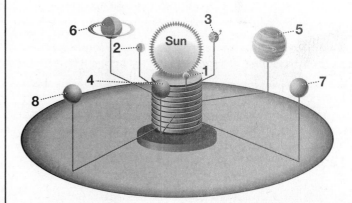

Which planet is identified by the number 5?

Ⓕ Mars            Ⓗ Saturn

Ⓖ Jupiter          Ⓙ Uranus

**Unit 25** Check for Understanding

**Use the model below and your knowledge of science to answer questions 1–3.**

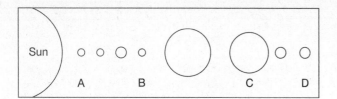

**1** A student draws this model of the solar system. What are the names, in order, of the first four planets from the Sun?

Ⓐ Mercury, Venus, Earth, Mars

Ⓑ Mars, Earth, Venus, Mercury

Ⓒ Venus, Mercury, Mars, Earth

Ⓓ Earth, Mercury, Venus, Mars

**2** Which planet is identified by the letter B?

Ⓕ Mercury

Ⓖ Mars

Ⓗ Saturn

Ⓙ Neptune

**3** Which planet is seventh from the Sun?

Ⓐ Venus

Ⓑ Jupiter

Ⓒ Uranus

Ⓓ Neptune

**4** Using acronyms is a technique that assists in memorizing many things. Which of the following acronyms would help students memorize the planets in order from the Sun?

Ⓕ My Very Easy Method Seems Just Uniquely Novel

Ⓖ My Very Excited Monkey Just Screams Until Noticed

Ⓗ My Very Unusual Mother Just Served Everyone Nachos

Ⓙ Most Eager Mothers View Jupiter Standing Upon Neptune

**5** Which lists the planets in the correct order in relation to the Sun?

Ⓐ Mercury, Mars, Earth, Venus, Jupiter, Saturn, Neptune, Uranus

Ⓑ Venus, Mercury, Mars, Earth, Saturn, Neptune, Uranus, Jupiter

Ⓒ Mars, Venus, Earth, Mercury, Saturn, Jupiter, Uranus, Neptune

Ⓓ None of the above

**6** Which planet is the sixth planet from the Sun?

Ⓕ Saturn

Ⓗ Earth

Ⓖ Jupiter

Ⓙ Mars

motivation**science**™ LEVEL 5

## Scientific Investigation and Reasoning Skills: Questions 7–14

**7** The diagram shows the inner planets and the Sun.

Which statement best describes the relationship between the planets and the Sun? **5.2(D)**

Ⓐ The planets rotate around the Sun in the same direction.

Ⓑ The planets revolve around the Sun in the same direction.

Ⓒ The Sun supplies the same amount of heat to all the planets.

Ⓓ The Sun's gravity provides gravity to all the planets.

**8** Many students have misconceptions about our solar system. Some students incorrectly believe Earth is the center of the solar system. Others believe the objects in the solar system are close together, when actually the solar system is so large that models are constructed to study it. All of the following are reasons why scientists use models **EXCEPT —** **5.3(C)**

Ⓕ to see an example

Ⓖ to visit the planets

Ⓗ to make predictions

Ⓙ to visualize their ideas

**Use the picture below and your knowledge of science to answer questions 9 and 10.**

**9** This picture shows the Sun and the eight planets. What would be beneficial for students to change about this picture to increase their knowledge of the solar system? **5.2(D)**

Ⓐ Position planets in a different order

Ⓑ Make all of the planets the same size

Ⓒ Identify each planet and the Sun

Ⓓ Show the other stars in the solar system

**10** Which planet shown in the picture above is the most massive planet? **5.2(D)**

Ⓕ Jupiter        Ⓗ Saturn

Ⓖ Earth          Ⓙ Venus

**Use the model below and your knowledge of science to answer questions 11–13.**

**11** What is one advantage of constructing a model like the one in the above picture? **5.3(C)**

Ⓐ To test the effects of the Sun's gravity on each planet

Ⓑ To identify and compare the order of the planets in the solar system

Ⓒ To show the distance of each planet from other stars

Ⓓ To form a hypothesis of how long it takes each planet to spin on its axis

**12** Which of the following is a question that can be answered by using the model constructed? **5.2(B)**

Ⓕ How long does it take the Moon to orbit Earth?

Ⓖ Which planet is closest to the Sun?

Ⓗ How far away is Earth from the Sun?

Ⓙ How long would it take a spacecraft to get to Neptune?

**13** Models often have limitations. All of the following are limitations shown in this model **EXCEPT —** **5.3(C)**

Ⓐ the planets are lined up in a straight line

Ⓑ the distance of each planet from the Sun

Ⓒ the order of each planet from the Sun

Ⓓ the size of each planet as compared to the Sun

**14** Students research the planets in Earth's solar system and share their findings with the class. Which of the following is **NOT** a valid reason for students to share their findings or conclusions? **5.2(F)**

Ⓕ Sharing findings provides an opportunity to expand the knowledge of other classmates.

Ⓖ Sharing conclusions provides students opportunities to ask questions and examine evidence.

Ⓗ Sharing findings provides students the opportunity to criticize other students.

Ⓙ Sharing conclusions provides students the opportunity to compare their own findings with the findings of others.

## Solar System Model

Develop a model of the solar system. Include the planets, their orbits, and the Sun. Be sure to label the planets correctly.

Describe the limitations of your model.

_____

_____

_____

Write the planets in order from the Sun.

1. _____    5. _____

2. _____    6. _____

3. _____    7. _____

4. _____    8. _____

## Formative Assessment

What are the advantages and disadvantages of using the image below to represent the solar system? Explain your reasoning.

_____

_____

_____

_____

_____

_____

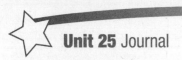

**Science Journal**

Plan a trip to Mars. What items would you take with you? What do you expect to find on Mars? Imagine the adventures you would have, and describe them.

_____

_____

_____

_____

_____

_____

_____

_____

_____

_____

_____

_____

_____

_____

_____

_____

_____

_____

_____

_____

 motivation**science** LEVEL 5 ©2011–2014 mentoring**minds**.com

**Science Vocabulary Builder**

Write information about each planet in the spaces below.

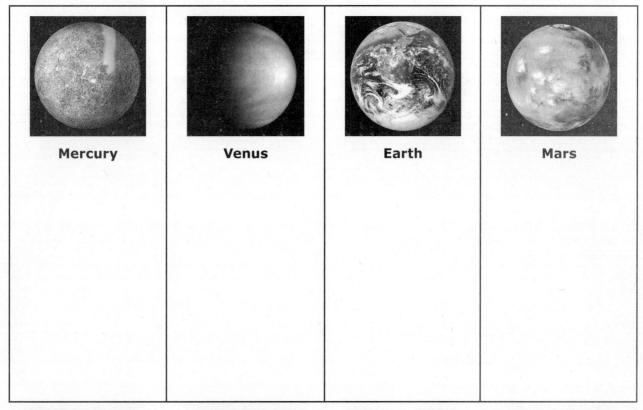

**Mercury**

**Venus**

**Earth**

**Mars**

**Jupiter**

**Saturn**

**Uranus**

**Neptune**

**Sing a Song of Planets**

Compose a song describing the eight planets. Include the order of the planets from the Sun. Use the space below to write the lyrics of your song.

✂ ------------------------------------------------------------

**Parent Activities**

1. Help your child compose a song about the planets.
2. Research the planets, and make a list of interesting facts to use for the song.
3. Try different tunes and rhythms to go with the song.

**1** Students create a model of sedimentary rock by mixing sand and plaster in a paper cup. After the mixture solidifies, students remove the paper. Then, students chip apart the rock using an iron nail to simulate weathering. Which piece of additional equipment should students use while breaking the rock model? **5.4(B)**

Ⓐ Triple beam balance

Ⓑ Fire extinguisher

Ⓒ Microscope

Ⓓ Goggles

**2** The Palo Duro Canyon near Amarillo, Texas, gets deeper ever year. Which of the following is most likely the cause of this process?

Ⓕ Soil deposition

Ⓖ Heat and pressure

Ⓗ Water erosion

Ⓙ Snowstorms

**3** Storms in the Gulf of Mexico are common during the summer when the Sun's rays hit Earth at a more direct angle. Which statement best explains the role the Sun plays in the summer storms?

Ⓐ The Sun's energy causes ocean water to evaporate into the air, which later condenses and forms storm clouds.

Ⓑ The Sun's energy causes ocean water to condense on nearby boats and ships.

Ⓒ The Sun's energy causes ocean water to create larger waves, which form thunderstorms and hurricanes.

Ⓓ The Sun's energy causes ocean water to transpire into the air and form storm clouds.

**4** This trilobite fossil was found in a dry region called the Permian Basin in West Texas. The fossil is very similar to a horseshoe crab currently living in the Gulf of Mexico.

What is the most likely reason that the trilobite fossil was found in the Permian Basin?

Ⓕ The Permian Basin used to be covered by a body of saltwater.

Ⓖ The Permian Basin used to be underneath a freshwater pond.

Ⓗ The Permian Basin trilobites were adapted to dry land.

Ⓙ The Permian Basin trilobites migrated from the Gulf of Mexico.

**5** The Moon is about one-fourth the size of Earth. It is spherical in shape and made of rock. Which of the following is **NOT** a characteristic of both the Moon and Earth?

Ⓐ Impact craters

Ⓑ Oceans

Ⓒ Trench-like valleys

Ⓓ Rocky surfaces

**6** How many times does the Sun appear to rise in a week?

Ⓕ One

Ⓖ Five

Ⓗ Seven

Ⓙ Not here

**7** Which of these can be used to complete the chart?

| Renewable | Nonrenewable |
|---|---|
| Crops | Coal |
| Livestock | Natural gas |
| Hydroelectricity | ? |

Ⓐ Wind

Ⓑ Oil

Ⓒ Wood

Ⓓ Grain

**8** What is necessary in order to have an accurate description of the climate during springtime in Texas?   **5.2(C)**

Ⓕ Take the temperature one day during springtime, and record it on a chart

Ⓖ Record the climate during fall because spring is the same

Ⓗ Record temperatures and weather conditions each spring over a period of many years

Ⓙ Record the climate every day because climate changes daily

**9** Students examine four different types of soil using hand lenses. They create a poster showing the properties of each soil. What is **NOT** a safe practice that should be used during this investigation?   **5.1(A)**

Ⓐ When observing the smell of each soil sample, use a hand to "waft" the odor toward your nose

Ⓑ Wash hands after handling soil samples

Ⓒ Taste a small sample of each soil to determine its texture

Ⓓ Follow the directions given by the teacher for proper disposal of soil samples

**10** In science class, students conduct an investigation to learn how biofuels provide energy. They mix 50 mL of corn syrup with a packet of yeast in a bottle, add warm water, replace the lid, and shake the mixture. Next, they take off the lid and replace it with a balloon. The balloon quickly inflates, and students record measurements. The activity is repeated 2 more times and additional data is recorded. Why do the students repeat the investigation?   **5.2(E)**

Ⓕ The investigation was so much fun they wanted to do it again and again.

Ⓖ Repeating an investigation increases the reliability of results.

Ⓗ The students forgot to measure the balloon the first two times.

Ⓙ Investigations never work the first time.

**11** During the month of January, students record the daily temperature, precipitation, and wind speed.

| Jan. 3 | Jan. 4 | Jan. 5 | Jan. 6 | Jan. 7 |
|--------|--------|--------|--------|--------|
| 5°C | 0°C | -1°C | -1°C | 0°C |
| 1.2 cm | 1.5 cm | 2.3 cm | 1.6 cm | 0.75 cm |
| 14 kph | 18 kph | 12 kph | 15 kph | 16 kph |

Based on the information shown above, what kind of weather will the students most likely see on January 8?

Ⓐ Windy and hot with small amounts of ice

Ⓑ Warm and calm with large amounts of rain

Ⓒ Cold and windy with small amounts of ice or snow

Ⓓ Warm and windy with large amounts of rain

**12** Which planet in the solar system has the shortest year?

Ⓕ Neptune          Ⓗ Mars

Ⓖ Saturn           Ⓙ Mercury

**13** Before beginning an experiment to test evaporation and the water cycle, a student proposes that the water will turn into gas after it is heated. What did the student formulate?  **5.2(B)**

Ⓐ A conclusion

Ⓑ A hypothesis

Ⓒ An observation

Ⓓ All of the above

**14** As Earth spins on its axis traveling around the Sun, the amount of light Earth receives changes. The picture below shows the position of Earth as the seasons change. The X on each globe represents a country in South America, which is located in the Southern Hemisphere.

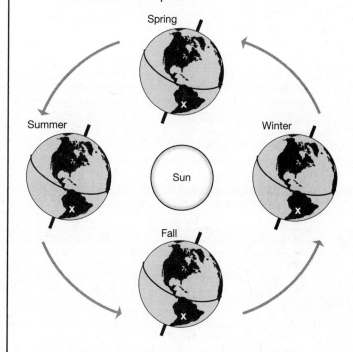

Based on the picture, which season will it be in South America during summer in North America?

Ⓕ Spring          Ⓗ Fall

Ⓖ Summer          Ⓙ Winter

**15** Students make piles of soil and place several small objects along the sides and top. Then they pour water on the top of the soil. They notice that the soil and small objects slide when water is poured. What does this model represent?

Ⓐ Earthquake

Ⓑ Landslide

Ⓒ Volcanic eruption

Ⓓ High winds

⭐ **Reporting Category 3** Assessment

**16** Which is **NOT** necessary for the formation of sedimentary rocks?

Ⓕ Sediment   Ⓗ Pressure

Ⓖ Time       Ⓙ Wood

**17** After creating a model of a sand dune, a student concludes that wind is a major cause of the formation of sand dunes. Is the student's conclusion accurate?   **5.3(A)**

Ⓐ No, because water is the main cause of the formation of sand dunes.

Ⓑ No, because ice is the major cause of the formation of sand dunes.

Ⓒ Yes, because a conclusion is a guess, and all guesses are valid.

Ⓓ Yes, because wind causes the formation of sand dunes.

**18** Large turbines can be seen from the highway in West Texas.

Which kind of energy are the turbines using to generate electrical power?

Ⓕ Water   Ⓗ Solar

Ⓖ Wind    Ⓙ Heat

**19** Students design an experiment to investigate the water cycle in wet and dry environments. The students make 2 terrariums, one representing a desert and another representing a rainforest. They add 100 mL of water to the desert terrarium and 50 mL of water to the rainforest terrarium. The students observe that the desert terrarium looks too wet, so they remove the lid. They keep the rainforest terrarium enclosed. How can students design a more valid investigation?   **5.2(A)**

Ⓐ Students should test only one variable at a time and keep all other conditions the same.

Ⓑ Students should test other environments, such as ocean environments.

Ⓒ The investigation should be conducted outside so that the extra water in the desert terrarium evaporates faster.

Ⓓ The desert terrarium should be placed outside, and the rainforest terrarium should be placed inside.

**20** In an activity, students record the position of the Sun in the sky. They notice the Sun appears low in the sky in the morning, high in the sky in the afternoon, and low in the sky in the evening. Why does the Sun appear to move across the sky?   **5.2(D)**

Ⓕ Earth is tilted and spins around the Sun each day.

Ⓖ Earth rotates around the Sun each day.

Ⓗ Earth rotates on its axis once each day.

Ⓙ Earth changes position on its axis each day.

**21** Smooth-edged leaves are usually found in areas with warm temperatures, while tooth-edged leaves are found in areas with colder temperatures. A scientist finds a fossil of a leaf with tooth-like edges in the middle of the rainforest. Which conclusion can be made based on the leaf edges of the fossil? **5.2(F)**

Ⓐ The area where the rainforest is located used to have a much warmer climate.

Ⓑ The area where the rainforest is located used to have more rainfall.

Ⓒ The area where the rainforest is located used to have a much colder climate.

Ⓓ The area where the rainforest is located used to have less rainfall.

**22** Satellite photographs such as the image shown help meteorologists predict tomorrow's —

Ⓕ climate          Ⓗ weather

Ⓖ season          Ⓙ meteors

**23** Students perform an investigation in which they place ice in a pan on a hot plate. They hold a lid several inches above the pan and observe changes. Eventually the ice melts, and they notice drops of water forming on the lid of the pan. What part of the water cycle do the drops on the pan represent?

Ⓐ Condensation          Ⓒ Collection

Ⓑ Evaporation          Ⓓ Runoff

**24** Engineers are developing alternative energy sources for powering engines. The hydrogen-powered engine, an engine that uses hydrogen gas as a power source, is one type of alternative energy being developed. Which statement is **NOT** a reason why it is important to find new renewable energy sources to fuel cars and other gasoline-powered engines?

Ⓕ Digging for fossil fuels is harmful to the environment.

Ⓖ Burning fossil fuels creates pollution.

Ⓗ More fossil fuels are being created every year.

Ⓙ Fossil fuel supplies are limited.

**25** The San Andreas Fault in California is an area where the Pacific and North American tectonic plates meet. What occurrence is caused by the plate movement along the San Andreas Fault?

Ⓐ Tornadoes          Ⓒ Tsunamis

Ⓑ Earthquakes          Ⓓ Volcanoes

**26** Meteorologists make predictions every day using maps, satellites, and computers. What area of science is the specialization of meteorologists? **5.3(D)**

Ⓕ Fossils          Ⓗ Weather

Ⓖ Forces          Ⓙ Meteors

**27** A student draws a solar system model and used the labels in the order shown.

> Sun, Mars, Venus, Earth, Mercury, Neptune, Jupiter, Saturn, Uranus

How should the labels be corrected on the solar system model?

Ⓐ  Venus should be before Mars, and Neptune should be between Saturn and Uranus.

Ⓑ  Mars should be after Venus, and Jupiter should be after Saturn.

Ⓒ  Earth should be after Mercury, and Saturn should be before Jupiter.

Ⓓ  None of the above

**28** In an activity, students compare the Sun, Moon, and Earth. They describe each by its size on a scale of 1–3, with 1 being the greatest and 3 being the least. Which chart correctly shows these comparisons?  **5.2(G)**

Ⓕ

|       | Size |
|-------|------|
| Sun   | 1    |
| Moon  | 3    |
| Earth | 2    |

Ⓖ

|       | Size |
|-------|------|
| Sun   | 1    |
| Moon  | 2    |
| Earth | 3    |

Ⓗ

|       | Size |
|-------|------|
| Sun   | 3    |
| Moon  | 2    |
| Earth | 1    |

Ⓙ

|       | Size |
|-------|------|
| Sun   | 3    |
| Moon  | 1    |
| Earth | 2    |

**29** A student reads the following information in a textbook related to soils.

> Soil that is rich in humus is able to hold water and has plenty of nutrients.

Desert soil is loose and dry soil with very little humus. Which correctly describes desert soil?

Ⓐ  Desert soil allows for good drainage and retains nutrients because it does not have much humus.

Ⓑ  Desert soil retains very little water and nutrients because it is not rich in humus.

Ⓒ  Desert soil holds water but has very few nutrients because it does not have much humus.

Ⓓ  Desert soil allows water to drain away and nutrients to be lost because it is rich in humus.

**30** Students create various ocean models to demonstrate tides. After building the models, which student makes the right choice before leaving class?  **5.1(B)**

Ⓕ  Student 1 efficiently gathers his books and leaves.

Ⓖ  Student 2 disposes of the extra materials by washing them down the sink, gathers his books, and leaves.

Ⓗ  Student 3 places the extra sand back into the container and disposes of the water and wet sand as directed by the teacher.

Ⓙ  Student 4 leaves the extra sand out but puts the wet sand back in its container.

# Chart Your Success

## Sedimentary Rocks and Fossil Fuels

Question 1 | Question 16

Total Correct | Total Possible | 2

## Landforms

Question 2 | Question 17

Total Correct | Total Possible | 2

## Alternative Energy

Question 10 | Question 18

Total Correct | Total Possible | 2

## Fossils

Question 4 | Question 21

Total Correct | Total Possible | 2

## Weather and Climate

Question 8 | Question 22

Total Correct | Total Possible | 2

## Sun, Ocean, and the Water Cycle

Question 3 | Question 19

Total Correct | Total Possible | 2

## Earth's Rotation

Question 6 | Question 20

Total Correct | Total Possible | 2

## Sun, Earth, and Moon

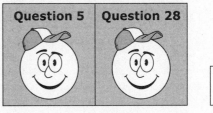
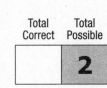

Question 5 | Question 28

Total Correct | Total Possible | 2

## Properties of Soil

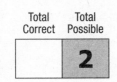
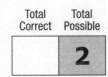

Question 9 | Question 29

Total Correct | Total Possible | 2

## Renewable/Nonrenewable Resources

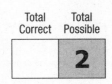

Question 7 | Question 24

Total Correct | Total Possible | 2

# Chart Your Success

Color Mike or Molly *green* if your answer was correct or *red* if your answer was incorrect.

### Weather Maps and Predictions

| Total Correct | Total Possible |
|---|---|
|  | 2 |

### Water Cycle

| Total Correct | Total Possible |
|---|---|
|  | 2 |

### Shadows, Tides, Seasons, and Moon

| Total Correct | Total Possible |
|---|---|
|  | 2 |

### Rapid Changes to Earth's Surface

| Total Correct | Total Possible |
|---|---|
|  | 2 |

### Solar System

| Total Correct | Total Possible |
|---|---|
|  | 2 |

 motivation**science**™LEVEL 5

Name _____

**Motivation Station: Molly's Cool Science Fact**

Scientists who study living things and how they interact and survive within ecosystems are called ecologists.

**After this lesson I will be able to:**

- **Observe** the way organisms live and survive in their ecosystems by interacting with the living and nonliving elements.

## Comparative Investigations

**Activity 1:** Ecosystem Demonstration

Observe and experience what happens when certain parts of ecosystems are removed. Participate in a demonstration to understand how components of an ecosystem rely on one another for survival.

1. Describe your part in the ecosystem demonstration.

_____

_____

_____

2. Which parts of the ecosystem were instructed to sit down? What happened when parts of the ecosystem were no longer available?

_____

_____

3. How do parts of an ecosystem rely on one another for survival?

_____

_____

_____

4. How did this demonstration symbolize the dependence plants, animals, and their environment have on one another?

_____

_____

_____

**Unit 26** Introduction

**Activity 2:** Observing an Ecosystem

There are ecosystems all around. Ecosystems can be found in forests, caves, rivers, ponds, and even your backyard. Observe and study an outdoor ecosystem. Record observations three times throughout the day in the space below.

**Observations**

| Observation 1 | Observation 2 | Observation 3 |
|---|---|---|
| | | |

List the living and nonliving components of the ecosystem.

| Living | Nonliving |
|---|---|
| | |

What changes, if any, occurred in the ecosystem throughout the day?

_____

Illustrate the ecosystem, and label the living and nonliving elements.

     motivation**science**™LEVEL 5   ©2011–2014 mentoring**minds**.com

**1** What is one observable interaction of how organisms live and survive in their environment?

Ⓐ Grass supplying food and oxygen to a rabbit

Ⓑ A deer providing oxygen and food to a shrub

Ⓒ Rocks and water eroding a hillside environment

Ⓓ A tree providing carbon dioxide for a squirrel

**2** Ecology is the study of how living and nonliving things interact.

Which statement describes the relationship between prairie dogs and the soil?

Ⓕ The prairie dogs provide oxygen for the soil.

Ⓖ The prairie dogs cause the soil to erode.

Ⓗ The soil provides a shelter for the prairie dogs.

Ⓙ The soil provides nutrients for the prairie dogs.

**3** Specific environments meet the needs of organisms. The school aquarium below shows what is needed for these organisms to survive in their environment.

The aquarium pictured is a good model of — **5.3(C)**

Ⓐ a terrarium      Ⓒ a tide pool

Ⓑ an ecosystem      Ⓓ a swamp

**4** A group of students wants to produce a project that displays the way organisms live and survive in their ecosystem. The group decides to construct a diorama as their representation of the relationships organisms have within an environment. The diorama is a/an —   **5.3(C)**

Ⓕ model      Ⓗ aquarium

Ⓖ diagram      Ⓙ experiment

**5** Which of the following nonliving elements do all living organisms depend on for survival?

Ⓐ Water, grass, air

Ⓑ Sun, air, water

Ⓒ Soil, Sun, rocks

Ⓓ Water, rocks, air

**6** How are the living and the nonliving things connected to one another in this diagram?

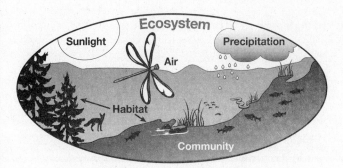

Ⓕ The Sun, water, and air provide necessary resources to the plants and animals.

Ⓖ The plants and animals receive oxygen from the Sun, water, and air.

Ⓗ The water and air recycle to help the Sun provide energy to plants and animals.

Ⓙ The animals provide shelter for the plants, enabling them to grow.

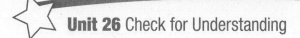
**Use the table below and your knowledge of science to answer questions 1 and 2.**

**Title A**

| Living Organisms | Title B |
| --- | --- |
| Prairie dog | Soil, water, air, food |
| Bison | Plants, water, air |
| Jackrabbit | Plants, water, air |
| Snake | Animals, water, soil, air |
| Grass | Water, soil, air |

1  Which title would be most appropriate for Title A above?

&#9398;  Prairie Ecosystem

&#9399;  Plants and Animals on a Prairie

&#9400;  Prairie Climate and Weather Conditions

&#9401;  Prairie Life Survival Skills

2  Which title would best replace Title B?

&#9403;  Animal Survival Needs

&#9404;  Competition between Living and Nonliving Elements

&#9405;  Survival Needs

&#9406;  Nonliving Elements

3  How does the Strangler Fig interact with its ecosystem in order to survive?

> In the rainforest, strangler fig seedlings begin growing on other trees, wrapping roots around the host tree. When the roots reach the ground, the strangler fig takes root and grows larger than the host tree, taking nutrients from the host tree and growing to the height of the rainforest canopy.

&#9398;  The fig produces its own food and does not use nutrients from other trees.

&#9399;  The rainforest floor does not receive much sunlight, so the fig must compete for sunlight and nutrients.

&#9400;  The fig roots rot in the wet rainforest.

&#9401;  None of the above

4  In Africa, lions chase and kill their prey. The lion family eats all it wants and then vultures come and finish the rest. The interaction between the lions and vultures is an example of —

&#9403;  the lions not being harmed by the relationship and the vultures benefiting

&#9404;  the lions benefiting from the relationship and the vultures being harmed

&#9405;  the lions benefiting by consuming the vultures as food

&#9406;  both the lions and the vultures competing with one another for food

5  Scientists observe that the deer population is growing and worry there will not be enough plants for the deer during the winter. Why are the scientists worried about the deer and not the plants?

&#9398;  The deer need plants to eat, but the plants only need sunlight and water.

&#9399;  The deer need water stored in the plants in the winter, but the plants do not.

&#9400;  The plants are nonliving elements.

&#9401;  The plants use oxygen which deer need in order to survive.

6  Colorado elk need food, water, and air to sustain their population. Based on this information, what statement is true regarding the elk's ecosystem?

&#9403;  Elk lack dependence on living and nonliving elements in their environment.

&#9404;  Too many factors limit the elk's survival within their ecosystem.

&#9405;  Living organisms are independent of nonliving elements within the ecosystem.

&#9406;  Living and nonliving factors work together to keep the elk's ecosystem functioning.

**Scientific Investigation and Reasoning Skills: Questions 7–14**

**7** What can be concluded using the data shown below? **5.2(G)**

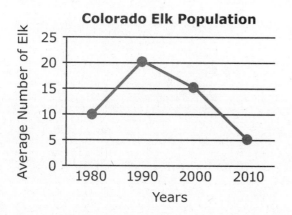

**Colorado Elk Population**

Ⓐ Elk population increased over a 30-year period.

Ⓑ Elk population decreased over a 20-year period.

Ⓒ Elk population decreased over a 30-year period.

Ⓓ Elk population increased over a 20-year period.

**8** When studying ecosystem interactions, students collected living and nonliving objects found in the schoolyard and took them back to the classroom to observe. Which science equipment would be important to use while collecting objects outdoors? **5.4(B)**

Ⓕ Terrariums

Ⓖ Gloves

Ⓗ Thermometers

Ⓙ Notebooks

**9** A group of students uses their outdoor classroom to investigate the way organisms live and survive in their ecosystem. They notice a trail of ants carrying bits of food into a mound of dirt. The students are making a/an — **5.2(C)**

Ⓐ hypothesis     Ⓒ conclusion

Ⓑ observation     Ⓓ graph

**10** A burrowing shrimp with poor eyesight digs a hole in the sand for both it and the goby fish to live. When danger approaches, the fish touches the shrimp's tail and they both hide in the hole.

| | 2007 | 2009 | 2011 | 2013 |
|---|---|---|---|---|
| Goby fish | 200 | 275 | 350 | 250 |
| Shrimp | 198 | 279 | 348 | ? |

Based on the population chart above, what will happen to the shrimp population in 2013? **5.2(A)**

Ⓕ It will increase.

Ⓖ It will decrease.

Ⓗ It will stay the same.

Ⓙ They will die out completely.

**11** Ecologists study the soil particles from a desert biome to better understand how the nutrients in the soil sustain plant survival. Which of the following tools is most beneficial for observing the particles of soil? **5.4(A)**

Ⓐ Collecting net

Ⓑ Magnet

Ⓒ Microscope

Ⓓ Telescope

**12** Dogs and ticks share the same ecosystem. How do dogs and ticks interact within an ecosystem? **5.2(D)**

Ⓕ Ticks benefit by feeding on dogs' blood.

Ⓖ Dogs benefit by obtaining nutrients from ticks.

Ⓗ Neither dogs nor ticks benefit from the relationship.

Ⓙ Both dogs and ticks benefit from the relationship.

**13** For protection, hermit crabs use gastropod shells to hide their bodies so that only their heads are visible. Students research why the population of hermit crabs has been decreasing.

One question they should ask is — **5.2(B)**

Ⓐ Who has a hermit crab for a pet?

Ⓑ Do hermit crabs make sounds?

Ⓒ What colors are hermit crabs?

Ⓓ Have any changes occurred in their ecosystem?

**14** After observing an outdoor ecosystem, a student writes the following conclusion in a science notebook.

> Ecosystems are only made of living things.

Is the student's conclusion logical? **5.3(A)**

Ⓕ Yes, because ecosystems are made of living things that interact.

Ⓖ No, because ecosystems are made of living and nonliving things that interact.

Ⓗ Yes, because ecosystem is another name for habitat.

Ⓙ No, because an ecosystem has nothing to do with living things.

       motivation**science** LEVEL 5

## Ecosystem Analogy

Compare and contrast an ecosystem to a school. For each, include two different living and nonliving components that make up the ecosystem and the school, and describe how they interact and rely on one another.

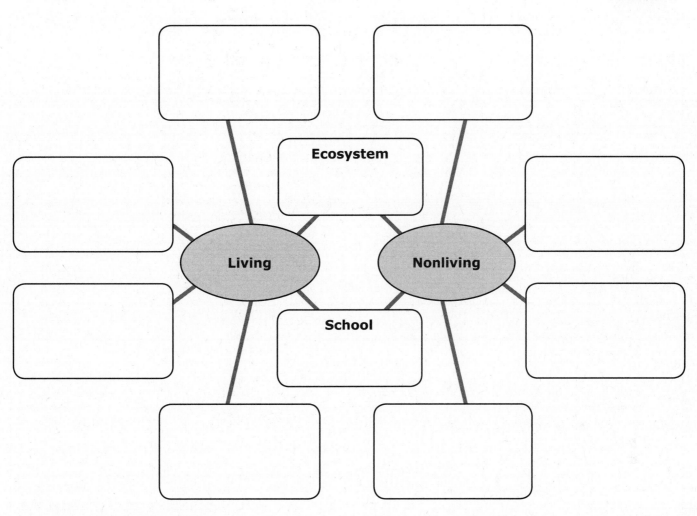

## Formative Assessment

Generate a list of the ways organisms interact with living and nonliving elements within an ecosystem.

### Ecosystem Interactions

| Interactions with Living Organisms | Interactions with Nonliving Organisms |
|---|---|
|  |  |

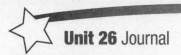

Name _____

**Science Journal**

Describe the ecosystem you live in, and compare it to an ecosystem you would like to visit.

_____

_____

_____

_____

_____

_____

_____

_____

_____

_____

_____

_____

_____

_____

_____

_____

_____

_____

_____

_____

_____

_____

_____

## Science Vocabulary Builder

Define and illustrate each vocabulary word in the boxes below.

| living | |
|---|---|
| definition | illustration |
| | |

| nonliving | |
|---|---|
| definition | illustration |
| | |

| ecosystem | |
|---|---|
| definition | illustration |
| | |

| survive | |
|---|---|
| definition | illustration |
| | |

| competition | |
|---|---|
| definition | illustration |
| | |

| interact | |
|---|---|
| definition | illustration |
| | |

| interdependence | |
|---|---|
| definition | illustration |
| | |

| species | |
|---|---|
| definition | illustration |
| | |

**Unit 26** Homework

## Using an Ethogram

Scientists observe animal behaviors using a tool called an ethogram. Observe a real life animal, such as a pet, to see how it interacts with other living things and its environment. Fill out the ethogram below to organize observations. Each minute, look to see what the animal is doing. Use tally marks to collect data. If unable to observe an animal, go to *http://nationalzoo.si.edu/Animals/WebCams/default.cfm*

| Time | Eating | Playing | Fighting | Resting | Bathing/Cleaning Themselves |
|---|---|---|---|---|---|
| 1 minute | | | | | |
| 2 minutes | | | | | |
| 3 minutes | | | | | |
| 4 minutes | | | | | |
| 5 minutes | | | | | |
| 6 minutes | | | | | |
| 7 minutes | | | | | |
| 8 minutes | | | | | |
| 9 minutes | | | | | |
| 10 minutes | | | | | |

Describe the ecosystem where the animal lives. _____

_____

Did anything surprise you about the animal? _____

_____

Which activity did the animal do the most/least? _____

_____

✂ - - - - - - - - - - - - - - - - - - - - - - - - - - - - - - - - - - - - - - - - - - - - - - - - - - - -

## Parent Activities

1. Discuss the observed animal with your child. Talk about living and nonliving parts of the ecosystem.

2. Visit a zoo with your child to see real life examples of ecosystems and the interactions between the plants and animals that live in them.

3. Go on a drive to view different environments. Help your child describe the ecosystem and the organisms living there.

 motivation**science** LEVEL 5

Readiness Standard 5.9(B)

**Motivation Station: Mike's Cool Science Fact**

Decomposers are a very <u>vital</u> part of an ecosystem. Without decomposers, the remains of dead organisms would never rot or decompose. Luckily, decomposers recycle nutrients back into food webs and food chains.

**After this lesson I will be able to:**

- **Describe** how the flow of energy derived from the Sun, used by producers to create their own food, is transferred through a food chain and food web to consumers and decomposers.

## Comparative and Experimental Investigations

**Activity 1:** What Did You Consume?

Think about the food you ate yesterday. What role did each item play in the food chain before it was consumed by you?

Fill in the data table below to classify the role of each food you ate as a producer, consumer, or decomposer.

| Producer | Consumer | Decomposer |
|----------|----------|------------|
| Plant | human | fungy |

What was your role? _Consumer_

**Activity 2:** Bread Mold Experiment

**Question:** Will mold grow faster on wet bread or dry bread?

**Hypothesis:** I believe mold will grow faster on _____ bread.

**Procedure:** Label one sealable bag *Dry* and the other *Wet*. Place one slice of white bread in each bag. Seal the dry bag. Add 5 mL water to the other bag and seal. Place in an undisturbed location, and observe every two days for eight days. To collect data, draw your observations below. When the investigation is complete, answer the questions that follow, and communicate your conclusion.

| | Day 2 | Day 4 | Day 6 | Day 8 |
|---|---|---|---|---|
| **Dry** |  |  |  |  |
| **Wet** |  |  |  |  |

What was your variable in the investigation?

_____

_____

Was your hypothesis correct?

_____

_____

What can you conclude about the growth of mold?

_____

_____

What role does mold serve in a food chain? Cite evidence from the investigation to support your answer.

_____

_____

**1** What source provides the energy to begin the food web shown below?

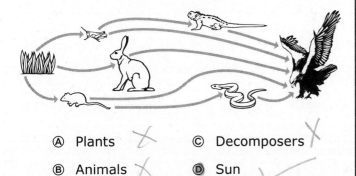

Ⓐ Plants ✗

Ⓒ Decomposers ✗

Ⓑ Animals ✗

Ⓓ Sun ✓

**Use your knowledge of science and the table below to answer questions 2 and 3.**

### Roles of Antarctic Organisms

| Organism | Niche | Prey | Predators |
|---|---|---|---|
| Algae | Producer | | Fish |
| Killer whales | Consumer | Fish, seals | |
| Fish | Consumer | Algae | Seals, killer whales |

**2** Which event below would affect the most organisms? **5.2(G)**

Ⓕ The extinction of killer whales ✗

Ⓖ Exhausting the fishery through overfishing ✗

Ⓗ Removing the algae from the ocean ✓

Ⓙ A decrease in the bird population ✗

**3** If the organisms in the table were placed in their correct places on a food web, which organism would start the flow of energy?

Ⓐ Killer whales

Ⓒ Algae

Ⓑ Seals

Ⓓ Birds

**Use the diagram below to answer questions 4 and 5.**

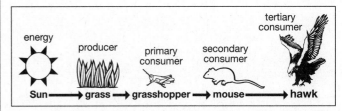

**4** What do the arrows represent in the food chain above?

Ⓕ The direction of energy flow

Ⓖ The type of food each organism prefers

Ⓗ The organism's place in the ecosystem

Ⓙ The space separating each organism on a food chain

**5** Which question below cannot be answered using the diagram above? **5.2(B)**

Ⓐ What would happen if one of the organisms was removed from the food chain?

Ⓑ What are consumers?

Ⓒ Which organism is a producer?

Ⓓ What might a food chain from a marine environment look like?

**6** Which statement below best describes how energy flows in a food chain or food web?

Ⓕ Energy from the Sun is used by consumers and transferred to producers and decomposers.

Ⓖ Energy from the Sun is used by producers and transferred to consumers and decomposers.

Ⓗ Energy from the Sun is used by decomposers and transferred to producers and consumers.

Ⓙ Energy from the Sun is used by producers and transferred to scavengers and decomposers.

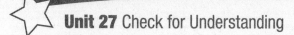

**Unit 27** Check for Understanding

**1** Which statement correctly describes the role of bacteria as part of the food chain?

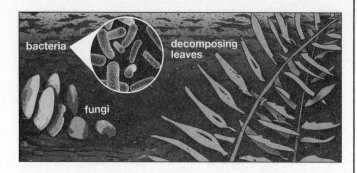

Ⓐ Bacteria are decomposers that break down waste and remains of dead animals and plants.

Ⓑ Bacteria cause plant and animal illnesses which are always harmful to the environment.

Ⓒ Bacteria are predators which catch and consume their prey.

Ⓓ Bacteria are producers that make their own food from the Sun's energy.

**2** The Sun is important in many ways. What is the purpose of the Sun in a food chain?

Ⓕ The Sun provides energy for animals to stay warm.

Ⓖ The Sun provides light for animals to see.

Ⓗ The Sun provides warmth for plants to survive.

Ⓙ The Sun provides energy for plants to make food.

**3** What happens to plants and animals when they die?

Ⓐ They become food for decomposers.

Ⓑ They become food for producers.

Ⓒ They make their own food.

Ⓓ They provide energy for the Sun.

**4** Why is the Sun an important factor in the transfer of energy in an ecosystem?

Ⓕ The Sun supplies nutrients to consumers to be transferred to producers.

Ⓖ The Sun supplies energy to consumers so they can create their own food.

Ⓗ The Sun provides energy to producers so they can create their own food.

Ⓙ The Sun provides nutrients so consumers and scavengers can create their own food.

**Use the diagram below and your knowledge of science to answer questions 5 and 6.**

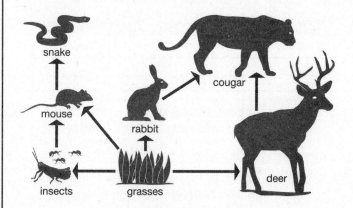

**5** The diagram above is an example of —

Ⓐ interconnected food chains

Ⓑ multiple food webs

Ⓒ a single food chain

Ⓓ all of the above

**6** Which organism above is both predator and prey?

Ⓕ Grass      Ⓗ Mouse

Ⓖ Cougar      Ⓙ Insect

## Scientific Investigation and Reasoning Skills: Questions 7–14

**7** Which of the following would best complete the food chain shown?  **5.2(D)**

Ⓐ Producer   Ⓒ Decomposer

Ⓑ Consumer   Ⓓ Sun

**8** Several animals are kept as pets in the classroom. Students are responsible for feeding, watering, and cleaning their cages. What rule best reflects the science safety rule students should remember to do upon entering the room?  **5.1(A)**

Ⓕ Sharpen pencils

Ⓖ Write in science notebooks

Ⓗ Visit quietly with neighbors until the bell rings

Ⓙ Ask permission before working with the animals

**9** A food web is a more realistic model of the flow of energy through an ecosystem than a food chain because —  **5.3(C)**

Ⓐ most organisms depend on more than one species for food

Ⓑ each organism in a food chain represents multiple feedings

Ⓒ most organisms depend on just one species for food

Ⓓ each organism in a food web represents a single feeding

**10** Students grow mold on bread to learn about the role of decomposers in a food web. For two weeks, students record their observations by taking pictures of the changes in mold growth.

When conducting an investigation with decomposers, it is important for the students to —  **5.4(B)**

Ⓕ keep a fire extinguisher nearby

Ⓖ wear gloves and other protective equipment

Ⓗ taste samples of the mold growth

Ⓙ feed the molded bread to the classroom pet

**11** The flyer shown below is advertising an all-you-can-eat special. People ordering the special will be consuming — **5.3(B)**

TODAY'S SPECIAL
**Grilled Mushrooms**

**ALL YOU CAN EAT!**

ⓐ a producer

Ⓑ a consumer

Ⓒ a decomposer

Ⓓ a scavenger

**12** Students create food chains to learn how energy flows through an ecosystem. After completing several chains, students notice some of the same animals appear on several food chains. The students conclude that within an ecosystem, food chains combine to create food webs. Do the students reach a logical conclusion? **5.3(A)**

Ⓕ No, because most animals only eat one type of food.

Ⓖ Yes, because most living things consume a variety of foods in order to survive.

Ⓗ No, because producers make their own food.

Ⓙ Yes, because food chains and food webs are the same.

**13** In an investigation, students grow mold on bread to learn about decomposers. They place 20 mL of water into two bags. In one of the bags, they place a slice of white bread. In the other bag, they place a slice of wheat bread. The bags are sealed, and students record notes about the growth of the mold in science notebooks. What is the variable in the investigation? **5.2(A)**

ⓐ Amount of water used

Ⓑ Type of bread used

Ⓒ Amount of time bread was left in the bags

Ⓓ Number of mold spots that grew

**14** Which organisms in the food web below would be most affected by the removal of insects? **5.2(D)**

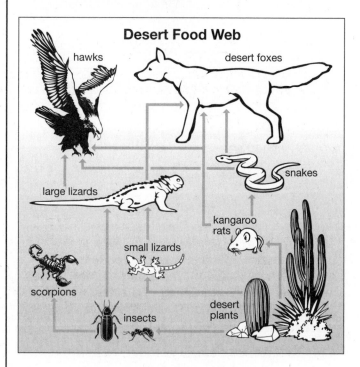

**Desert Food Web**

hawks
desert foxes
large lizards
snakes
kangaroo rats
small lizards
scorpions
insects
desert plants

Ⓕ Hawks and desert foxes

Ⓖ Desert plants and snakes

Ⓗ Large lizards and scorpions

Ⓙ Small lizards and desert plants

motivation**science**™LEVEL 5

## Creating a Food Web

Circle an ecosystem below.

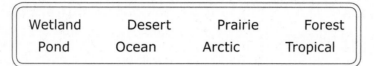

| Wetland | Desert | Prairie | Forest |
|---------|--------|---------|--------|
| Pond | Ocean | Arctic | Tropical |

Using the chosen ecosystem, illustrate and label a food web in the space below.

Which organisms in the food web above represent producers? Which organisms represent consumers? Which organisms represent decomposers?

_____

_____

What is the difference in a food chain and a food web?

_____

_____

_____

## Formative Assessment

Compare and contrast the roles of producers, consumers, and decomposers.

| Producers | |
|-----------|---|
| **Consumers** | |
| **Decomposers** | |

**Science Journal**

Using pictures and words, describe how energy in food chains and food webs flows through an ecosystem. Begin your description with the Sun.

_____

_____

_____

_____

_____

_____

_____

_____

_____

_____

_____

_____

_____

_____

_____

## Science Vocabulary Builder

Write a description, and create an illustration for each vocabulary term. Use the three vocabulary terms and information in the graphic organizer to write a summary of the information learned during this unit.

| **Term** producer | **Illustration** |
|---|---|
| **Description** | |

| **Term** consumer | **Illustration** |
|---|---|
| **Description** | |

| **Term** decomposer | **Illustration** |
|---|---|
| **Description** | |

**Summary**

_____

_____

_____

## Producers, Consumers, and Decomposers

Label the images as producers, consumers, or decomposers.

corn

_____

chicken

_____

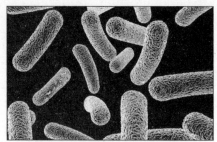

bacteria

_____

mushroom

_____

flower

_____

cow

_____

1. What is a producer? Give examples of producers. _____

_____

2. What is a consumer? Give examples of consumers. _____

_____

3. What is a decomposer? Give examples of decomposers. _____

_____

4. What is the Sun's role in the food chain? _____

_____

_____

-----------------------------------------------------------------

### Parent Activities

**1.** Discuss producers, consumers, and decomposers with your child. How would humans be classified?

**2.** Discuss how the Sun provides energy to plants, which enables them to grow.

**Motivation Station: Molly's Cool Science Fact**

Human activities, such as fishing and pollution, have affected at least 40% of the world's oceans. Humans impact the world's forests, too. Each second, over two acres of forests are destroyed on Earth.

**After this lesson I will be able to:**

- **Predict** the effects of changes in ecosystems caused by living organisms, including humans, such as the overpopulation of grazers or the building of highways.

## Descriptive and Experimental Investigations

**Activity 1:** Changes in Ecosystems

Place an animal in each square below. In groups, take turns rolling the die. If you roll an odd number, take an animal off a square, and draw a house in its place. Continue playing until every group member has had 6 turns, and then answer the questions.

| Animal Habitat |
|:---:|
|  |

How many houses were built in the habitat?

_____

If the number of houses built was 3 or greater, the habitat would not be able to support the animal population. According to the data you collected, was the animal habitat destroyed?

_____

**Activity 2:** Overpopulation

**Question:** What changes are caused by overpopulation?

**Hypothesis:** _____

_____

**Procedure:**

- Take two foam cups and use a pencil to poke a small drainage hole in the bottom of each. Label one *Normal* and the other *Overpopulated*. Fill each about $\frac{3}{4}$ full with potting soil. In the cup labeled normal, plant 2 radish seeds, spaced apart. In the cup labeled overpopulated, plant 25 radish seeds. Place both cups on a tray in a sunny location. Water both cups with 50 mL of water.

- Continue watering every 3 days, or as needed. Make sure both cups get watered equally and receive the same amount of sunlight.

- Collect data in the calendar below for a month. Record the height of each plant daily as well as any other important observations.

| Monday | Tuesday | Wednesday | Thursday | Friday |
|--------|---------|-----------|----------|--------|
|        |         |           |          |        |
|        |         |           |          |        |
|        |         |           |          |        |
|        |         |           |          |        |
|        |         |           |          |        |

What can you conclude from the results of your investigation?

_____

_____

What problems are caused by overpopulation? How is the food chain affected by overpopulation?

_____

_____

_____

 motivation**science**™LEVEL 5 ©2011–2014 mentoring**minds**.com

1   Humans are part of the ecosystem and therefore impact it. Which of the following events in an ecosystem may produce a negative effect?

Ⓐ   Preventing deer from depleting food resources

Ⓑ   Restoring a natural habitat

Ⓒ   Wildlife rangers minimizing disturbances

Ⓓ   A lumber company clearing a forest

2   Scientific research shows that as tundra vegetation zones continue to move northward with the changing climate, caribou and reindeer may have a more difficult time finding food. Which prediction below best explains the effect of this change on caribou and reindeer?   **5.3(D)**

Ⓕ   Caribou and reindeer populations may increase because of their dependence on tundra vegetation.

Ⓖ   Caribou and reindeer populations will not be affected by this change to the ecosystem.

Ⓗ   Caribou and reindeer populations may decline because of their dependence on tundra vegetation.

Ⓙ   Caribou and reindeer populations will increase as the food supply decreases.

3   All the following are ways humans can adversely change the ecosystem **EXCEPT** —

Ⓐ   waste dumping

Ⓑ   using biodegradable products

Ⓒ   overhunting animals

Ⓓ   industrial pollution

4   What effect would building a highway have on an ecosystem?

Ⓕ   Increase in butterfly migration

Ⓖ   Decrease in destruction of habitat

Ⓗ   Increase in carbon dioxide

Ⓙ   Increase in oxygen

5   Scientific evidence predicts events that will occur because of the overpopulation of grazers. Which of the following is **NOT** a change caused by the overpopulation of grazers?   **5.3(A)**

Ⓐ   Grazers have less food to eat.

Ⓑ   Grazers wander into unnatural habitats.

Ⓒ   Grazers have access to unlimited resources.

Ⓓ   Grazers are susceptible to more diseases.

6   Overpopulated animals cause severe damage to an ecosystem and the surrounding landscape. Additionally, overpopulation can affect the food chain, water routes, and land. Based on the information provided, which of the following is the best conclusion about the effects of overpopulation?

Ⓕ   Overpopulation is destroying the entire United States.

Ⓖ   Overpopulation does not impact the food chain.

Ⓗ   Overpopulation can change the entire structure of an ecosystem.

Ⓙ   Overpopulation causes serious issues with the water cycle.

Name _____

1  Hunting is an environmental management tool that helps control wildlife populations. Hunting is an example of —

Ⓐ the deer population creating change in an ecosystem

Ⓑ the food chain creating change in an ecosystem

Ⓒ humans creating change in an ecosystem

Ⓓ a cycle creating change in an ecosystem

2  Which of the following is a positive effect of building highways in an ecosystem?

Ⓕ Enhancing access between existing communities

Ⓖ Destruction of existing homes and businesses

Ⓗ Prohibiting some species from migrating

Ⓙ Increase in noise and air pollution

3  Which human activity puts the greatest number of animals at risk for becoming endangered?

Ⓐ Starting forest fires

Ⓑ Destruction of habitat

Ⓒ Hunting and fishing

Ⓓ Making pets of wild animals

4  What is an effect of cutting down forests for the development of land and cities?

Ⓕ Increase in amount of oxygen for animals

Ⓖ Decrease in energy provided for producers

Ⓗ Lack of habitat areas for plants and animals

Ⓙ Gain of habitat areas for new species of animals and plants

5  The Texas blind salamander lives in the underwater caves of the Edwards Aquifer, which is used to provide drinking water for many Texans. The Texas blind salamander has been on the endangered list since 1967. Which could **NOT** be a possible cause for the salamanders being on the endangered list?

Ⓐ Motor oil draining into the sewer

Ⓑ Using lots of water for irrigation

Ⓒ Lower average rainfall totals

Ⓓ Swimming and fishing activities

6  Biologists observe and record the deer population. They notice that the population is four times larger than the habitat can support. Which is least likely to occur from the overpopulation of deer?

Ⓕ The grass population in the deer's habitat will begin to decrease.

Ⓖ The deer population will be stronger and healthier.

Ⓗ The area's water source will be reduced or depleted.

Ⓙ The deer will spread disease to other animals and humans.

   motivation**science**™ LEVEL 5

## Scientific Investigation and Reasoning Skills: Questions 7–14

**7** Which of these activities is most likely to have a negative impact on Earth's environment?  **5.1(B)**

Ⓐ Planting trees

Ⓑ Constructing highways

Ⓒ Recycling paper and plastics

Ⓓ None of the above

**8** Based on the information given in the table, why do overpopulated animals wander?  **5.2(G)**

### Effects of Overpopulation of Grazers

| |
|---|
| 1. Wander into areas populated by humans |
| 2. Wander onto roads and highways and get killed |
| 3. Rummage through garbage and kill farm animals |

Ⓕ Their natural ecosystem can no longer support them.

Ⓖ They migrate to compete with other species for garbage.

Ⓗ Their natural ecosystem has a vast supply of food and water.

Ⓙ They migrate to areas where there are fewer producers.

**9** Students are given an assignment to research and document the negative and positive effects of changes in ecosystems caused by humans. Which of the following tools would be most appropriate to use for this assignment?  **5.4(A)**

Ⓐ Notebook

Ⓑ Calculator

Ⓒ Hand lens

Ⓓ Aquarium

**10** A group of students is exploring the causes of change in the physical structure of a forest ecosystem. Each student in the group makes a prediction of how changes will impact the ecosystem. The students have each —  **5.2(B)**

Ⓕ made a table

Ⓖ formed a hypothesis

Ⓗ developed a model

Ⓙ planned an experiment

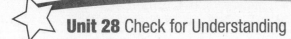

**Unit 28** Check for Understanding

**11** The Texas kangaroo rat, native to north-central Texas, makes its home in mesquite bushes.

If the mesquite bushes are cleared for human homes, which of the following is the most probable result? **5.2(D)**

Ⓐ The rat population will rise.

Ⓑ The rat population will decrease.

Ⓒ The rat population will stay the same.

Ⓓ The rat population will double.

**12** In order to reduce the negative impact on the ecosystem, it is important that people — **5.1(B)**

Ⓕ make informed choices in conservation

Ⓖ demonstrate safety practices

Ⓗ record data using technology

Ⓙ neglect wildlife regulations

**13** In class, students learn that conserving water reduces the human impact on area watersheds. Students investigate whether 4th graders or 5th graders use the most water when washing their hands. Which part of the investigation should be recorded? **5.2(A)**

Ⓐ Height of the students

Ⓑ Time the faucet is turned on and off

Ⓒ Size of the sink

Ⓓ Grade level of the students

**14** Students conduct outdoor investigations in a marshy area. They collect water samples for viewing under the microscope to determine if pollution has impacted the health of the pond. The water is oily and shiny, and students are not sure what is in the water. All are good precautions to use while gathering the water samples **EXCEPT** — **5.4(B)**

Ⓕ wearing rubber gloves

Ⓖ running around the pond

Ⓗ keeping long hair tied back

Ⓙ staying with the group

 motivation**science**™ LEVEL 5

## Human Impact

Humans impact ecosystems in many ways. Some of the ways people cause changes to ecosystems include urban development, building roads, water development, pollution, and starting forest fires.

For each of the activities listed below, describe how the event impacts people. Then predict how the event changes ecosystems.

| Event | Urban Development |
|---|---|
| Impact to People | |
| Changes to Ecosystem | |

| Event | Building Roads |
|---|---|
| Impact to People | |
| Changes to Ecosystem | |

| Event | Pollution |
|---|---|
| Impact to People | |
| Changes to Ecosystem | |

| Event | Starting Forest Fires |
|---|---|
| Impact to People | |
| Changes to Ecosystem | |

## Formative Assessment

Discuss the impact of deforestation on an ecosystem and the environment.

_____

_____

_____

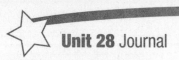
**Science Journal**

Can the changes to ecosystems caused by living organisms be prevented? Why or why not?

_____

_____

_____

_____

_____

_____

_____

_____

_____

_____

_____

_____

_____

_____

_____

_____

_____

_____

_____

_____

_____

_____

_____

_____

## Science Vocabulary Builder

Complete the graphic organizer below.

| Overpopulation | | |
|---|---|---|
| **Definition** | **Visual Representation** | **Association** <br> *This word reminds me of...* |
| | | |

| Human Impact | | |
|---|---|---|
| **Definition** | **Visual Representation** | **Association** <br> *This word reminds me of...* |
| | | |

| Grazers | | |
|---|---|---|
| **Definition** | **Visual Representation** | **Association** <br> *This word reminds me of...* |
| | | |

| Non-Native Species | | |
|---|---|---|
| **Definition** | **Visual Representation** | **Association** <br> *This word reminds me of...* |
| | | |

## Persuasive Poster

Imagine that your neighborhood park was one of the locations being considered for the building of a new highway. Decide whether you would be for or against this change. Design a persuasive poster supporting your point of view.

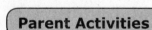

## Parent Activities

1. As a family, observe your neighborhood and note new housing developments. How did the developments change the local ecosystem?

2. Help wildlife in your area by installing a bird feeder or a hummingbird feeder.

3. Participate in an insect count, such as the Journey North Monarch Butterfly Tracking Project or the Museum of Science in Boston Firefly Watch. Links to each can be found below.

   - Journey North Monarch Butterfly Tracking Project: *http://www.learner.org/ jnorth/monarch/*

   - Firefly Watch: *https://legacy.mos.org/fireflywatch/*

**Motivation Station: Mike's Cool Science Fact**

A scientist named Joseph Priestly discovered oxygen in 1744. He also discovered photosynthesis when he conducted an experiment. Priestly found out a burning candle would go out if a jar was placed inside an inverted jar. When he placed a plant and a burning candle under the jar, the candle stayed lit, proving plants produce oxygen.

**After this lesson I will be able to:**

- **Identify** the significance of the carbon dioxide-oxygen cycle to the survival of plants and animals.

## Descriptive and Experimental Investigations

**Activity 1:** Photosynthesis

Using reference materials, label the diagram below using the following terms:

| oxygen | carbon dioxide | glucose (sugar) | water | sunlight |
|---|---|---|---|---|

**Photosynthesis Diagram**

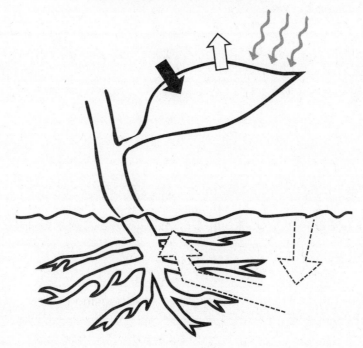

Fill in the equation below:

_____ + Water + _____ = Glucose (sugar) + _____

## Activity 2: What is Carbon?

All living things contain carbon. Illustrate before and after pictures of the items used in the demonstration.

| Bread | |
|---|---|
| Before | After |
| | |

| Hot Dog | |
|---|---|
| Before | After |
| | |

## Activity 3: What is the Carbon Dioxide-Oxygen Cycle?

With your group members, brainstorm ideas about how the carbon dioxide-oxygen cycle works. Write your ideas in the space below.

Research the following words with your group. Record the definitions of each word below.

Carbon dioxide _____

_____

Oxygen _____

_____

Carbon dioxide-oxygen cycle _____

_____

_____

 motivation**science**™LEVEL 5

**1** Which of the cycles below recycles air needed by animals and plants?

Ⓐ Life cycle

Ⓑ Plant and animal cycle

Ⓒ Carbon dioxide-oxygen cycle

Ⓓ Environmental cycle

**2** Sunlight and the continuous movement through the environment of carbon dioxide are important factors in the growth of —

Ⓕ Plants  Ⓗ Humans

Ⓖ Animals  Ⓙ Minerals

**3** Scientists consider 99.9% of all organisms on the planet need carbon to survive. However, Earth has only a fixed amount of carbon. The carbon dioxide-oxygen cycle is the vital because carbon is — **5.3(A)**

Ⓐ created in a unlimited amount

Ⓑ continuously cycled and reused

Ⓒ interrupted through the cycling process

Ⓓ mixed evenly with oxygen

**4** What is the relationship of plants and animals within the carbon dioxide-oxygen cycle?

Ⓕ Plants take in carbon dioxide needed by animals, and animals release oxygen needed by plants.

Ⓖ Plants release oxygen needed by animals, and animals release carbon dioxide needed by plants.

Ⓗ Animals inhale oxygen needed by plants, and plants release carbon dioxide needed by animals.

Ⓙ All of the above

**5** Which of the following could be used to investigate, through observation, the importance of the carbon dioxide-oxygen cycle on the survival of plants and animals? **5.4(A)**

Ⓐ Terrarium

Ⓑ Beaker

Ⓒ Microscope

Ⓓ Collecting net

**6** The diagram above shows how oxygen moves from —

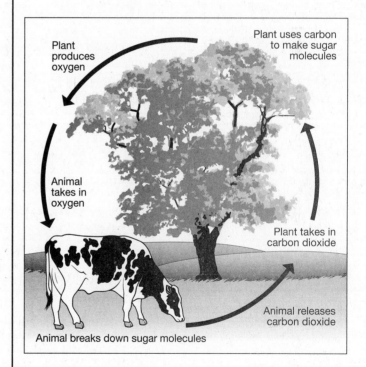

Ⓕ grass to tree

Ⓖ plants to animals

Ⓗ animals to animals

Ⓙ plants to plants

motivation**science**™LEVEL 5

**Unit 29** Check for Understanding

**1** This illustration best shows —

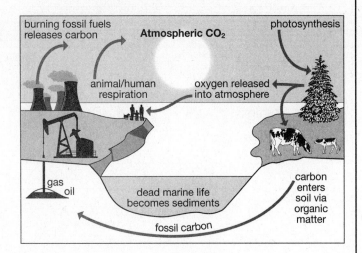

burning fossil fuels releases carbon

**Atmospheric CO₂**

photosynthesis

animal/human respiration

oxygen released into atmosphere

gas oil

dead marine life becomes sediments

carbon enters soil via organic matter

fossil carbon

Ⓐ the cycling of nutrients

Ⓑ where fossils and fossil fuels come from

Ⓒ how pollution gets into the air

Ⓓ the exchange of carbon dioxide and oxygen

**2** Plants use the energy from sunlight to convert carbon dioxide and water into oxygen. Animals use the oxygen for a process called respiration. In other words, animals use oxygen for —

Ⓕ creating food

Ⓖ breathing

Ⓗ transpiration

Ⓙ making glucose

**3** What causes an increase in the oxygen level in the atmosphere?

Ⓐ Oxygen released by plants

Ⓑ Oxygen taken in by plants

Ⓒ Oxygen released by animals

Ⓓ Oxygen inhaled by animals

**4** All of the following add carbon to the atmosphere **EXCEPT** —

Ⓕ constructing new highways

Ⓖ building more factories

Ⓗ planting more trees

Ⓙ burning wood

**5** The Amazon Rainforest produces more than 20% of Earth's oxygen. During photosynthesis, plants use what gas to make glucose?

Ⓐ Helium

Ⓑ Carbon Dioxide

Ⓒ Oxygen

Ⓓ Nitrogen

**6** What is happening in Step 2?

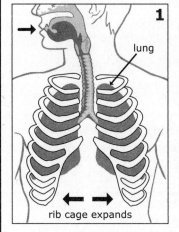
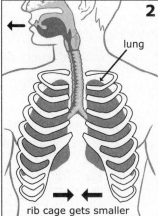

lung

**1**

rib cage expands

lung

**2**

rib cage gets smaller

Ⓕ Exhaling carbon dioxide

Ⓖ Exhaling oxygen

Ⓗ Inhaling oxygen

Ⓙ Inhaling carbon dioxide

Scientific Investigation and Reasoning Skills: Questions 7–14

**7** Scientists feel that human activity has affected and possibly altered the natural process of the carbon dioxide-oxygen cycle that nature had previously kept in balance. In recent history, how have humans added to the carbon dioxide-oxygen cycle? **5.3(D)**

Ⓐ Releasing massive amounts of oxygen

Ⓑ Preventing heat from escaping Earth

Ⓒ Burning fossil fuels like coal and oil

Ⓓ Rapid growth of plant producing farms

**8** In an activity, students research how the Sun's energy is used by plants. They write the following hypothesis.

> If the Sun stopped shining, Earth's plants and animals would not survive.

Which statement correctly supports the students' hypothesis? **5.3(A)**

Ⓕ Plants use the Sun's energy and oxygen to make glucose, which animals eat.

Ⓖ Plants use the Sun's energy and carbon dioxide to make glucose, and release oxygen, which is used by animals.

Ⓗ Plants use the Sun's energy to make water and release oxygen, which is used by animals.

Ⓙ Plants use the Sun's energy to make carbon dioxide and release glucose.

**9** Students conduct an investigation to determine how much oxygen is in the water of a nearby lake.

| Trial | Amount of Oxygen in Water (mg/L) |
|-------|----------------------------------|
| A | 7.6 |
| B | 11.3 |
| C | 8.0 |
| D | 7.9 |

According to the table, which of these trials is most unusual? **5.2(E)**

Ⓐ Trial A     Ⓒ Trial C

Ⓑ Trial B     Ⓓ Trial D

**10** What do the arrows represent in the diagram below? **5.2(D)**

Ⓕ The cycling of water through the environment

Ⓖ The cycling of nitrogen gases through the environment

Ⓗ The cycling of carbon dioxide and oxygen through the environment

Ⓙ The cycling of energy through the nonliving parts of an environment

**11** High levels of oxygen are usually found in streams where the water runs over rocks and oxygen is mixed with the water. Students took samples of water at different places along the stream.

| Location | Amount of Oxygen (mg/L) |
|----------|-------------------------|
| A | 5.9 |
| B | 7.2 |
| C | 6.0 |
| D | 13.8 |

Based on the table, from where would you expect Sample D to have been taken? **5.2(G)**

Ⓐ Near the bank

Ⓑ In the middle of a big pool

Ⓒ In the shade

Ⓓ Near a lot of rocks

**12** Joseph Priestly was a scientist who made an important discovery. He noticed that a candle placed in a closed container would quickly go out. However, if a sprig from a mint plant was placed inside the jar with a lighted candle, the candle stayed lit. Why did the mint sprig keep the candle ignited? **5.3(D)**

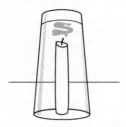

Ⓕ The candle flame burned the sprig of mint as fuel.

Ⓖ The candle produced oxygen, which the plant needs for photosynthesis.

Ⓗ The plant produced oxygen, which fire needs in order to burn.

Ⓙ The candle produced carbon, which was removed by the plant.

**13** A group of students uses resources to construct a model of the carbon dioxide-oxygen cycle.

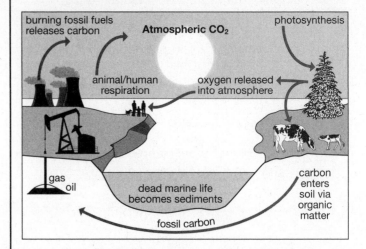

Which question below can be answered using the carbon dioxide-oxygen cycle model? **5.3(C)**

Ⓐ What gas do humans and animals exhale?

Ⓑ Why is it important to identify nitrogen?

Ⓒ How does water cycle through the atmosphere?

Ⓓ How long is the life cycle of a tree?

**14** The class had a small fish bowl with rocks on the bottom in the science lab. During the past few weeks, all the plants in the fish bowl died. As students watched the fish, they noticed that they started swimming very rapidly, and their gills were opening and closing very quickly. Based on observations, the best conclusion from the fish's behavior is that — **5.2(F)**

Ⓕ the fish were exercising

Ⓖ the fish were hungry

Ⓗ the fish needed more carbon dioxide

Ⓙ the fish needed more oxygen

## Carbon-Dioxide Oxygen Cycle

Using the diagram, describe the role of the carbon dioxide-oxygen cycle parts in the space below.

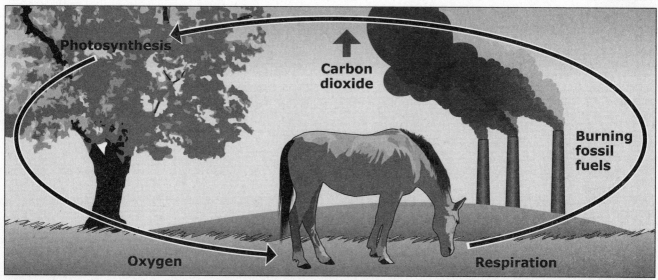

| Roles | |
|---|---|
| Carbon dioxide | |
| Plants | |
| Oxygen | |
| Animals | |
| Photosynthesis | |
| Respiration | |
| Burning fossil fuels | |

## Formative Assessment

Name 4 other cycles. What characteristics do all cycles have in common?

_____  _____  _____  _____

_____

_____

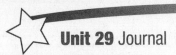

**Science Journal**

How do plants and animals depend on the carbon dioxide-oxygen cycle for survival?

_____

_____

_____

_____

_____

_____

_____

_____

_____

_____

_____

_____

_____

_____

_____

_____

_____

_____

_____

_____

_____

## Science Vocabulary Builder

Describe the relationships by completing the graphic organizers.

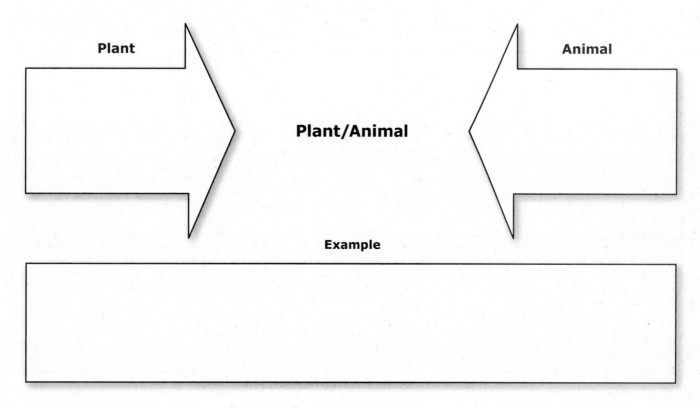

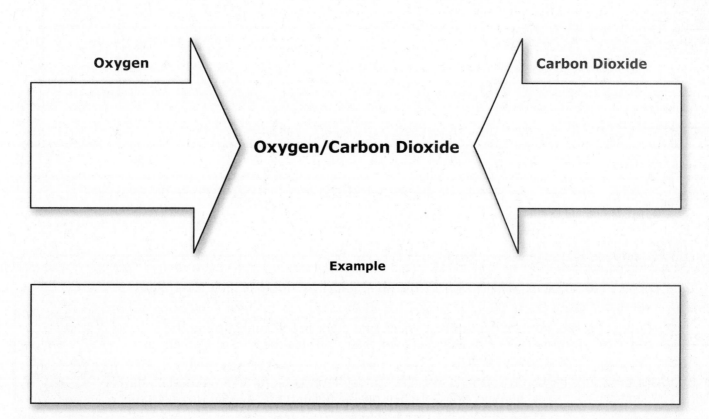

## Cycle Diagram

Draw a picture of the carbon dioxide-oxygen cycle. Explain what is happening, and use arrows to show how the cycle moves through the environment. Include labels in your diagram.

## Parent Activities

1. Plant a seed, and watch it grow. As the plant develops, discuss photosynthesis with your child.

2. Conduct a simple plant experiment. Place one plant in the sunlight and the other in the closet. Observe changes over time. Discuss the role of sunlight in the process of photosynthesis.

3. Discuss how carbon is released into the atmosphere. Look for examples such as exhaust from cars, burning wood or charcoal, or pollution from a nearby factory.

motivation**science**™ LEVEL 5
©2011–2014 mentoring**minds**.com

**Motivation Station: Molly's Cool Science Fact**

Some herbivores, such as cows and giraffes, chew their cud. When they eat, the food passes to one of their stomachs. They are able to burp up the food to chew it at a later time. This special adaptation allows them to get a meal quickly and then enjoy their dinner in a safe place away from predators.

**After this lesson I will be able to:**

- **Compare** the structures and functions of different species that help them live and survive such as hooves on prairie animals or webbed feet in aquatic animals.

## Comparative Investigations

**Activity 1:** Webbed Feet

Investigate the function of webbed feed in an aquatic environment. Place a rubber glove on your hand. Move your hand through the water. Describe your observations.

_____

_____

_____

_____

_____

_____

Put a plastic bag over your hand. Wrap a rubber band around your wrist to seal the bag around your wrist. Move your hand through the water again. Describe your observations.

_____

_____

_____

_____

_____

_____

**Activity 2:** Comparing Structures and Functions

Using research materials, find a special adaptation for an organism that fits each classification below. Under the classification column, list the name of the organism, and draw a picture. Then name and illustrate the special structure in the structure column. In the function column, explain the purpose of the structure and how it helps the organism survive in its environment.

| Classification | Structure | Function |
|---|---|---|
| Mammal: | | |
| Bird: | | |
| Reptile: | | |
| Amphibian: | | |
| Fish: | | |
| Desert Plant: | | |

motivation**science** LEVEL 5

**1** Hooves on buffalo and webbed feet on ducks are —

Ⓐ structures on the same species

Ⓑ behaviors of different species

Ⓒ structures on different species

Ⓓ behaviors of the same species

**2** Compare the different species pictured below.

What is the purpose of their webbed feet?

Ⓕ Structural adaptation for survival

Ⓖ Behavioral adaptation for survival

Ⓗ Competition between species

Ⓙ Learned behavior of species

**3** Colorado has a large population of bighorn sheep. They are herbivores and have hooves with specialized claws or toenails adapted for running and helping them escape predators. Mountain lion, elk, chipmunks, and black bears also live in Colorado. Which of the animals below has feet that are most similar to the Colorado bighorn sheep? **5.2(D)**

Ⓐ Mountain lion  Ⓒ Chipmunk

Ⓑ Elk  Ⓓ Black bear

**4** Biologists study the structural adaptation of animals, such as marine birds with webbed feet, to understand the function of their feet and how they help them live and survive. Which of the following questions below can best be answered from a biologist's study? **5.2(B)**

Ⓕ How do birds use webbed feet to nest high in trees?

Ⓖ What causes marine birds to stay dry in water?

Ⓗ How do the feathers of marine birds help them fly?

Ⓙ Can all birds with webbed feet swim?

**5** Which of the following would be best to use for sorting these animals into two groups?

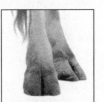
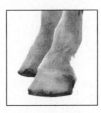

Ⓐ Animals with lungs and animals with gills

Ⓑ Prairie animals and aquatic animals

Ⓒ Saltwater animals and freshwater animals

Ⓓ Mammals and amphibians

**6** Which of the following is a structural adaptation of a cow?

Ⓕ Having hooved feet

Ⓖ Possessing sharp teeth

Ⓗ Coming when called

Ⓙ None of the above

**Unit 30** Check for Understanding

**1** A student reads the following information.

> 1. Feet covered in hair for good grip and protection against extreme temperatures
>
> 2. Thickly callused pads for protection from sharp edges and extreme temperatures
>
> 3. Long claws for climbing and digging

Which animal most likely has the characteristics described?

- Ⓐ Polar bear
- Ⓑ Red kangaroo
- Ⓒ Desert fox
- Ⓓ Western gorilla

**2** Cows and deer are herbivores. They have an adaptation which helps them cover enough ground to find food and water. This adaptation is called —

- Ⓕ hooves
- Ⓖ paws
- Ⓗ claws
- Ⓙ toenails

**3** Many animals are aquatic, such as a platypus and frog. A structure that is beneficial for both of these aquatic animals is —

- Ⓐ down feathers
- Ⓑ long tail
- Ⓒ webbed feet
- Ⓓ scaly skin

**4** Elk and bighorn sheep are grazers. A structural adaptation that helps meet the needs for this type of diet is —

- Ⓕ camouflaged fur
- Ⓖ flat teeth
- Ⓗ webbed feet
- Ⓙ good eyesight

**5** Bactrian camels have special features that allow them to live in harsh, hot climates. These camels have long eyelashes and ears lined with hair. They also have nostrils that they can close when needed. Which is most likely the reason camels have these adaptations?

- Ⓐ Protection from hot weather
- Ⓑ Protection from sandstorms
- Ⓒ Protection from rainstorms
- Ⓓ Protection from predators

**6** The kangaroo rat lives in the drier areas of the western and southwestern United States. It is very small and has a long tail and large back legs that allow it to jump up to 2.7 meters.

These animals most likely use their back legs to —

- Ⓕ dig burrows
- Ⓖ leap away from predators
- Ⓗ listen for danger
- Ⓙ attract a mate

 ©2011–2014 mentoring**minds**.com

## Scientific Investigation and Reasoning Skills: Questions 7–14

**7** In an activity, students observe and record information about bird feet. Four students write explanations telling why geese have webbed feet.

| Bird Footprint | Type of Bird | Environment | Diet |
|---|---|---|---|
| | Bald eagle | Near large bodies of water<br><br>Tall trees for nesting and sleeping | Fish and small animals |
| | Pheasant | Medium-high grass<br><br>Fields of grain | Seeds, grains, and insects |
| | Goose | Rivers, ponds, and lakeshores | Water plants, grass roots, and grain |

Which student's statement is the best reason why geese have webbed feet? **5.3(A)**

Ⓐ Geese live in muddy areas. Webbed feet keep them from sinking in the mud.

Ⓑ Geese fly south each winter. Webbed feet can be used to steer when flying.

Ⓒ Geese spend most of their time around water. Webbed feet help geese swim.

Ⓓ Geese live in cold areas. Webbed feet keep them from getting stuck in snow.

**8** Groups of students select a topic for research. A group wants to study the adaptations of animals in the desert. One question they should ask is — **5.2(B)**

Ⓕ how long do the animals live?

Ⓖ how do the animals satisfy their need for water?

Ⓗ how many offspring do the animals have?

Ⓙ can you buy the animals in pet stores?

**9** Students collect data about the arctic fox. They learn it can change colors from brown to white.

**Number and Color of Arctic Foxes**

| | Jan. | May | Aug. |
|---|---|---|---|
| **White** | 15 | 0 | 0 |
| **Brown and white** | 0 | 13 | 0 |
| **Brown** | 0 | 0 | 18 |

What conclusion can be drawn from the table about the color change? **5.2(F)**

Ⓐ Color changes help the fox with camouflage.

Ⓑ Color changes help the fox find shelter.

Ⓒ Color changes help the fox stay cooler.

Ⓓ Color changes help the fox move faster.

**10** A group of students compares the hooves of deer and buffalo. They construct a diorama to display a real-life representation of how these two species use this structural adaptation to survive in their environment. The students are constructing a — **5.3(C)**

Ⓕ diagram          Ⓗ sculpture

Ⓖ model          Ⓙ cast mold

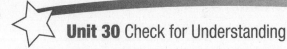

**11** The main purpose for the flyer below is to — **5.3(B)**

### City of Cadott Bird Watchers Society

| Bird Beaks and Bird Feet | | | |
|---|---|---|---|
| You can tell a lot about what a bird eats by its beak! | | You can tell a lot about where a bird lives by its feet! | |
| **probing** | **scooping** | **perching** | **paddling** |
| hummingbird | pelican | crow | mallard |
| **straining** | **tearing** | **grasping** | **climbing** |
| mallard | eagle | eagle | woodpecker |

Ⓐ encourage students to join a club

Ⓑ compare the structures and functions of beaks and feet

Ⓒ persuade others to fight against habitat destruction

Ⓓ list the names of all the birds living in the city

**12** Students are to research a scientist who has worked with animals. One scientist they might choose would be — **5.3(D)**

Ⓕ Thomas Edison

Ⓖ Jane Goodall

Ⓗ Benjamin Franklin

Ⓙ Isaac Newton

**13** Everything in nature has a reason for how it is structured and how it behaves. It is important to learn about animals and how they survive in their environments. Which of the following questions **CANNOT** be answered from studying animal structures and their functions? **5.2(B)**

Ⓐ How do animals instinctively survive changes made within an ecosystem?

Ⓑ What are some structural adaptations for living on water and on land?

Ⓒ What observations can be made about body parts of aquatic animals?

Ⓓ What are some physical features of prairie animals that help them adapt to climate?

**14** Students conduct an investigation to learn about bird beaks. They use different tools to represent different bird beaks, such as tweezers, straws, and spoons. When they finish the investigation, the teacher instructs the students to conduct a second trial. Why does the teacher want students to do the same investigation two separate times? **5.2(E)**

Ⓕ The students did not listen to directions the first time.

Ⓖ Birds in the natural world eat two times a day.

Ⓗ Data tables look better when they have more than one column.

Ⓙ Two trials are needed to make the investigation valid.

### New Animal Discovery

Imagine you have discovered a new animal. Complete the animal information sheet below to share the new creature with the world.

| | |
|---|---|
| Animal Name | |
| Animal Classification | |
| Animal Habitat | |
| Diet | |
| Structural Adaptations | |
| Illustration of Animal | |

### Formative Assessment

Construct an explanation to describe how the structures and functions of a species help them live and survive. Use evidence to support your answer.

| What is your explanation? | What is your evidence? |
|---|---|
| | |

Name _____

**Science Journal**

Write about your favorite zoo animal. Explain special structures of the animal and the function of the structures.

_____
_____
_____
_____
_____
_____
_____
_____
_____
_____
_____
_____
_____
_____
_____
_____
_____
_____
_____
_____
_____
_____
_____

ILLEGAL TO COPY  motivation**science**™LEVEL 5  ©2011–2014 mentoring**minds**.com

**Science Vocabulary Builder**

In each of the bubbles below, list structural adaptations for the animals given.

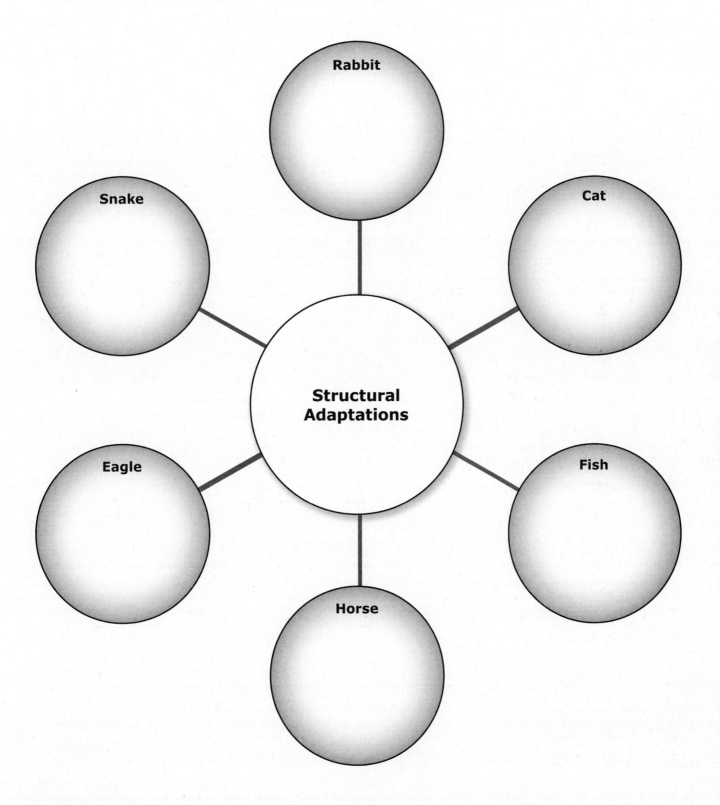

**Hooves, Paws, and Webbed Feet**

Using the Venn diagram below, compare and contrast the structures and functions for each type of animal foot.

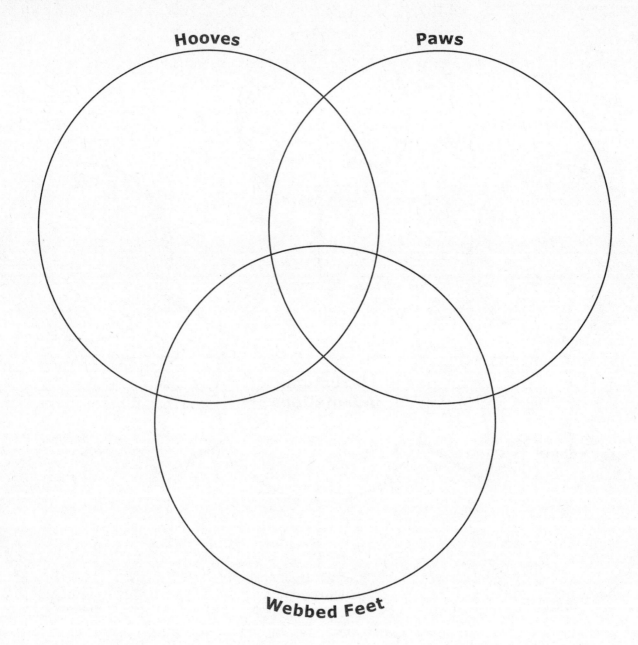

Hooves          Paws

Webbed Feet

**Parent Activities**

1. Discuss the adaptations of the family pet. How do the adaptations help the animal survive?

2. Look around your yard for plants with special adaptations, such as thorns on a rose bush or spines on a cactus.

**Motivation Station: Mike's Cool Science Fact**

Instincts, like hibernation and migration, are inherited traits. These inherited traits help animals survive in their environment.

**After this lesson I will be able to:**

- **Differentiate** between inherited traits of plants and animals such as spines on a cactus or shape of a beak and learned behaviors such as an animal learning tricks or a child riding a bicycle.

## Comparative Investigations

**Activity 1:** Class Survey

How many of your classmates share the same traits as you? Take the survey below to find out. Use a tally mark to record how many in your class have each inherited trait.

| Dominant Traits | Recessive Traits |
|---|---|
| Right handed | Left handed |
| | |
| Widow's peak | No widow's peak |
| | |
| Longer second toe | Longer big toe |
| | |
| Crooked pinky | Straight pinky |
| | |
| Long eyelashes | Short eyelashes |
| | |
| Can roll tongue | Cannot roll tongue |
| | |
| Free earlobes | Attached earlobes |
| | |

Which characteristics do you have? _____

_____

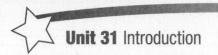
## Activity 2: Inherited Traits of Plants and Animals

Select an ecosystem.

| desert | arctic | rainforest | prairie | marine |

With your group, research one plant and one animal that lives in the chosen ecosystem. For each organism, find 5 examples of inherited traits, and list them in the circles below.

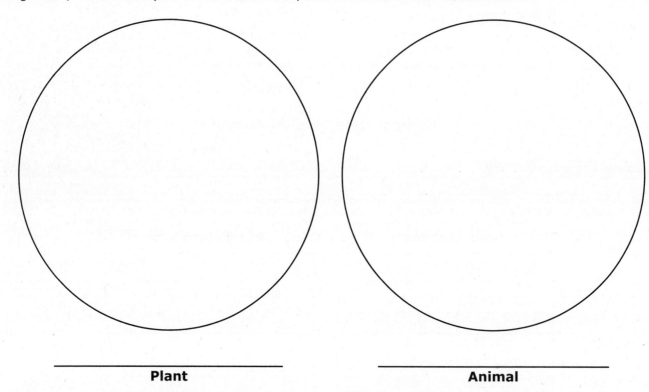

**Plant**                                    **Animal**

## Activity 3: Learned Behaviors in Animals

The animal listed above has many inherited traits but also has learned many things which help it survive. Write a paragraph explaining the learned behaviors of your chosen animal and how those behaviors help the animal survive.

_____

_____

_____

_____

_____

_____

_____

Name _____

**1** Some traits and behaviors are learned and some are inherited. Which of the following traits are inherited?

Ⓐ Speaking Spanish

Ⓑ Bird saying hello

Ⓒ Cat using a litter box

Ⓓ Spines on a cactus

**2** Which of the following is a behavior that is learned?

Ⓕ Shape of a beak

Ⓖ Monkey riding a bicycle

Ⓗ Horse eating hay

Ⓙ Snake eating mice

**3** What is the difference between a learned behavior and an inherited trait?

Ⓐ Learned behaviors are taught, and inherited traits are passed down from parent to child.

Ⓑ Learned behaviors take years to acquire, and inherited traits take only a short period of time to accomplish.

Ⓒ Learned behaviors are difficult to accomplish, and inherited traits are easy to accomplish.

Ⓓ Learned behaviors are passed down from parent to child, and inherited traits are taught to children by parents.

**4** When danger approaches, a black bear mother will send a warning call to her cubs. The cubs will then climb a tree. This response is —

Ⓕ an environmental trait

Ⓖ an inherited trait

Ⓗ a learned behavior

Ⓙ a personality trait

**Use the picture below and your knowledge of science to answer questions 5 and 6.**

Students take a trip to the zoo to observe animals in their natural habitats. At the zoo, they research different species to determine the differences in their inherited traits and learned behaviors. Data was collected on 11 species and recorded on a table the students constructed.

**5** After collecting the data, what is the next step students should take? **5.2(F)**

Ⓐ Form a hypothesis

Ⓑ Gather materials

Ⓒ Put away all the tools used

Ⓓ Discuss results, and form conclusions

**6** Which of the following would be the most beneficial for maintaining the collected data for future reference? **5.4(A)**

Ⓕ Textbook

Ⓖ Tape recorder

Ⓗ Camera

Ⓙ Notebook

Name _____

**1** Which of the following is an inherited trait?

Ⓐ Swimming

Ⓑ Eye color

Ⓒ Skateboarding

Ⓓ Callused fingers

**2** Aquarena Springs in San Marcos, Texas, had a diving pig for over 20 years named Ralph the Diving Pig. The pig was taught to swim and dive as a park attraction. Which statement correctly describes Ralph?

Ⓕ The pig knew how to dive as instinct, which is an inherited trait.

Ⓖ The diving pig had an inherited trait for being a good swimmer.

Ⓗ The diving pig had an inherited talent for being easy to train.

Ⓙ The pig learned to dive over time, which is an acquired trait.

**3** In an activity, students learn about inherited and acquired traits. They record what they discover in a chart.

| Inherited | Acquired |
| --- | --- |
| Person's hairline | Musical ability |
| Tree height | Scars |
| Flower color | Mouse learning a maze |
| Earlobe shape | ??? |

Which trait completes the chart?

Ⓐ Color blindness

Ⓑ Leaf shape

Ⓒ Scientific knowledge

Ⓓ Animal warning sound

**4** The shape of a bird's beak is a body structure that the bird has at birth. This body structure is a/an —

Ⓕ learned trait

Ⓖ special trait

Ⓗ inherited trait

Ⓙ developed trait

**5** It takes a child several hours of practice to be able to ride a skateboard successfully. This is an example of —

Ⓐ learned behavior

Ⓑ inherited behavior

Ⓒ good behavior

Ⓓ childish behavior

**6** Proboscis monkeys live on the island of Borneo in forests near freshwater. These monkeys are named for their large, fleshy noses that turn red and swell when they are angry or excited. They also make loud honking sounds as a warning when danger is near. Proboscis monkeys have large pot bellies that are divided into two chambers for digestion. When babies are born, proboscis mothers teach their young which leaves are safe to eat. Which proboscis monkey trait is a learned behavior?

Ⓕ Finding safe leaves

Ⓖ Large, fleshy noses

Ⓗ Loud honking sounds

Ⓙ Two-chamber stomach

Scientific Investigation and Reasoning Skills: Questions 7–14

**7** Two categories of desert plants are called drought resisters and drought evaders.

| Drought Resisters | Drought Evaders |
|---|---|
| Store water in roots, leaves, or stems | Survive as seeds until heavy rain |
| Have deep taproots | Have a short life span or very slow growth |
| Have widespread, shallow roots | Lose leaves and flowers during hot periods |
| Have a waxy coating | Grow in caves and crevices |

What can be concluded about drought resisters and drought evaders? **5.2(F)**

Ⓐ Both types of plants have acquired traits that allow them to survive in extreme conditions.

Ⓑ Drought resisters have inherited traits, while drought evaders have acquired traits that allow them to survive.

Ⓒ Both types of plants have inherited traits that allow them to survive in extreme conditions.

Ⓓ Drought resisters have acquired traits, while drought evaders have inherited traits that allow them to survive.

**8** Students pull strands of their hair to view under the microscope. They know that hair color is an inherited trait. One of the students has red hair. Neither parent has red hair. From where did the student inherit the red hair? **5.2(D)**

Ⓕ The student's ancestors

Ⓖ The student's father

Ⓗ The student's mother

Ⓙ All of the above

**9** The class has a pet gerbil that runs inside a large, plastic ball that moves around the room. When the gerbil bumps into furniture, he stops and runs another direction inside the ball to keep going. Students construct four obstacle courses and watch the gerbil successfully navigate the course each time. Students conclude this is — **5.2(F)**

Ⓐ an inherited trait

Ⓑ a learned behavior

Ⓒ a physical trait

Ⓓ an adaptation

**10** Students want to collect data on the behavior of ducks. Each day after school the students approach the pond, call to the ducks, and throw handfuls of corn on the ground. The ducks learn to come eat the corn. The best tool for recording the ducks' behavior would be a — **5.4(A)**

Ⓕ stopwatch

Ⓖ camera

Ⓗ calculator

Ⓙ beaker

**11** The pictures below display — **5.2(D)**

&#9398; inherited traits

&#9399; instinctive traits

&#9400; innate abilities

&#9401; learned traits

**12** Biologists study the structural adaptations of organisms, which are — **5.3(D)**

&#9403; inherited behaviors

&#9404; learned behaviors

&#9405; inherited traits

&#9408; learned traits

**13** A group of students visits the botanical gardens to study the inherited traits of tropical plants. Before the students and teachers explore the gardens, the trained instructor, who is a botanist, discusses important guidelines and expectations of behavior for the students. She tells students these rules are for their protection as well as for the protection of the plants housed in the garden. The instructor talked to the students about these things because students are expected to — **5.1(A)**

&#9398; ask good questions

&#9399; wait their turn

&#9400; speak softly

&#9401; demonstrate safe practices

**14** At the zoo, students are allowed to touch a bearded dragon. What should the students do after this experience? **5.1(A)**

&#9403; Put on rubber gloves

&#9404; Shake the zookeeper's hand

&#9405; Wash hands

&#9408; Get a drink of water

## My Characteristics

Inside the star, fill in an inherited trait to match each characteristic 1–5. Outside the star, fill in a learned behavior to match each characteristic 6–10.

Application
*i*
Apply

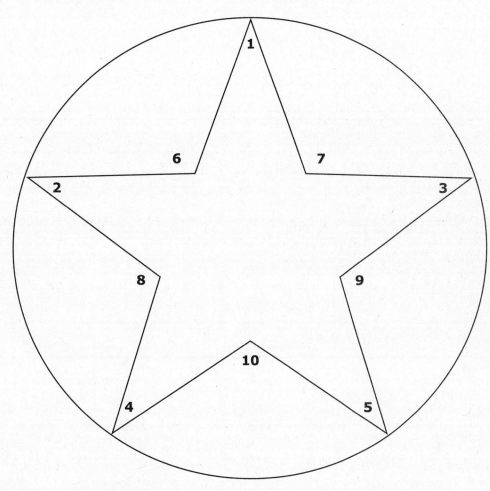

1. Trait inherited from mother
2. Trait inherited from father
3. Trait shared with a grandparent
4. Trait shared with an aunt
5. Trait shared with a sibling

6. Best subject
7. Favorite food
8. Favorite music
9. Languages spoken
10. Talent

## Formative Assessment

Differentiate between the inherited traits and learned behaviors of your family pet or favorite animal.

_____

_____

_____

_____

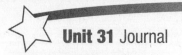

Name _____

**Science Journal**

How do traits of desert plants and animals help them survive the dry desert conditions?

_____

_____

_____

_____

_____

_____

_____

_____

_____

_____

_____

_____

_____

_____

_____

_____

_____

_____

_____

_____

_____

_____

_____

_____

_____

_____

_____

_____

ILLEGAL TO COPY motivation**science**™ LEVEL 5 ©2011–2014 mentoring**minds**.com

**Science Vocabulary Builder**

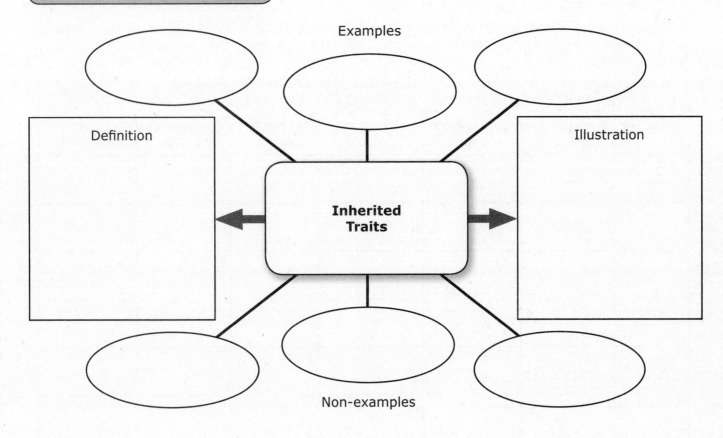

Examples

Definition

Illustration

**Inherited Traits**

Non-examples

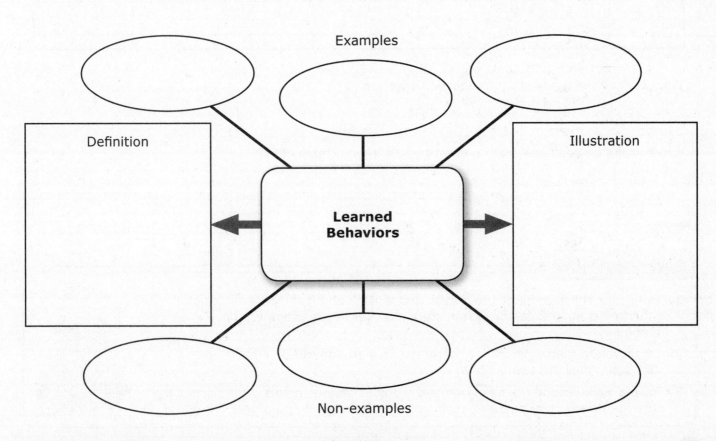

Examples

Definition

Illustration

**Learned Behaviors**

Non-examples

**Unit 31** Homework

## Family Survey

Conduct a survey of your family members to find how many of them share the traits below. Write your family members' names in the first column. For each trait, write the characteristic for each family member.

| Family Member | Attached earlobes/ Free earlobes | Widow's peak/ No widow's peak | Longer second toe/ Longer big toe | Crooked pinky/ Straight pinky | Can roll tongue/ Cannot roll tongue | Short eyelashes/ Long eyelashes |
|---|---|---|---|---|---|---|
| Self | | | | | | |
| | | | | | | |
| | | | | | | |
| | | | | | | |
| | | | | | | |
| | | | | | | |
| | | | | | | |

What traits do you have in common with your family?_____

_____

Which traits do you have that no other person in your family has?_____

_____

✂ - - - - - - - - - - - - - - - - - - - - - - - - - - - - - - - - - - - - - - - - - - - - -

## Parent Activities

1. Help your child complete the survey above. Talk about the differences in inherited traits and learned characteristics that family members have in common.

2. Observe the family pet. What characteristics are inherited? What characteristics are learned?

3. Take a walk around the neighborhood. Look at various plants, and discuss the inherited traits they possess, such as flower color or shape of leaf.

motivation**science**™ LEVEL 5

| **Motivation Station: Molly's Cool Science Fact** |
| --- |
| Earth is home to some really big insects! The longest insect is the female giant walking stick, who can grow up to 55.5 cm. The giant walking stick is long, but very light. The heavyweight of all insects is the goliath beetle, who can grow up to 11.43 cm and can weigh as much as 85 grams! |

**After this lesson I will be able to:**

- **Describe** the differences between complete and incomplete metamorphosis of insects.

## Comparative and Experimental Investigations

**Activity 1:** Complete or Incomplete?

Research the insects below. One goes through complete metamorphosis, and the other goes through incomplete metamorphosis. Determine which insect goes through each form of metamorphosis. Draw and label the stages of each insect's life cycle.

**Dragonfly**

**Darkling Beetle**

- - - - - - - - - - - - - - - - - - - - - - - - - - - - - - - - - - - - - - - - - - - - - -

**Complete Metamorphosis**     Name of Insect _____

| | | | |
| --- | --- | --- | --- |
| | | | |

**Incomplete Metamorphosis**     Name of Insect _____

| | | |
| --- | --- | --- |
| | | |

Name _____

## Unit 32 Introduction

Supporting Standard 5.10(C)

**Activity 2:** Catching Insects

**Question:** Will different types of insects be attracted to different baits?

**Hypothesis:** _____

**Procedure:** As a group, choose two baits to use from the materials provided by your teacher. Take the materials outside, and dig two holes in the same area. Place a cup in each hole, so that the top of the cup is even with the ground. In each cup, drop in a different kind of bait. Use rocks to prop a cardboard cover over the cups. Weight down the top with more rocks. Leave the insect catchers overnight, and check the next day. Research and record types and numbers of insects found. Identify the insects as going through complete or incomplete metamorphosis. Repeat for two more nights, re-baiting the trap and checking it the following day. After the third day, share and analyze results with your class. Form a conclusion based on your data.

**Name of Bait:** _____   **Location:** _____

| Day | Insect | Number Caught | Complete or Incomplete Metamorphosis |
|---|---|---|---|
| 1 | | | |
| 2 | | | |
| 3 | | | |

**Name of Bait:** _____   **Location:** _____

| Day | Insect | Number Caught | Complete or Incomplete Metamorphosis |
|---|---|---|---|
| 1 | | | |
| 2 | | | |
| 3 | | | |

**Conclusion:** _____

342   ILLEGAL TO COPY   motivation**science**™LEVEL 5   ©2011–2014 mentoring**minds**.com

**1** How is incomplete metamorphosis different than complete metamorphosis?

Ⓐ Incomplete metamorphosis is an unfinished life cycle.

Ⓑ Incomplete metamorphosis is the undeveloped growth of organisms.

Ⓒ Incomplete metamorphosis has fewer life cycle stages.

Ⓓ Incomplete metamorphosis is the partial body development of organisms.

**2** What are the distinct life cycle stages of complete metamorphosis?

Ⓕ Seed, seedling, baby plant, adult

Ⓖ Egg, larva, pupa, adult

Ⓗ Seed, pupa, larva, adult

Ⓙ Birth, growth, maturity, death

**3** Incomplete metamorphosis has only 3 life cycle stages: egg, nymph, adult. The nymph looks similar to a smaller version of the —

Ⓐ adult

Ⓑ egg

Ⓒ pupa

Ⓓ larva

**4** Crickets, grasshoppers, cockroaches, and dragonflies are examples of organisms that go through incomplete metamorphosis. A physical characteristic that distinguishes the nymph from the other two stages would be that it is —

Ⓕ wingless

Ⓖ worm-like

Ⓗ colorless

Ⓙ developed

**5** Students want to examine the differences of insects that go through incomplete and complete metamorphosis. Which tool would be most helpful? **5.4(A)**

Ⓐ Telescope

Ⓑ Stopwatch

Ⓒ Hand lens

Ⓓ Beaker

**6** Entomology is the scientific study of insects. Entomologists study the way insects develop, grow, and change form. Some insects go through three stages of development, while others go through four stages. The development, growth, and form change of insects is called — **5.3(D)**

Ⓕ ecosystems

Ⓖ metamorphosis

Ⓗ photosynthesis

Ⓙ classification

**Unit 32** Check for Understanding

**1** Which describes a characteristic of nymphs in incomplete metamorphosis?

Ⓐ Nymphs molt their exoskeletons as they grow.

Ⓑ Nymphs reproduce to make more of their kind.

Ⓒ Nymphs protect the egg and hold it together.

Ⓓ Nymphs do not eat or move.

**2** Which best explains what is shown in the diagram below?

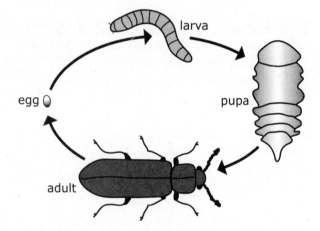

Ⓕ Larval stage of a common beetle

Ⓖ Complete metamorphosis of a beetle

Ⓗ Pupa stage of a common beetle

Ⓙ Incomplete metamorphosis of a beetle

**3** Which statement about the differences between complete metamorphosis and incomplete metamorphosis is **NOT** correct?

Ⓐ Both have four stages.

Ⓑ Both have an egg stage.

Ⓒ Both have an adult stage.

Ⓓ Both are cycles of insects.

**4** The praying mantis life cycle is shown in the diagram below.

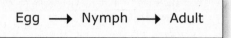

Egg ⟶ Nymph ⟶ Adult

Which statement best describes the life cycle of a praying mantis?

Ⓕ The praying mantis grows from egg to adult by complete metamorphosis.

Ⓖ The praying mantis grows to adult size by the pupa stage.

Ⓗ The praying mantis grows from egg to adult by incomplete metamorphosis.

Ⓙ The praying mantis grows to adult size by the larval stage.

**5** If an insect forms a chrysalis during the third stage of complete metamorphosis, the adult will be a —

Ⓐ moth          Ⓒ dragonfly

Ⓑ mosquito      Ⓓ butterfly

**6** Which stage is missing from the diagram below?

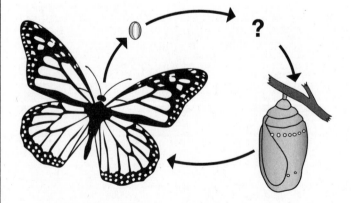

Ⓕ Egg           Ⓗ Pupa

Ⓖ Adult         Ⓙ Not here

| Scientific Investigation and Reasoning Skills: Questions 7–14 |
| --- |

**7** A fifth grade class receives a lady bug kit with 10 live larvae. Students make daily observations and record how many of the pupas hatch each day. At the end of the investigation, students make a table to display the data.

| Date | 10 | 11 | 12 | 13 | 14 | 15 |
| --- | --- | --- | --- | --- | --- | --- |
| Number hatched | 1 | 2 | 4 | 2 | 0 | 0 |

What title should they give the table? **5.2(G)**

Ⓐ Life of a Lady Bug

Ⓑ Weekly Observations

Ⓒ Lady Bug Pupa Hatchings

Ⓓ Incomplete Metamorphosis Table

**8** Students design an investigation to see what impact temperature might have on the length of time it takes for painted lady butterflies to go through a complete metamorphosis. Based on the purpose of the investigation, what should their variable be? **5.2(A)**

Ⓕ The number of specimens

Ⓖ The amount of time it takes the butterflies to transform

Ⓗ The location of the hatchery

Ⓙ The temperature of the hatchery

**9** Students go outside in the fall and collect crickets from the grass around the building. They notice that some of the crickets have wings and some of the smaller ones do not. Based on what they know about the different stages of metamorphosis, what do the students conclude about the crickets with no wings? **5.2(F)**

Ⓐ The crickets are old and have lost their wings.

Ⓑ The crickets are immature and have not developed wings yet.

Ⓒ A predator tried to eat the cricket and broke its wings.

Ⓓ The crickets are a species that does not develop wings.

**10** The diagram shows the life cycle of a mosquito.

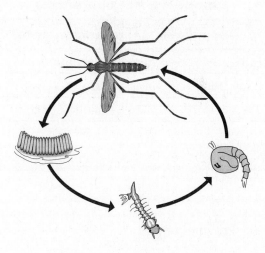

What is represented in the diagram? **5.2(D)**

Ⓕ Complete metamorphosis

Ⓖ Incomplete photosynthesis

Ⓗ Complete development

Ⓙ Incomplete metamorphosis

**11** Students observe the changes in the life cycle stages of a beetle and a grasshopper. What should the students do to remember what they observed? **5.2(C)**

Ⓐ Repeat the experiment one more time

Ⓑ Record their information in a science notebook

Ⓒ Analyze the information using a computer

Ⓓ Discuss their observations with other students

**12** Which of the following best completes the table below? **5.2(G)**

**Organisms that
Experience Metamorphosis**

| Complete | Incomplete |
|---|---|
| Butterfly | Grasshopper |
| Lady bug | Cricket |
| ??? | Walking stick |

Ⓕ Ant

Ⓖ Cockroach

Ⓗ Dragonfly

Ⓙ Praying mantis

**13** In an activity, students make a chart describing complete and incomplete metamorphosis.

| Complete Metamorphosis | Incomplete Metamorphosis |
|---|---|
| 4 stages | 3 stages |
| Egg, larva, pupa, adult | Egg, nymph, adult |
| Complete change in body structure | ??? |

Which information best completes the chart? **5.2(G)**

Ⓐ Incomplete change in body structure

Ⓑ Similar body structure, different sizes

Ⓒ Different body structure, same size

Ⓓ Complete change in body structure

**14** Which tool would be most helpful for students to measure the differences between the nymph and adult stages of a grasshopper? **5.2(C)**

Ⓕ Meter stick

Ⓖ Triple beam balance

Ⓗ Calculator

Ⓙ Metric ruler

           motivation**science**™LEVEL 5

## Insect Design

Use the parts below to design an insect. Illustrate your insect in the space below. Give your insect a name, tell whether it goes though complete or incomplete metamorphosis, and draw the stages of its life cycle.

Circle your choices.

| **Eyes** | **Antennae** | **Mouth Parts** | **Wings** |
|---|---|---|---|

Insect Name _____

Life Cycle_____

Illustration of Insect

Life Cycle Illustration

## Formative Assessment

Students find a female praying mantis and place it in a terrarium. The female lays eggs, which hatch several months later. The young insects that emerge from the eggs look like miniature versions of the adult. The students conclude that a praying mantis goes through incomplete metamorphosis. Did the students make a valid conclusion? Why or why not?

_____

_____

_____

_____

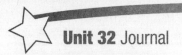

Name _____

**Science Journal**

Describe how insects protect themselves while in the larval stage.

_____
_____
_____
_____
_____
_____
_____
_____
_____
_____
_____
_____
_____
_____
_____
_____
_____
_____
_____
_____
_____
_____
_____
_____
_____
_____
_____

motivation**science**™ LEVEL 5

**Science Vocabulary Builder**

Fill in the Venn diagram to compare and contrast complete and incomplete metamorphosis. In the circles above and below the Venn, give four examples of insects which go through each change.

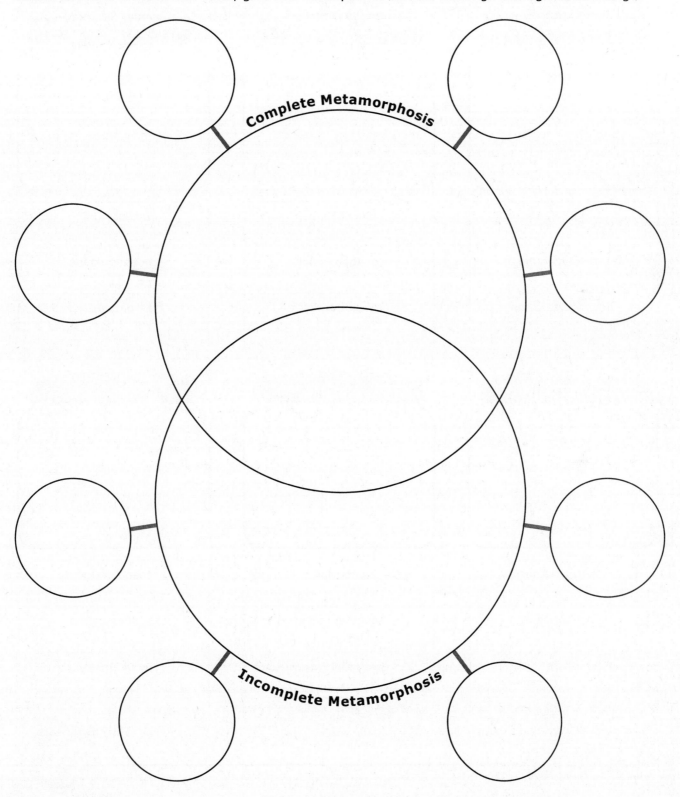

Complete Metamorphosis

Incomplete Metamorphosis

## Illustrated Bug Collection

Find 6 examples of insects in your neighborhood. In each jar below, illustrate the insect. Below the jar, complete the information about each insect.

Insect Name
_____
Location Found
_____
Type of Life Cycle
_____

Insect Name
_____
Location Found
_____
Type of Life Cycle
_____

Insect Name
_____
Location Found
_____
Type of Life Cycle
_____

Insect Name
_____
Location Found
_____
Type of Life Cycle
_____

Insect Name
_____
Location Found
_____
Type of Life Cycle
_____

Insect Name
_____
Location Found
_____
Type of Life Cycle
_____

✂ - - - - - - - - - - - - - - - - - - - - - - - - - - - - - - - - - - - - - - - - - - - - - - - - - -

## Parent Activity

Help your child find and identify insects for the project above.

| **Motivation Station: Mike's Cool Science Fact** |
| :-- |
| Antarctica, the coldest place on Earth, is actually considered a desert. Each year, Antarctica receives slightly more rain than the Sahara Desert. |

**After this lesson I will be able to:**

• **Observe** and **describe** the physical characteristics of environments and how they support populations and communities within an ecosystem.

## Descriptive and Comparative Investigations

### Activity 1: Populations

Each seed in the jar represents an individual ant in a population of ants living in a forest community. The forest community is home to many other populations of animals and plants, which make up the ant's environment. The living and nonliving components within the forest are all a part of the ant's ecosystem.

The group's assignment is to determine the population of ants in the jar. Your group will have three minutes to make an estimation. Four tools are available to assist your group in making an estimation: a beaker, a portion cup, a measuring spoon, and a ruler. When time is up, write your estimate in the space below.

We estimate the population of ants is _____.

Describe the method your group used to calculate your answer.

_____

_____

Count the actual number of ants. Record the number. _____.

How close was your estimate?

_____

Can scientists count every ant in a forest to determine the population?

_____

_____

How could counting a sample be used to determine the population?

_____

_____

**Unit 33** Introduction

**Activity 2:** Physical Characteristics of Environment

Use reference materials to complete the chart by describing the six different environments listed below. In the first column, include a graphic representation of each environment.

| Environment | Physical Characteristics | Native Plants and Animals | Climate |
|---|---|---|---|
| Grassland | | | |
| Desert | | | |
| Pond | | | |
| Ocean | | | |
| Forest | | | |
| Arctic | | | |

How do grassland, forest, and ocean environments support the populations and communities living within the ecosystem? Describe below.

**Grassland:** _____

_____

**Forest:** _____

_____

**Ocean:** _____

_____

 motivation**science**™ LEVEL 5 ©2011–2014 mentoring**minds**.com

**1** Plants are able to grow in the desert because of special adaptations that allow them to collect and store water. This adaptation is most beneficial in —

Ⓐ wet climates

Ⓑ dry climates

Ⓒ windy climates

Ⓓ humid climates

**2** Tundra plants are often dark in color because dark colors absorb more heat from the Sun. This adaptation helps them survive in the tundra's —

Ⓕ blazing atmosphere

Ⓖ dramatic climatic changes

Ⓗ frigid temperatures

Ⓙ changing land surface

**3** Marsh ecosystems provide habitats for a variety of plants and animals. All of the following animals are supported by the marsh **EXCEPT** —

Ⓐ frogs

Ⓑ whales

Ⓒ salamanders

Ⓓ fish

**4** Changes in other parts of the world can affect an environment. For example, a volcano erupting in Mexico can decrease the temperature of the entire world for several years. This is why it is important to take care of our environment through —   **5.1(B)**

Ⓕ exploration

Ⓖ transpiration

Ⓗ destruction

Ⓙ conservation

**5** Tundra animals have adaptations such as thick coats that allow them to survive in the vast tundra. Why does the musk ox have a thick coat of fur?

Ⓐ To insulate from the cold tundra wind and water

Ⓑ To blend in with the snow and water

Ⓒ For protection against predators

Ⓓ To attract a mate during the winter season

**6** Which question is vital for understanding environments and their ability to support populations and communities within an ecosystem?   **5.2(B)**

Ⓕ What types of fossil fuels are found in the environment?

Ⓖ What is the climate and geography like in the environment?

Ⓗ What is the ratio of human and animal populations?

Ⓙ How far is the environment from the equator?

**Unit 33** Check for Understanding

**1** The spadefoot toad has an adaptation for burrowing in the desert. Why does the spadefoot toad live underground for nine months out of the year in the desert ecosystem?

Ⓐ To hunt prey in the darkness

Ⓑ To hunt for water

Ⓒ To hide from predators

Ⓓ To avoid the hot Sun

**2** Coral reefs and the fish that live in them are very delicate. Reefs will not form or survive in water that is below 17°C or above 30°C.

What possible effect could a steep rise in water temperature have on animals living in a coral reef?

Ⓕ Coral will not survive, and other marine life will compete for the use of the existing coral.

Ⓖ Coral will survive, and animals will have a place to live.

Ⓗ Coral will grow out of control, and food sources will run low.

Ⓙ Coral will grow very rapidly, and the animals that live in it will leave due to overpopulation.

**3** A forest is teaming with life. Birds, insects, fungi, plants, and other animals all depend on their forest home. Which inhabitant of the forest is most dependent on the decaying plant and animal life of the forest?

Ⓐ Reptiles          Ⓒ Mammals

Ⓑ Insects          Ⓓ Fish

**4** What would a group of five cats living in the same environment be called?

Ⓕ An ecosystem of cats

Ⓖ A community of cats

Ⓗ A bunch of cats

Ⓙ A population of cats

**5** Which type of vegetation will most likely be supported in an environment that has very low precipitation in summer and winter and a very cold climate?

Ⓐ Barrel cactus     Ⓒ Kapok tree

Ⓑ Arctic moss      Ⓓ Buffalo grass

**6** Which of the following animals will most likely be supported in an environment that has a high temperature and rainfall year round?

Ⓕ Poison dart frog

Ⓖ Polar bear

Ⓗ Kangaroo rat

Ⓙ None of the above

motivation**science**™ LEVEL 5

## Scientific Investigation and Reasoning Skills: Questions 7–14

**7** Students read information about alligator gars. After reading the information, the teacher asks students to conclude why the alligator gar is now found in different habitats.

### The Alligator Gar

The alligator gar is a long fish with a snout and large teeth on either side of the upper jaw. It lives in fresh, slow-running water found throughout Texas and the southeastern United States. Adult gars eat mostly fish, but also some water birds. Their only natural predators are the American alligator and humans. Alligator gar used to prefer to live in very large rivers with large areas for flooding. The gar is most commonly found in much smaller rivers now with smaller floodplains.

Which of the conclusions is the most logical reason gars are found more often in smaller rivers? **5.3(A)**

Ⓐ The smaller rivers were once larger rivers.

Ⓑ The smaller rivers have larger populations of organisms for the gar to eat.

Ⓒ The building of dams and levees for flood control of large rivers forced the gar to find new habitats.

Ⓓ As the gars were swimming, they lost their way and could not find the large rivers.

**8** All of the following are reasons why it is important to care for the environment **EXCEPT** — **5.1(B)**

Ⓕ to support life

Ⓖ to neglect wildlife

Ⓗ to prevent extinction

Ⓙ to protect animals

**9** Students take a field trip to the woods to study the different communities on a rotting log. They expect to find many different insects. A safety rule to remember when they investigate the log is — **5.1(A)**

Ⓐ always wear sandals in the woods

Ⓑ scream when an insect is seen

Ⓒ do not pick up insects with bare fingers

Ⓓ talk quietly so the animals will not be frightened

**10** Students take a walk one day to a pond near the school to look for turtles. They see no turtles. The students decide there are no turtles at the pond. What is wrong with their conclusion? **5.2(E)**

Ⓕ Only the boys looked for turtles.

Ⓖ They only looked for turtles one day.

Ⓗ They did not go to the right place.

Ⓙ The turtles moved to a new pond.

**11** A student notices this label on a tuna can.

Why did the tuna company add the dolphin friendly logo to its label? **5.3(B)**

Ⓐ To show the other ingredients included in the tuna can

Ⓑ To show the friendly relationship between tuna populations and dolphin populations

Ⓒ To convince dolphin populations that Tuna Chunks tuna fish is the nicest

Ⓓ To convince consumers that dolphin populations were not harmed when fisherman caught the tuna

**12** Which of the following would be most useful in determining the number of ants in a forest population? **5.2(C)**

Ⓕ Collecting each ant, counting it, then releasing it

Ⓖ Counting a sample of ants and then using the number to estimate the population

Ⓗ Collecting data by taking pictures of each ant with a night-vision camera

Ⓙ Counting the number of predators which rely on the ant for food and using that number to make an estimation

**13** Students set up two environments to see which one best supports the growth of hibiscus flowers. One environment is created as a desert, using sandy soil. The plant is exposed to high temperatures. The other environment is created as a tropical forest, using loamy soil and exposing the plant to high temperatures. What is the variable used in the investigation? **5.2(A)**

Ⓐ The temperature

Ⓑ The environment

Ⓒ The type of flower

Ⓓ The amount of sunlight

**14** In groups, students create dioramas to depict different ecosystems and their physical characteristics. One of the dioramas is pictured.

Why are dioramas useful for studying environments? **5.3(C)**

Ⓕ The model gives students an idea of how different environments appear.

Ⓖ The diorama is a useful chart for collecting data on environments.

Ⓗ A diorama is an accurate tool for measuring environmental changes.

Ⓙ Students can use a diorama to set up an investigation that tests one variable.

 motivation**science**™ LEVEL 5

## Home for Sale

Create a classified advertisement to sell an animal habitat in a specific environment. Include a picture and description of the habitat, the physical characteristics of the habitat's location, and any other information which would help the habitat sell.

# CLASSIFIEDS
## SELL IT OR FIND IT HERE FIRST

| Habitat Illustration | Habitat Description | Reason to Buy |
|---|---|---|
|  |  |  |

## Formative Assessment

Describe a wetland ecosystem, and explain how the ecosystem supports the populations and communities that live there.

| What is your explanation? | What is your evidence? |
|---|---|
|  |  |

**Science Journal**

If you were an animal, and could live in any environment, which environment would you choose and why?

_____

_____

_____

_____

_____

_____

_____

_____

_____

_____

_____

_____

_____

_____

_____

_____

_____

_____

_____

_____

_____

_____

motivation**science**™LEVEL 5

©2011–2014 mentoring**minds**.com

**Science Vocabulary Builder**

In the boxes below, list four examples of physical characteristics of the Taiga, and name four organisms that live there.

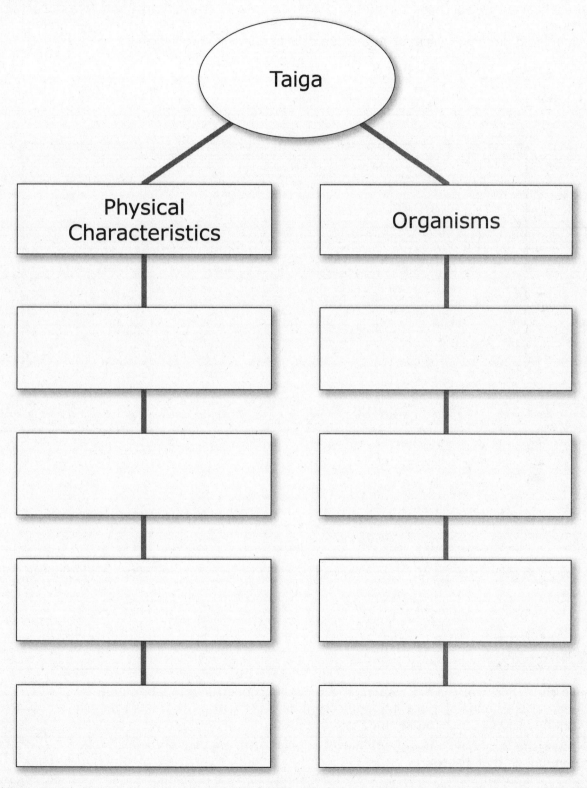

Taiga

Physical Characteristics

Organisms

**Unit 33** Homework

## Environment Diorama

A diorama is a type of three-dimensional model, usually made using a cardboard box, such as a shoebox. Build a diorama representing a specific environment. In your diorama, include objects to represent the physical characteristics of the environment. Your diorama should also contain representations of the native plants and animals which would be found in the environment. Bring your completed diorama to school on the due date and share with the class.

Plan your diorama in the space below.

**Environment:** _____

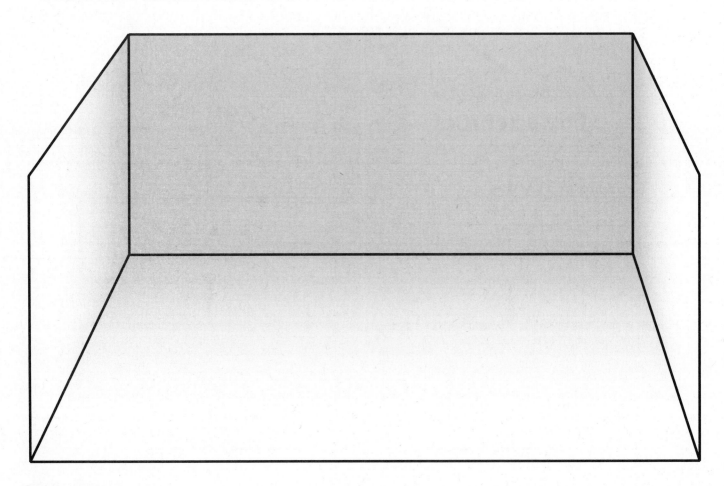

## Parent Activities

1. Help your child create a diorama of an ecosystem. Construction paper, pipe cleaners, dry beans or macaroni, and cotton balls are just a few items that could be used to create a diorama.

2. Discuss the local environment and how it supports the populations and communities that live there.

3. On your next visit to the zoo, discuss the habitats and environments of different animals.

   motivation**science**™LEVEL 5  ©2011–2014 mentoring**minds**.com

### Motivation Station: Molly's Cool Science Fact

One reason frogs need to live near water is because they absorb water through their skin instead of drinking it. Frogs also take in extra oxygen through their skin, a process that works better when the frog's skin is wet.

### After this lesson I will be able to:

- **Investigate** and **compare** how animals and plants undergo a series of orderly changes in their diverse life cycles such as tomato plants, frogs, and lady bugs.

## Descriptive and Experimental Investigations

**Activity 1:** Frog Life Cycle

Use research materials to investigate the life cycle of a frog. In the space below, draw a diagram of the metamorphosis of a frog, and label each stage.

How is metamorphosis of frogs similar and different to metamorphosis of insects?

_____

_____

_____

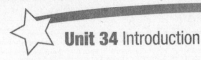
**Activity 2:** Comparing Plant Life Cycles

**Question:** How is the life cycle of a tomato plant different from the life cycle of a bean plant?

**Hypothesis:** _____

**Procedure:** Fill two Styrofoam cups $\frac{3}{4}$ full of potting soil. In one cup, plant 2 tomato seeds. In the other cup, plant 2 bean seeds. Label the cups. Water with 30 mL of water, and place cups in a sunny location. Record the growth of the plants in the data table for eight weeks. Use the collected data to create a graph of the results. Use your results to form a conclusion.

| Week | Tomato Plant | Bean Plant |
|------|--------------|------------|
| 1 | | |
| 2 | | |
| 3 | | |
| 4 | | |
| 5 | | |
| 6 | | |
| 7 | | |
| 8 | | |

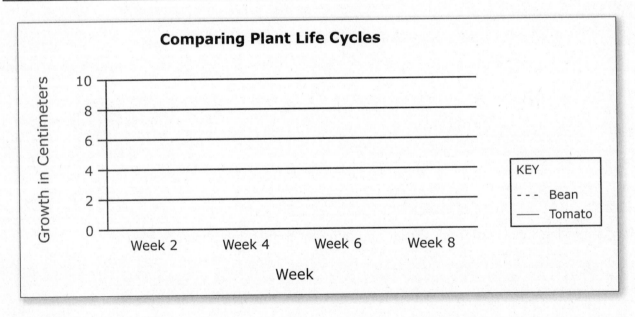

**Conclusion:** _____

**1** What is the same about plant and animal life cycles?

Ⓐ The offspring grow into adults.

Ⓑ Both go through the same stages.

Ⓒ Each requires water and soil.

Ⓓ Both are forms of metamorphosis.

**2** Students investigate the changes in the life cycle of a frog. What is the difference between tadpoles and adult frogs?

Ⓕ Tadpoles live in water, breathe with gills, have legs, and have no tail. Adults live on land, breathe with lungs, have legs, and have a tail.

Ⓖ Frogs breathe with gills while living in water and breathe with lungs while living on land.

Ⓗ Tadpoles live in water, breathe with gills, have no legs, and have a long tail. Adult frogs live on land and in water, breathe with lungs, have legs, and have no tail.

Ⓙ Tadpoles breathe with lungs while living in water and breathe with gills while living on land.

**3** Which of the following are the central components of the life cycles of both plants and animals?

Ⓐ Birth and death

Ⓑ Growth and reproduction

Ⓒ Height and length

Ⓓ Seedling and adult

**4** Investigating the series of orderly changes in the life cycle of a plant helps scientists understand —

Ⓕ how difficult it is being a plant

Ⓖ why change is important

Ⓗ how a plant grows

Ⓙ how plants go through metamorphosis

**5** Which experiment will help students understand the changes that a bean plant goes through during its life cycle? **5.2(A)**

Ⓐ Germinate a seed in a bag

Ⓑ Plant an adult bean plant in soil, and add water

Ⓒ Prepare the soil, and add water

Ⓓ Cut and replant the bean plant leaves

**6** What do these two life cycles have in common? **5.2(D)**

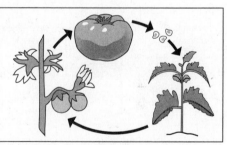

**Tomato Plant Life Cycle**

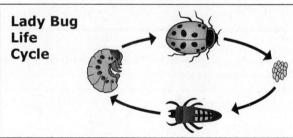

**Lady Bug Life Cycle**

Ⓕ Both make their own food.

Ⓖ Both take in carbon dioxide through respiration.

Ⓗ Both grow, change, and reproduce.

Ⓙ Both retain water through transpiration.

**Unit 34** Check for Understanding

**1** Which of the following is the correct sequence of changes in the life cycle of a plant?

Ⓐ Germination, seed, growth, reproduction, maturity

Ⓑ Seed, germination, growth, maturity, reproduction

Ⓒ Growth, germination, seed, maturity, reproduction

Ⓓ Seed, growth, germination, reproduction, maturity

**2** There are comparable stages in the life cycles of plants and animals.

Which plant picture below corresponds to the stage of animal development above?

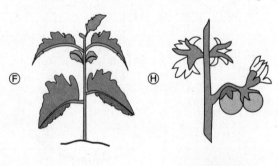

Ⓕ    Ⓗ

Ⓖ    Ⓙ

**3** In the life cycle of the frog, what stage comes after tadpole?

Ⓐ Egg          Ⓒ Larva

Ⓑ Adult        Ⓓ Froglet

**4** Most animals including fish, mammals, birds, and reptiles have very simple life cycles. The young are similar to the parent, only —

Ⓕ wiser        Ⓗ larger

Ⓖ older        Ⓙ smaller

**5** Peaches are one of the largest fruit crops grown in Texas. They have a pit or large seed in the center that, when planted, begins life for a new tree.

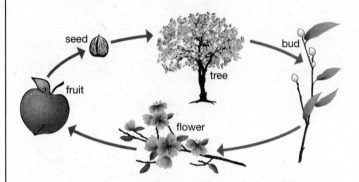

What must occur for a peach flower to grow into a peach with a seed in the center?

Ⓐ The flower must fall off the tree to make room for the seed.

Ⓑ The flower must get lots of water to grow into a fruit.

Ⓒ The flower must be pollinated by animals, insects, wind, or water.

Ⓓ The flower must use the Sun's energy to turn into a seed.

**6** What keeps the life cycle of humans going?

Ⓕ Recreation       Ⓗ Reproduction

Ⓖ Maturation       Ⓙ Pollination

  motivation**science**™ LEVEL 5

## Scientific Investigation and Reasoning Skills: Questions 7–14

**Use the picture below and your knowledge of science to answer questions 7 and 8.**

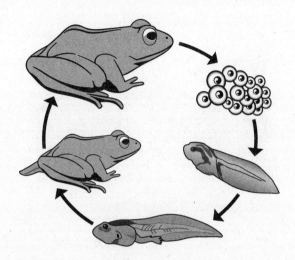

**7** Which of the following would be an appropriate investigation on the life cycle of a frog?  **5.2(A)**

Ⓐ Create a habitat, and watch the frogs change from larva stage to pupa stage

Ⓑ Acquire spawn, and observe the transformation into air-breathing amphibians

Ⓒ Draw a picture of an adult frog in its natural environment

Ⓓ Catch flies to lure a frog into a shoebox

**8** Which tool is best for observing the actual life cycle of a frog?  **5.4(A)**

Ⓕ Terrarium

Ⓖ Planetarium

Ⓗ Aquarium

Ⓙ Diorama

**9** This graph shows how tall a tomato plant has grown each week.

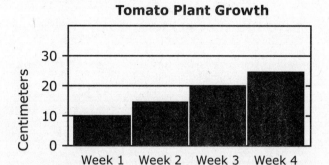

**Tomato Plant Growth**

If the plant continues to grow at the same rate, how tall will it be by week 5? Record and bubble in your answer to the nearest centimeter.  **5.2(G)**

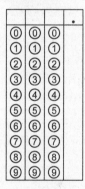

**10** Students find frog eggs in the school pond. One mass is put in an aquarium in the room. Students check daily and discover that the temperature of the water in the pond is warmer than in the aquarium. The tadpoles in the pond become frogs faster than the tadpoles in the aquarium. What conclusion can students make from this observation?  **5.2(F)**

Ⓕ The eggs in the pond are better than the ones in the aquarium.

Ⓖ The eggs in the pond are a different species.

Ⓗ Warmer temperature make the eggs grow faster.

Ⓙ Tadpoles in the pond change faster so they do not get eaten by the fish.

**11** Veggie Cage advertises a tomato plant support system.

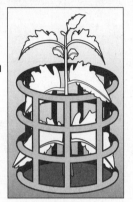

# The Fabulous Veggie Cage

**TURN THOSE SEEDS INTO HEALTHY PLANTS!**

Use the Veggie Cage Support System after the vegetables sprout.

The vegetables you grow using the Veggie Cage Support System will impress your friends and neighbors.

**Buy Veggie Cages for all your gardening needs.**

What information do consumers know about the Veggie Cage from reading the advertisement?  **5.3(B)**

Ⓐ Tomato seeds will instantly turn into tomato plants.

Ⓑ The support system is used after the seeds germinate.

Ⓒ Tomato plants will not grow properly without the Veggie Cage.

Ⓓ Everyone thinks the Veggie Cage is a wonderful product.

**12** Students grow frogs from tadpoles to adults. Each week, they take turns cleaning the aquarium. After cleaning the aquarium, students should remember to —  **5.1(A)**

Ⓕ scrub the aquarium rocks with soap and rinse with water

Ⓖ dry their hands thoroughly with paper towels

Ⓗ bathe the frogs before returning them to the aquarium

Ⓙ wash their hands with soap and water

**13** Students compare the life cycle of a chicken with the life cycle of a butterfly. After completing their observations, the students write conclusions about the difference between the chicken and butterfly life cycles.

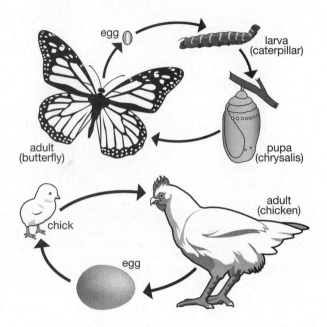

Which best explains how the two life cycles are different?  **5.3(A)**

Ⓐ The chicken has a long life span, but the butterfly has a short life span.

Ⓑ A newborn chick is similar in structure to an adult, but the grown butterfly looks very different from a newly hatched caterpillar.

Ⓒ A butterfly egg has a longer incubation period than a chicken egg.

Ⓓ None of the above

**14** Students want to investigate lady bug larva more closely. Which is the best tool to observe the larva? **5.4(A)**

Ⓕ A ruler

Ⓗ A hand lens

Ⓖ A telescope

Ⓙ A balance scale

## Lady Bug Party

Lady bugs, like butterflies and darkling beetles, go through complete metamorphosis. Imagine you are the proud, older sibling of a lady bug. Design a party invitation to celebrate one of the lady bug's stages (egg, larva, pupa, or adult) in the space below.

Write a speech to read at the party explaining how your sibling has changed throughout his/her life.

**Invitation**                              **Speech**

_____

_____

_____

_____

_____

_____

_____

_____

_____

_____

_____

_____

_____

## Formative Assessment

Think of a question that could be used to investigate life cycles of plants or animals. Then, form a hypothesis, and generate a list of equipment that would be needed to test the hypothesis.

| Question | |
| --- | --- |
| **Hypothesis** | |
| **Equipment** | |

**Science Journal**

How does the life cycle of a plant compare to the life cycle of an animal?

_____

_____

_____

_____

_____

_____

_____

_____

_____

_____

_____

_____

_____

_____

_____

_____

_____

_____

_____

_____

_____

_____

_____

_____

_____

_____

Supporting Standard 3.10(C)

## Science Vocabulary Builder

Using the words in the box at the bottom of the page, decide the correct sequence for the words, and place in the graphic organizer.

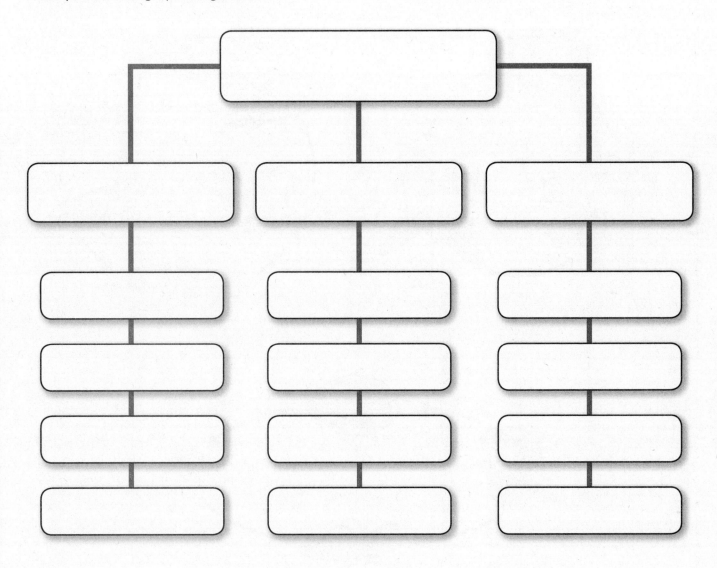

eggs     seed     eggs     tadpoles     froglet     larva

seedlings     adult     lady bug     frog     flowers

fruit     Life Cycles     adult     pupa     tomato

motivation**science**™ LEVEL 5

## Unit 34 Homework

Supporting Standard 3.10(C)

### Labeling Life Cycles

Label the stages of the life cycles shown below.

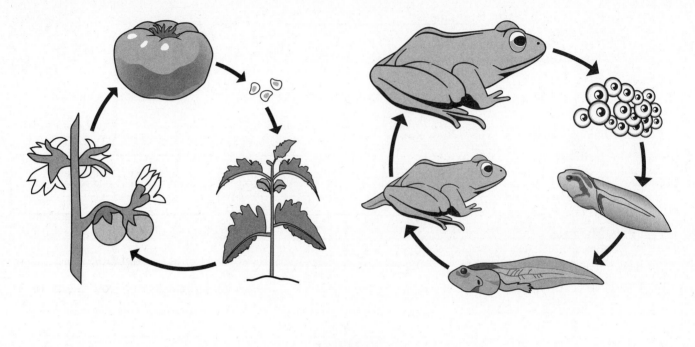

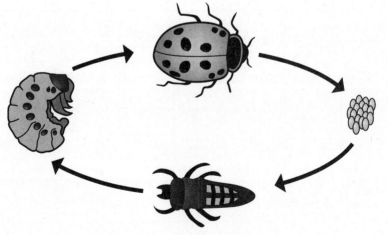

✂ ------------------------------------------------------------

### Parent Activities

1. Grow a family pizza garden by growing tomatoes, peppers, onions, garlic, and basil, or a taco garden with peppers, tomatoes, lettuce, and cilantro. When the vegetables are ready to harvest, cook together as a family to share your garden's bounty. Discuss the life cycles of the plants in the garden.

2. You can order a butterfly or lady bug kit and enjoy watching the life cycle of these amazing insects. Kits can be purchased using the link below.

 • Insect Lore–*http://www.insectlore.com/*

**1** During outdoor observations of a pond ecosystem, students are given safety precautions to follow. Which safety rule should students follow while visiting a pond ecosystem?  **5.1(A)**

Ⓐ Have a fire extinguisher close during observations

Ⓑ Do not put anything but feet and hands in the pond

Ⓒ Wear sandals or open-toed shoes

Ⓓ Do not get in the water

**2** To help sustain our environment for future generations, it is important to preserve and protect our natural resources. Which is **NOT** an example of a way humans can positively impact ecosystems?  **5.1(B)**

Ⓕ Reducing or eliminating the use of pesticides and household chemicals

Ⓖ Recycling as much waste as possible and reducing the amount of garbage produced

Ⓗ Using reusable bags at the grocery store rather than using paper or disposable plastic bags

Ⓙ Changing the motor oil in a car and disposing of the used oil on the ground behind the garage

**Use the information below and your knowledge of science to answer questions 3 and 4.**

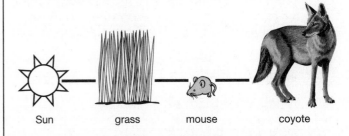

Sun          grass        mouse        coyote

**3** Students create models of food chains to show how energy is transferred. Which of the questions below could **NOT** be answered using the food chain model shown?  **5.2(B)**

Ⓐ What would happen if there was an overpopulation of mice?

Ⓑ How do producers get their food?

Ⓒ How many mice can a coyote eat in a day?

Ⓓ What would happen if the producers were removed from the food chain?

**4** How can students improve the food chain model?  **5.3(C)**

Ⓕ Include more producers, such as bushes and trees

Ⓖ Replace the grass in the food chain with a wheat plant

Ⓗ Remove the lines, and replace with arrows to show the direction energy is being transferred

Ⓙ Add another consumer that eats mice, and remove the Sun from the model

**5** Zookeepers make sure the animals at the zoo are safe and healthy. For instance, an elephant must be trained to walk onto a scale to be weighed or to lift its foot in the air to be examined. An elephant lifting its foot in the air to be checked is an example of — **5.3(D)**

Ⓐ an instinct

Ⓑ an inherited trait

Ⓒ a learned behavior

Ⓓ an adaptation

**6** Students study the role of plants in the carbon dioxide-oxygen cycle. They place a sprig of elodea in a test tube and a feather in another tube. An equal amount of water is added to each test tube, and they are corked with rubber stoppers. They place both test tubes in the Sun. At the end of four hours, the students notice the tube containing elodea has formed bubbles of oxygen, but the tube containing the feather has not.

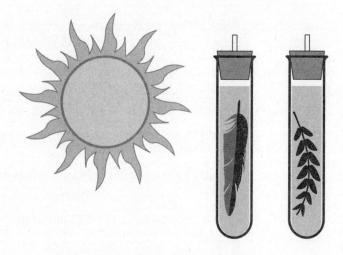

What is the variable tested in the experiment? **5.2(A)**

Ⓕ The amount of water

Ⓖ The formation of bubbles

Ⓗ The type of test tube

Ⓙ The material placed in test tube

**7** Students place a hula hoop outside on the ground and observe the populations and communities found inside the circle of the hoop. They leave the hoop outside and come back every day for a week to investigate the environment. Each day, they record the results in a science notebook. Why is it important to observe the same area for a week? **5.2(E)**

Ⓐ Checking the environment over several days allows students to collect more accurate information about the organisms living there.

Ⓑ The hula hoop is moved each day, so students have to keep re-doing the investigation.

Ⓒ By checking the environment all week, students collect enough information to fill the data tables given to them by the teacher.

Ⓓ Observations of environments are always conducted over a one-week time period by scientists.

**8** Which of the following is best for observing a radish plant as it undergoes changes in its life cycle? **5.4(A)**

Ⓕ Planetarium

Ⓖ Diorama

Ⓗ Aquarium

Ⓙ Terrarium

**9** How long is the darkling beetle?  **5.2(C)**

Ⓐ  1 m          Ⓒ  5 cm

Ⓑ  3 cm         Ⓓ  10 mm

**10** A class orders a Lady Bug Luxury Habitat to observe the life cycle of a lady bug.

> **Lady Bug Luxury Habitat includes:**
> • Lady bug habitat
> • Live lady bug larvae mail-in certificate
> • Lady bug care information
> • Eyedropper to water your lady bugs

When the lady bug habitat arrives, it will come complete with —  **5.3(B)**

Ⓕ  water for the lady bugs

Ⓖ  live lady bug larvae

Ⓗ  an eyedropper

Ⓙ  all of the above

**11** Students use research to compare the structures of webbed feet on a platypus and a duck. Which of the research collected below is **NOT** empirical evidence?  **5.3(A)**

Ⓐ  The back feet of a platypus are partially webbed.

Ⓑ  Duck feet have no nerves or vessels.

Ⓒ  A duck swims better than a platypus.

Ⓓ  A platypus has claws on its webbed feet.

**12** A science class conducts an investigation to see if people exhale carbon dioxide or oxygen. They use a liquid indicator called Bromothymol blue, which turns yellow when it detects carbon dioxide or blue when oxygen is present. They add 5 drops of Bromothymol blue to a cup of water. The teacher blows gently into the water using a straw, and the water turns yellow. What is a safety precaution the class should use during this investigation?  **5.4(B)**

Ⓕ  Wear gloves and goggles

Ⓖ  Conduct the investigation outdoors

Ⓗ  Put on a protective face mask

Ⓙ  Stir the mixture with the straw

**13** Which trait did the student inherit from the father?  **5.2(G)**

| Family Member | Earlobes | Toes | Tongue Roll | Eyelashes |
|---|---|---|---|---|
| Student | Free | Larger second toe | Can roll tongue | Short eyelashes |
| Mother | Free | Larger big toe | Can roll tongue | Short eyelashes |
| Father | Attached | Larger second toe | Cannot roll tongue | Long eyelashes |

Ⓐ  Free earlobes

Ⓑ  Larger second toe

Ⓒ  Can roll tongue

Ⓓ  Not here

**14** Students find the following things outside when observing the schoolyard ecosystem: grass, soil, flowers, ants, grasshoppers, rocks, sticks, and centipedes. Based on the information collected, students know —

Ⓕ the ecosystem observed is only made of living things

Ⓖ the ecosystem observed contains living things and nonliving elements

Ⓗ the ecosystem observed has more grasshoppers than ants

Ⓙ the ecosystem observed does not have enough plants for the grasshoppers to survive

**15** Below is a hand and a foot model of an animal.

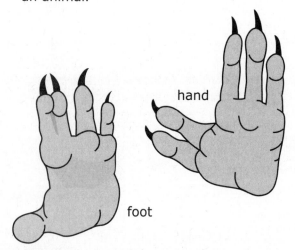

hand

foot

Where is an animal that has feet and hands like the picture above most likely to live? **5.2(D)**

Ⓐ In water

Ⓑ In a cave

Ⓒ In the ocean

Ⓓ In a tree

**16** Which student correctly classified producers, consumers, and decomposers?

| Student | Producers | Consumers | Decomposers |
|---|---|---|---|
| 1 | • trees<br>• tomato plant<br>• grass | • tiger<br>• human<br>• dog | • bacteria<br>• worms<br>• fungus |
| 2 | • grass<br>• fungus<br>• tomato plant | • human<br>• dog<br>• tiger | • trees<br>• worms<br>• bacteria |
| 3 | • tiger<br>• human<br>• dog | • trees<br>• tomato plant<br>• grass | • bacteria<br>• worms<br>• fungus |
| 4 | • bacteria<br>• fungus<br>• grass | • worms<br>• human<br>• dog | • tiger<br>• trees<br>• tomato plant |

Ⓕ Student 1   Ⓗ Student 3

Ⓖ Student 2   Ⓙ Student 4

**17** Which is an example of how living organisms interact with nonliving parts of their ecosystem?

Ⓐ A bear living in a cave

Ⓑ A lion eating a zebra

Ⓒ Humans having pets

Ⓓ Cows eating grass

**18** All the following are changes to ecosystems. Which is **NOT** an example of a change caused by humans?

Ⓕ Building roads and highways

Ⓖ Cutting down trees in the rain forest

Ⓗ Building new houses

Ⓙ Overpopulation of grazers

**374**     motivation**science**™ LEVEL 5

**19** What does the diagram show?

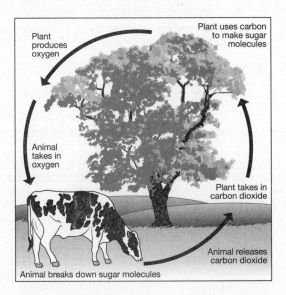

Ⓐ The carbon dioxide-oxygen cycle

Ⓑ A life cycle

Ⓒ A food web

Ⓓ All of the above

**20** Animals that live in the tundra have special adaptations, such as short ears and thick coats, that help them survive the extreme temperatures and conditions. This body structure helps —

Ⓕ minimize exposure to frigid air

Ⓖ maximize exposure to tropical air

Ⓗ minimize exposure to humidity

Ⓙ maximize exposure to diseases

**21** Which of the following is **NOT** an example of an acquired trait?

Ⓐ Playing basketball

Ⓑ Hair between knuckles

Ⓒ Riding a bicycle

Ⓓ Hairstyle

**22** A mite known as the Varroa mite is a small Asian mite that kills European honeybees. The mite has caused the loss of entire wild bee colonies. Commercial beekeepers have also seen losses of up to 30% of their colonies due to the Varroa mite. What effect might the declining bee populations have on crops and other plants?

Ⓕ Pollination of plants will not occur, and food will become scarce for carnivores.

Ⓖ Bees will no longer be a food source for other consumers.

Ⓗ Pollination of plants will not occur, and food will become scarce for herbivores.

Ⓙ Bees will no longer produce honey as a food source for other consumers.

**23** Which statement correctly explains why the metamorphosis of an ant is called a complete metamorphosis?

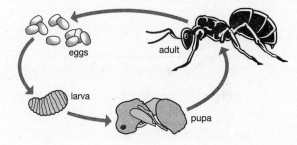

Ⓐ It has three stages of growth in which the body is completely reorganized to form the adult.

Ⓑ It has four stages of growth in which the body of the young ant is very similar to the adult body.

Ⓒ It has three stages of growth in which the body of the young ant is very similar to the adult body.

Ⓓ It has four stages of growth in which the body is completely reorganized to form the adult.

**24** Animals, insects, and plants all have unique life cycles. Which part is important for continuing the life cycle?

Ⓕ Population    Ⓗ Precipitation

Ⓖ Reproduction    Ⓙ Adaptation

**25** What is **NOT** a likely effect of a forest ecosystem that has been changed by the building of homes?

Ⓐ Animals losing their homes

Ⓑ Trees being cut down

Ⓒ Oceans becoming contaminated

Ⓓ Animals moving to different locations

**26** About 12% of all insects go through incomplete metamorphosis. How many stages are there in incomplete metamorphosis?

Ⓕ 2    Ⓗ 4

Ⓖ 3    Ⓙ 5

**27** Which is an example of a decomposer?

Ⓐ Worm    Ⓒ Tiger

Ⓑ Tree    Ⓓ Dog

**28** The coldest ecosystem that has permanently frozen subsoil called permafrost is the —

Ⓕ Taiga

Ⓖ equator

Ⓗ temperate forest

Ⓙ tundra

**29** The animals and plants in the desert depend on one another. Which statement does **NOT** describe how the cacti interact with the animals in the desert?

Ⓐ Cacti provide shelter for certain animals living in the desert.

Ⓑ Cacti provide food, including cactus fruit, for the animals living in the desert.

Ⓒ Cacti provide water in their fleshy stems for the animals living in the desert.

Ⓓ Cacti provide shade for other cacti and plants living in the desert.

**30** The function of this structure is to —

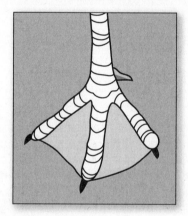

Ⓕ capture prey

Ⓖ perch on limbs

Ⓗ swim in water

Ⓙ climb on trees

**31** Learned behaviors are acquired through memory or experience, but instincts are behaviors that come naturally to an organism because they are —

Ⓐ important    Ⓒ memorized

Ⓑ taught    Ⓓ inherited

# Chart Your Success

**Color Mike or Molly *green* if your answer was correct or *red* if your answer was incorrect.**

## Ecosystem Interactions

| Question 1 | Question 14 | Question 17 | Question 29 |

| Total Correct | Total Possible |
| --- | --- |
| | 4 |

## Food Chain/Food Web

| Question 3 | Question 4 | Question 16 | Question 27 |

| Total Correct | Total Possible |
| --- | --- |
| | 4 |

## Changes to Ecosystems

| Question 2 | Question 18 | Question 25 |

| Total Correct | Total Possible |
| --- | --- |
| | 3 |

## Carbon Dioxide-Oxygen Cycle

| Question 6 | Question 12 | Question 19 |

| Total Correct | Total Possible |
| --- | --- |
| | 3 |

## Structures and Functions

| Question 11 | Question 15 | Question 20 | Question 30 |

| Total Correct | Total Possible |
| --- | --- |
| | 4 |

# Chart Your Success

### Inherited Traits/Learned Behaviors

| Total Correct | Total Possible |
|---|---|
|  | 4 |

### Complete/Incomplete Metamorphosis

| Total Correct | Total Possible |
|---|---|
|  | 3 |

### Characteristics of Environments

| Total Correct | Total Possible |
|---|---|
|  | 3 |

### Life Cycles

| Total Correct | Total Possible |
|---|---|
|  | 3 |

     motivation**science**™ LEVEL 5

# Science Glossary

## A

**absorb** – to soak up or take in

**accumulation** – a part of the water cycle in which water collects in large bodies of water

**accuracy** – being error free, exact, or precise

**accurate** – error free, exact, or precise

**acquired trait** – a trait that occurs in response to the environment

**adaptation** – a structure or behavior that helps an organism survive in its environment

**adult** – a fully grown plant or animal

**aftershock** – a smaller earthquake which comes after a larger earthquake, occurring in the same area as the original quake

**air** – a natural resource that people breathe, but cannot see, taste, or smell

**air mass** – a large body of air having similar temperature and moisture content

**air pressure** – a force exerted by the weight of air pressing down on everything

**air resistance** – a force that opposes the motion of an object through the air

**alternative energy** – a form of energy used to replace fossil fuels

**amphibian** – a cold–blooded vertebrate that starts life in water and lives on land as an adult

**analyze** – to study the parts of something carefully

**animal** – an organism made of many cells that moves on its own and eats other organisms

**apparent movement** – seeing movement of an object when no movement is actually taking place

**aquarium** – a tank, usually filled with water, that is used to hold live organisms

**aquatic** – to live in or be connected with water

**Arctic** – the area near the North Pole that is covered with ice and snow most of the year

**asteroid** – a large rocky object that orbits the Sun

**astronomer** – a scientist who studies the celestial bodies in the universe

**astronomy** – the study of celestial bodies in the universe

**atmosphere** – the layer of air that surrounds Earth

**attract** – to pull toward

**attribute** – a property or characteristic of an object such as color, size, or shape

**autumn** – the season following summer, also known as fall

**axis** – an imaginary line around which a planet rotates

## B

**bacteria** – one-celled organisms with no nucleus

**balance scale** – a tool used to compare the mass of two objects

**basic needs** – the things an organism needs to live such as air, water, food, and shelter

**beaker** – a container with a pouring spout and measurement marks, used to measure volume

**behavioral adaptation** – something an organism does to survive, such as migration or hibernation

**biofuel** – a type of fuel made from living or recently living organisms

**biologist** – a scientist who studies plants and animals

**biology** – the study of plants and animals

**biomass** – organic matter that contains stored energy

**biome** – a large region that has a specific climate and specific types of plants and animals

**blizzard** – a heavy snowstorm with strong winds

**boiling point** – the temperature at which a liquid changes to a gas

**botanist** – a scientist who studies plants

**botany** – the study of plants

**buoyancy** – the ability of an object to float or rise in a liquid or gas

**by-product** – a product created as a result of making something else

# C

**calculator** – a tool used to perform mathematical operations

**camera** – a tool used to take photographs

**camouflage** – a color, shape, or pattern that helps an animal blend into its surroundings

**canyon** – a valley between steep cliff sides formed by running water, such as a river or stream

**capacity** – the amount that can be held by a container

**carbon** – a nonmetallic element found in all organisms

**carbon dioxide** – a colorless, odorless gas that animals breathe out and plants use to produce food

**carbon dioxide-oxygen cycle** – the movement of carbon dioxide and oxygen among plants, animals, and nonliving parts of the environment

**carnivore** – an animal that eats other animals for food

**Celsius** – a unit of measure for temperature

**centimeter** – a metric unit used to measure short lengths

**change** – to make or become different

**chaparral** – a thicket of dense shrubs, bushes, and small trees

**characteristic** – a trait or feature

**chart** – a table or diagram that shows recorded data

**chemist** – a scientist who studies the properties of matter

**chemistry** – the study of matter and its properties

**chlorophyll** – the green substance in plants that captures sunlight and makes food

**chrysalis** – the pupa stage of a butterfly, occurring between the larva and adult stages

**circuit** – the path of an electric current

**classify** – to sort objects into groups that are alike in some way

**clay** – a type of soil with very fine particles that is pliable when wet and hard when dry

**climate** – the general pattern of weather conditions in a region over a period of many years

**clock** – a tool used to measure time

**closed circuit** – an electrical path with no breaks or gaps

**cloud** – a group of water droplets or ice crystals floating in the air

**cloudy** – a weather condition in which clouds are present

**coal** – a fossil fuel used for energy which was formed from decomposed plant material

**cocoon** – a case which holds the larva of some insects during the pupa stage

**cold front** – the leading edge of a cooler air mass

**collect** – to gather or assemble

**collecting net** – a tool used for gathering living organisms

**collection** – a group of things that have been gathered together

**color** – a property of reflecting light

**communicate** – to give information

**community** – a group of organisms that live together in the same environment and depend on one another

**comparative investigation** – a type of investigation in which collected data is used to compare two or more things or conditions

**compare** – to look for ways that objects are alike or different

**compass** – a tool with a needle that always points to magnetic north

**competition** – a contest between organisms for food, territory, or other resources

**complete metamorphosis** – the life cycle of an organism whose appearance changes substantially at each of the four stages

**compost** – dead and decaying plant matter broken down by decomposers to provide nutrients for plants

**computer** – a tool that performs calculations and organizes and stores data

**concave** – a type of lens which is thinner in the middle

**conclusion** – a statement telling the results of an investigation based on data and observations

**condensation** – the change from gas to liquid as a result of cooling

**conductor** – a material that easily transfers heat or electricity

**conservation** – the wise use of natural resources in order to protect them

**conserve** – to use only what you need

**construct** – to build or form

**consumer** – an organism that receives energy by eating other organisms

**contribution** – the role or influence of an individual

**control** – a condition or factor that is kept the same throughout an experiment

**convection zone** – a layer of the Sun in which energy is transferred by convection

**convex** – a type of lens which is thicker in the middle

**cooling** – to make or become colder

**core** – the innermost layer of Earth, Sun, or Moon

**corona** – the atmosphere of gas surrounding the Sun

**craters** – bowl–shaped holes

**critique** – to analyze

**crust** – the outermost, rocky layer of the Earth or the Moon

**current** – the flow of electricity through a conductor

**cycle** – a sequence of events that is repeated over and over

# D

**data** – facts or information

**data table** – a table used to record facts or information

**day** – a period of time lasting 24 hours; the amount of time it takes Earth to make one complete rotation on its axis

**decibel** – a unit used to measure the loudness of sound

**deciduous forest** – a forest containing trees which lose their leaves in fall

**decomposer** – an organism that receives energy by breaking down dead matter, returning nutrients to the environment

**deforestation** – to cut down trees in a forest

**delta** – soil which is deposited at the mouth of a river, usually in a triangular shape

**density** – the amount of matter compacted into a given volume of a substance

**deposition** – a process by which wind or water drops sediment in a new location

**descriptive investigation** – a type of investigation which involves describing or quantifying parts

**desert** – an environment with very little rain

**develop** – to form into a more complex state

**direct** – straightforward and readily observed

**disposal** – the action of getting rid of something

**dissolve** – to mix completely with another substance to form a solution

**dominant trait** – the characteristic visible when at least one dominant allele for a trait is inherited

**drought** – a long period of little or no rain

# E

**Earth** – the third planet from the Sun; a small, rocky planet that is unique because it has liquid water which enables it to support life

**earthquake** – a sudden tremor of Earth's surface caused by movement of the crust and mantle, usually along a fault line

**eclipse** – when one object in space blocks light from reaching another object

**ecologist** – a scientist who studies the relationships between living organisms and their environments

**ecology** – the study of the relationships between living organisms and their environments

**ecosystem** – all living and nonliving things in a certain environment

**egg** – the first stage in the life cycle of some animals

**electric circuit** – the path of an electric current

**electrical energy** – the form of energy that consists of a flow of electric charges through a conductor

**electricity** – energy created by charged particles

**electromagnet** – a temporary magnet that works by the flow of electric current

**electromagnetic wave** – energy waves that can travel through matter or empty space

**emerge** – to come out or appear

**empirical evidence** – evidence which would yield the same results for any observer, such as a specific measurement

**endangered** – in danger of dying off or becoming extinct

**energy** – the ability to work or cause change

**environment** – the surroundings of an organism

**environmentalist** – a scientist who studies and works to solve environmental problems

**epicenter** – the point on the surface of Earth directly above an earthquake's starting point or focus

**equipment** – tools used in science investigations

**erosion** – the movement of sediment by wind, water, or ice

**eruption** – an ejection of material, such as lava

**ethogram** – a tool used to record animal behavior and activity

**evaluate** – to judge or examine

**evaporation** – the process by which a liquid changes to a gas

**evidence** – information or proof which helps form a conclusion

**examine** – to inspect or investigate

**exhale** – to breathe out

 motivation**science**™ LEVEL 5 ©2011–2014 mentoring**minds**.com

**experiment** – a test conducted to discover something

**experimental investigation** – a type of investigation in which variables are tested

**extinct** – a species that is no longer in existence

**extinction** – the death of all members of a species

# F

**fall** – the season following summer

**fault** – a place where a break in Earth's crust causes movement

**filter** – a tool used to separate smaller particles from larger particles

**First Quarter Moon** – a Moon phase occurring after Waxing Crescent in which the right half is lit and visible from Earth

**float** – to stay on top of a liquid or a gas

**flood** – an event which occurs when a large amount of water overflows onto a normally drier area

**flow** – the movement of energy, water, mud, or lava

**flower** – the part of a plant that makes seeds

**fog** – water vapor which has condensed close to the ground

**food chain** – the sequence that traces food energy in an ecosystem from producers to consumers

**food web** – a system of overlapping and connecting food chains in an ecosystem

**force** – a push or pull that causes an object to move, stop, or change direction

**forecast** – a prediction of the weather

**forest** – a place with many trees growing close together

**formation** – the way something is structured or created

**fossil** – the traces or remains of ancient organisms preserved in rock

**fossil fuel** – a nonrenewable resource formed from the remains of prehistoric plants and animals

**fossilization** – the process by which remains of organisms are preserved as fossils

**freeze** – to change a liquid to a solid

**freezing point** – the temperature at which a liquid changes to a solid

**freshwater** – water that is not salty

**friction** – the force that resists motion when two surfaces rub against each other

**fruit** – the part of a flowering plant that contains seeds

**Full Moon** – a Moon phase occurring after Waxing Gibbous in which the entire side of the Moon facing Earth is visible from Earth

**function** – the job or work done by a particular structure

# G

**gas** – a state of matter that does not have a shape of its own

**gas giant** – a large, gaseous planet in the outer solar system

**generation** – a group or level of offspring exhibiting traits inherited from parent organisms

**genetic trait** – an inherited characteristic determined by the combination of genes from the parent organisms

**geologic fault** – a break in Earth's crust along which movement occurs

**geologist** – a scientist who studies the structure of Earth

**geology** – the study of the structure of Earth

**geothermal** – heat energy from inside Earth

**germinate** – to begin sprouting from a seed

**geyser** – a hot spring that erupts by throwing a column of hot water into the air at various intervals

**glacier** – a large mass of slowly moving ice and snow that carves new features and deposits sediments

**gloves** – a type of safety equipment used to protect the hands

**glucose** – sugar produced by plants through photosynthesis

**goggles** – a pair of glasses worn for protection during science investigations

**graduated cylinder** – a container marked with a graded scale and used to measure the volume of liquids

**gram** – the basic unit of mass in the metric system

**graph** – a diagram that shows information; to plot information on a diagram showing the relationship between two variable qualities

**grassland** – an area of land consisting mainly of grasses, such as a prairie, meadow, or savanna

**gravel** – a type of soil made of large-sized particles and pebbles

**gravity** – a force that pulls objects toward each other

**grazers** – herbivores that usually feed on grass

**greenhouse effect** – heating that occurs when gases in Earth's atmosphere trap heat

**groundwater** – water that percolates, or drains, through soil and rocks and collects in underground reservoirs

**growth** – increase in size

# H

**habitat** – the place in an ecosystem where an organism lives

**hail** – a form of precipitation made from lumps of ice

**hand lens** – a hand–held magnifying glass

**hardness** – the ability of a material to resist being scratched

**hatch** – to break out of an egg

**hazard** – a possible source of danger

**hearing** – the sense that receives sound

**heat** – a type of energy that makes things warm

**heating** – to make or become warmer

**herbivore** – a consumer that eats only plants

**heredity** – the passing of genetic traits from parent organisms to offspring

**hibernate** – to go into a deep sleep for the winter

**hibernation** – a survival behavior in which some animals go into a deep sleep for the winter

**high pressure** – an area where the atmospheric pressure is greater than the pressure of the surrounding areas

**high tide** – the time when the inflowing water reaches its highest level

**homogeneous** – the same in composition, as in a mixture in which the solute is evenly distributed throughout the solvent

**hooves** – structures covering the feet of certain animals

**hot plate** – a burner used for heating materials

**human impact** – the effect humans have on the environment

**humidity** – the amount of moisture in the air

**humus** – a rich, dark layer of soil made of decaying plants and animals

**hurricane** – a powerful storm with strong winds and heavy rains

**hydroelectric energy** – electrical energy produced using the power of moving water

**hypothesis** – a statement that can be tested by an investigation or observation

# I

**igneous rock** – a rock that forms when magma or lava cools and hardens

**incomplete metamorphosis** – the life cycle of an organism whose appearance does not change substantially and has three growth stages

**indirect** – inferred; not readily observed

**individual** – a single member of a population of organisms

**infer** – to reach a conclusion based on something known or assumed

**information** – knowledge learned through the five senses

**ingredient** – a component of a mixture

**inhale** – to breathe in

**inherited trait** – a characteristic passed from parents to offspring through genes

**insect** – an invertebrate that has three body parts and six legs

**insoluble** – a substance that will not dissolve in a liquid

**instinct** – a behavior that is inherited by an organism

**insulator** – a material that stops or slows the flow of heat, electricity, or sound

**interact** – to work together

**interdependent** – when organisms depend on each other for survival

**invasive species** – an organism that is introduced to an area in which it would not have naturally lived

**investigation** – the act or process of using inquiry to gather facts

**iron filings** – small pieces of iron

# J

**Jupiter** – a gas planet, fifth from the Sun, and the largest of all planets

# L

**lake** – a large body of water with land all around it

**landform** – a physical feature on Earth's surface

**landslide** – sudden collapse of land causing a rapid change to Earth's surface

**larva** – an early stage in the life cycle of an insect

**lava** – molten rock that erupts from a volcano

**leaf** – the part of the plant that makes food for the plant

**learned behavior** – behavior that is taught or acquired through experience

**lenses** – transparent pieces of glass or plastic used for refracting light

**life cycle** – the sequence of stages or changes in the life of an organism

**light** – a form of energy that can be seen

**lightning** – electricity that moves between clouds or between clouds and the ground

**limited consumption** – controlling or limiting the amount of resources used

**liquid** – matter that flows and takes the shape of its container

**liter** – the basic unit of capacity in the metric system

**litter** – trash that is thrown around carelessly

**living organism** – something that grows, changes, and makes other living things

**loam** – a type of soil containing a mixture of other soils and rich in humus and nutrients

**logical** – makes sense based on information learned previously

**low pressure** – an area where the atmospheric pressure is lower than the pressure of the surrounding areas

**low tide** – the time when ocean water reaches its lowest level

**lunar cycle** – the different appearances of the Moon caused by the Moon's orbit around Earth

# M

**magma** – liquid, molten rock beneath Earth's surface

**magnet** – an object that attracts iron or steel

**magnetism** – the pulling force of a magnet

**magnify** – to make an object appear larger than it is using a science tool

**maintain** – to continue or keep going

**mantle** – the thick layer of rock between Earth's crust and core

**map** – a visual representation that shows features of an area

**map key** – a part of a map explaining what each symbol on the map represents

**marine biologist** – a scientist who studies organisms living in saltwater ecosystems

**marine biology** – the study of organisms living in saltwater ecosystems

**Mars** – a small, rocky planet; fourth from the Sun

**marsh** – an area of water-logged land

**mass** – the amount of matter in an object

**matter** – anything that takes up space and has mass

**measure** – to use tools to find the length, mass, capacity, or temperature of an object

**mechanical** – the energy in an object due to its position or motion

**medium** – a substance through which energy or waves travel

**melt** – to change from a solid to a liquid

**melting point** – the temperature at which a solid changes to a liquid

**Mercury** – the smallest planet and closest in relation to the Sun

**metals** – elements that are usually hard, shiny solids and good conductors of heat and electricity

**metamorphic rock** – a rock that has been changed by heat or pressure into another kind of rock

**metamorphosis** – a change in the way an organism looks as it grows

**meteorologist** – a scientist who studies weather, climate, and Earth's atmosphere

**meteorology** – the study of weather, climate, and Earth's atmosphere

**meter** – the basic unit of length in the metric system

**meter stick** – a science tool used to measure length

**method** – a process used for doing something

**microscope** – an instrument that uses lenses to make small objects look larger

**migration** – the seasonal movement of some animals from one place to another for survival

**milliliter** – a small unit of capacity in the metric system

**mimicry** – an animal's resemblance to another organism or object in color, shape, or design in order to escape predators or to attract prey

**mineral** – a nonliving solid object with a crystal structure found in nature

**mirror** – a reflective surface, usually silver in color

**mixture** – a combination of two or more substances that keep their own properties

**model** – a copy or replica of an object

**molt** – to shed skin, fur, or feathers

**moon** – a natural satellite in space that revolves around a planet

**Moon phases (waxing, waning)** – the changes in the appearance of the Moon as seen from Earth

**motion** – movement of an object

 motivation**science** LEVEL 5

# N

**natural gas** – a fossil fuel used for energy which was formed, through heat and pressure, from the remains of ancient plants and animals

**natural resource** – a material found in nature that is useful to humans

**neap tide** – a tide with the smallest difference between high and low tides, occurring during First and Third Quarter Moon phases

**Neptune** – a gas planet, eighth from the Sun, made primarily of methane gas

**New Moon** – a Moon phase occurring after Waning Crescent in which none of the side of the Moon facing Earth can be seen

**newton** (N) – the SI unit of force

**Newton's Laws of Motion** – three laws that are used to explain the movement of all objects in the universe

**niche** – the special role that a species fills in its habitat

**night** – the period of darkness which occurs each day when the opposite side of Earth is facing the Sun

**nocturnal** – active at night

**nonliving object** – an object that is not alive

**non-native species** – a species introduced to an area in which it would not naturally be found

**nonrenewable resource** – a resource that cannot be readily replaced

**notebook** – a science tool used to record notes, findings, and information gathered during investigations

**nutrient** – a substance needed by an organism to grow and survive

**nutritional label** – an area on a product showing the nutritional value contained in the product

**nymph** – a stage of incomplete metamorphosis in which the insect resembles the adult but is not fully developed

# O

**observe** – to gather information using the senses

**ocean** – a large body of saltwater

**offspring** – the young of a person, animal, or plant

**oil** – a liquid fossil fuel used for energy which was formed, through heat and pressure, from the remains of ancient plants and animals

**omnivore** – an organism that eats both plants and animals

**open circuit** – a broken or incomplete electrical path

**orbit** – the path an object takes as it moves around another object in space

**organism** – any living thing

**overfishing** – to excessively exhaust the supply of fish

**overpopulation** – a situation that occurs when a population becomes too great in number for the area they occupy so that resources become scarce

**oxygen** – a colorless, odorless gas that makes up about one-fifth of Earth's atmosphere and is necessary for life

# P

**paleontologist** – a scientist who studies ancient life using fossils

**paleontology** – the study of ancient life using fossils

**parent** – an organism that brings forth offspring

**part** – a piece of a whole or a system

**particle** – a small piece or part of a substance

**path** – the course or route something travels

**pattern** – a repeating design or series of numbers or events

**percolation** – the downward movement of water through soil and rock as a result of gravity

**permeability** – the rate something passes through a medium

**petroleum** – a liquid fossil fuel, also known as oil, formed from the remains of ancient plants and animals

**photosphere** – the visible, outer layer of the Sun

**photosynthesis** – the process by which plants use light to produce food

**physical characteristic** – a physical feature of an object

**physical property** – a characteristic of a substance that can be observed or measured without changing the substance

**physical state** – a form of matter

**physicist** – a scientist who studies force, energy, and motion

**physics** – the study of force, energy, and motion

**physiological adaptation** – an adaptation which occurs as a response to an environmental change, such as an animal's heart rate lowering to conserve energy

**pitch** – how high or low a sound is, determined by the frequency of sound waves

**planet** – a large body that moves in an orbit around a star

**plant** – a living thing that makes its own food and does not move from place to place

**plate tectonics** – the movement of tectonic plates on the fluid mantle, causing major geological events such as ocean basins, earthquakes, volcanic eruptions, and mountain building

**poaching** – to hunt or fish illegally

**pole** – the place on a magnet where the force is the strongest

**pollen** – the powdery substance in flowers needed for fertilization

**pollination** – the movement of pollen from the stamen to the pistil of a flower

**pollution** – material that harms air, land, or water

**pond** – a small body of freshwater

**population** – all the members of a species living in the same environment

**porosity** – the ability to allow fluids to pass through

**position** – the location of an object

**potting soil** – a type of soil rich in nutrients

**prairie** – a grassland area found in North America

**precaution** – an action taken before a science investigation to guard against possible danger

**precipitation** – any form of water falling from the clouds to Earth

**predation** – the feeding relationship in which one species (prey) becomes a food source for another (predator)

**predator** – an animal that hunts other animals for food

**predict** – to tell what you think will happen

**prey** – an animal that is hunted and eaten by a predator

**primary consumer** – an organism in a food chain that eats plants

**prism** – a transparent, three-dimensional shape used to separate white light into the color spectrum

**process** – a method or series of steps

**producer** – an organism that makes its own food

**product** – a good or service provided by a company

**prominence** – a stream of gas that erupts from the surface of the Sun

 motivation**science** LEVEL 5

**promotional materials** – advertisements or items used to sell a product

**property** – a characteristic of an object or substance

**pull** – a force that moves something closer

**pulley** – a simple machine made of a rope or chain and a grooved wheel

**pupa** – the stage of metamorphosis in which an insect changes from a larva to an adult

**push** – a force that moves something away

# Q

**question** – the problem in an experimental investigation

# R

**radiative zone** – the layer of the Sun closest to the core in which energy is transferred to the outer layers

**rain** – water that falls from clouds to Earth in drops

**rainforest** – a tropical forest where rain falls almost every day

**rapid** – very quickly or swiftly

**recessive trait** – a characteristic that is visible only when two recessive alleles for the same trait are inherited

**reconstruction** – restoring an area to replace the resources used

**record** – to write or draw what has been observed

**recycle** – to take the resource from a product and use it to make a new product

**reflection** – light energy that bounces off a surface

**refraction** – the bending of light rays as they pass from one substance to another

**relationship** – a connection between two or more things

**reliability** – the degree to which the results of an investigation are valid and dependable

**renewable resources** – resources that can be replaced as they are used

**repeated investigation** – an experiment that is tested multiple times

**repel** – to push away

**represent** – to stand for something else

**reproduce** – to have offspring or to produce more of a given animal or plant

**resource** – anything people can use

**respiration** – breathing in and out

**result** – outcomes of an investigation

**retain** – to hold in or keep

**reusable resource** – a natural resource that can be used more than once

**reuse** – to use again

**revolve** – to travel in a path around another object

**Richter scale** – a scale used to measure an earthquake's strength or magnitude

**river** – a large body of flowing water

**rock** – a hard, nonliving thing made of minerals

**rock cycle** – the slow, continuous process by which rocks change from one type to another

**root** – the part of a plant that usually grows below the ground, holds the plant in place, and takes in water and minerals

**rotate** – to turn on an axis

**rotation** – the act of spinning or turning around a center or an axis

**ruler** – a tool used to measure the length of an object

**runoff** – water from rain or melted snow that flows along Earth's surface into bodies of water

# S

**safe practices** – procedures used to keep one safe from danger or harm

**safety** – freedom from danger or harm

**saltwater** – water that has salt in it

**sample** – a small part of something larger used for analysis

**sand** – tiny pieces of broken rocks

**sand dune** – a hill of sand created by the wind

**satellite** – an object that revolves around a larger object in space

**Saturn** – a gas planet, second largest and sixth from the Sun, with many rings encircling it

**savanna** – a flat grassland found in tropical and subtropical areas

**scarcity** – something that is in short supply

**scavenger** – an animal that feeds on the remains of dead animals or garbage

**science tools** – tools used in science investigations

**scientific evidence** – information that either supports or disputes a scientific theory or hypothesis

**scientific explanation** – an explanation of how or why something happens based on observations and investigations

**scientific method** – step-by-step process used to find answers to questions about the world around us

**scientist** – a person who investigates, researches, and studies processes, patterns, and events

**season** – one of four periods of the year caused by the tilt of Earth away or toward the Sun as it revolves around the Sun

**secondary consumer** – an organism in a food chain that eats primary consumers

**sediment** – small particles of rock, soil, sand, or shell deposited by water, wind, or ice

**sedimentary rock** – a type of rock formed when layers of sediment are pressed together and harden over time

**seed** – the part of a plant that can grow into a new plant

**seedling** – a young plant

**seeing** – receiving information through the sense of sight

**seismic wave** – a vibration that travels through Earth, usually caused by an earthquake

**seismograph** – a tool used to detect the seismic waves caused by an earthquake

**seismologist** – a scientist who studies earthquakes

**seismology** – the study of earthquakes

**senses** – how we gather information about our surroundings

**separate** – to take apart

**shadow** – an image cast when light is blocked by an opaque object

**shelter** – a place where an animal can be safe

**SI system of measurement** – the International System of Units developed by scientists as a worldwide standard of measurement

**silt** – a type of soil made of fine-grained sediment

**sink** – to drop to the bottom of a liquid

**sleet** – a form of precipitation made of ice pellets

**smelling** – the sense that detects odors

**snow** – ice crystals that form from water vapor in the air and fall to Earth

**soil** – the layer of Earth's surface consisting of small pieces of rock, decayed plant and animal matter, and minerals

**solar** – relating to the Sun

**solar energy** – energy from the Sun

**solar flare** – a burst of energy from the Sun's surface

 motivation**science** LEVEL 5

**solar system** – a star and all the objects in orbit around it

**solid** – matter that has a definite shape

**soluble** – able to be dissolved in or by a liquid

**solute** – the substance which is dissolved in the solvent

**solution** – a mixture of two or more substances that are evenly distributed throughout

**solvent** – in a solution, the part of the mixture in which other substances are dissolved

**sort** – to group things by an attribute

**sound** – a type of energy that can be heard, caused by vibrations

**sound wave** – a vibration that travels as a wave passing through air, liquid, or solids to cause a sound that can be heard

**species** – the smallest group of organisms of the same kind that are able to produce offspring

**spring** – the season following winter

**spring scale** – a tool to measure weight using the force of gravity

**spring tide** – high tide greater than the usual high tide, occurring at New and Full Moon phases when the Sun, Earth, and Moon are aligned

**sprout** – to begin to grow

**star** – a huge ball of gases in space that releases heat and light

**state of matter** – one of the forms of matter

**static electricity** – the buildup of electric charges on an object

**stationary front** – a weather front in which the line between a cold front and a warm front is immobile

**stem** – the part of a plant that holds it up and moves water and food to the other parts of the plant

**stopwatch** – a tool used to measure time

**stream** – a body of flowing water that is smaller than a river

**structural adaptation** – a physical feature of an organism

**structure** – relating to the physical composition of an object

**summer** – the season after spring

**Sun** – the star that is at the center of our solar system which provides energy for Earth

**sunspots** – dark spots on the Sun's surface

**surface water** – the usable freshwater that moves over Earth's surface and is located in creeks, rivers, ponds, lakes, and reservoirs

**survive** – to stay alive

**system** – a group of things or parts that work together

# T

**table** – a structure used to organize and record information in rows and columns

**Taiga** – a subarctic forest consisting mainly of coniferous evergreen trees

**tasting** – the sense that detects sweet, sour, salty, and bitter

**tectonic plate** – giant, irregular piece of Earth's outermost layer that moves around on the fluid mantle below

**telescope** – an instrument that magnifies distant objects and makes them appear closer

**temperate forest** – a forest with a moderate climate

**temperature** – how hot or cold something is; a measure of the average kinetic energy of the particles of matter

**terrarium** – a small, closed container in which organisms can be observed and kept

**tertiary consumer** – an organism in a food chain that eats secondary consumers

**testable** – a question or hypothesis which can be investigated through experimentation

**texture** – how something feels

**theory** – a set of principles that explains and predicts phenomena

**thermal energy** (heat energy) – the energy of moving particles that produces heat

**thermometer** – a tool used to measure temperature in degrees

**Third Quarter Moon** – a Moon phase occurring after Waning Gibbous, also called Last Quarter, when the left half of the Moon is visible from Earth

**threatened** – an organism which is at risk of becoming endangered

**thunderstorm** – a rainstorm with thunder and lightning

**tide** – the regular rise and fall of ocean levels

**time** – a measure of the past, present, and future

**timing device** – a tool used to measure time, such as a clock, stopwatch, or timer

**tool** – a piece of equipment used to observe, measure, or make a task easier

**topsoil** – the top layer of soil, often the richest in nutrients for plant growth

**tornado** – a powerful funnel of very strong winds that can form during a thunderstorm

**touching** – the sense by which one feels pressure, pain, heat, and cold

**trait** – a characteristic of an organism

**transpiration** – the release of water vapor by plants

**triple beam balance** – a scale that uses three bars to measure the mass of an object

**troposphere** – the lowest layer of Earth's atmosphere extending to about 16 km above Earth's surface

**tsunami** – a large wave caused by an underwater earthquake

**tundra** – a flat, cold area with no trees

# U

**unlimited consumption** – consuming a resource without limiting how much of the resource is used

**Uranus** – a gas planet, seventh from the Sun, that is tilted "sideways" so that the South Pole is pointed almost directly at the Sun

# V

**valid** – reasonable and justifiable

**variable** – a condition or factor that changes in an investigation so the effects can be observed

**Venus** – a rocky planet, second from the Sun, similar in size to Earth

**vibration** – a rapid back and forth movement

**volcanic** – relating to a volcano

**volcano** – an opening in Earth's crust through which lava and ash erupt

**volume** – the amount of space an object takes up or the loudness of a sound

# W

**Waning Crescent** – a Moon phase occurring after the Third Quarter, in which a crescent shape of light is visible on the left side of the Moon

**Waning Gibbous** – a Moon phase occurring after the Full Moon, in which over half of the Moon is visible on the left side

**warm front** – the leading edge of a warmer air mass

**water** – a clear liquid that falls from the sky and fills oceans, rivers, and lakes

**water cycle** – the movement of water through Earth's environment

**water vapor** – water that has changed into a gas

**watershed** – the region of land drained by a river system

 motivation**science** LEVEL 5

**Waxing Crescent** – a Moon phase occurring after New Moon, in which a crescent shape of light is visible on the right side of the Moon

**Waxing Gibbous** – a Moon phase occurring after First Quarter, in which over half of the Moon is visible on the right side

**weather** – what the air outside is like

**weather front** – the boundary between two air masses of different density, moisture, or temperature

**weather instruments** – tools used by meteorologists to gather data

**weather map** – a chart showing the weather conditions of a large area

**weather symbols** – an international set of symbols used to show atmospheric conditions

**weathering** – the breaking down of rocks by water, wind, and ice

**webbed feet** – feet with toes which are connected by a membrane

**wind** – the movement of air

**winter** – the season following fall

**work** – what occurs when forces move an object over a distance

# Z

**zoologist** – a scientist who studies animals

**zoology** – the study of animals

motivation**science**™LEVEL 5

## Science Vocabulary Builder

Look at the following vocabulary chart. Draw a picture to help you remember what the word means. Cut the squares apart, and practice matching the words with the correct definitions and pictures.

### Mixture Mix-Up

| Vocabulary Word | Definition | Picture |
|---|---|---|
| Mixture | A combination of two or more substances that keep their own properties. | |
| Magnetism | The pulling force of a magnet. | |
| Combine | To put two or more substances together. | |
| Separate | To take apart. | |
| Iron filings | A small piece of shaved iron. | |
| Physical property | A characteristic of a substance that can be observed or measured without changing the substance. | |

motivation**science**™LEVEL 5

### Science Vocabulary Builder

Cut along the outside edges of the design. Then, fold the triangular flaps along the dotted line. On the outside of the flap, write the word. On the inside, write a sentence using the word, and draw a picture describing the word.

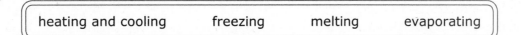

| heating and cooling | freezing | melting | evaporating |

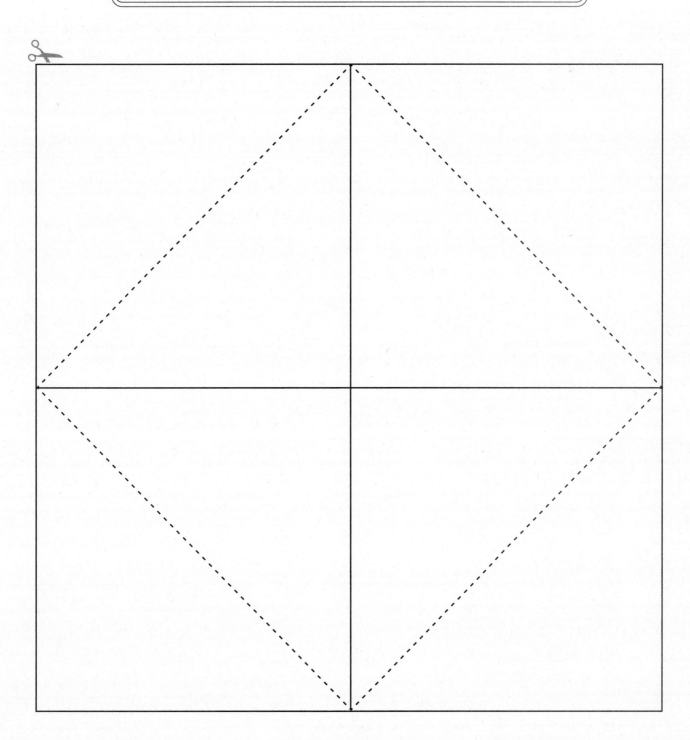

motivation**science**™ LEVEL 5

## Science Vocabulary Builder

Design a board game to play with partners or groups. Create a title for the game. Play the game with the following cards. When playing the game, you must draw cards and answer correctly. The winner gets to keep the board game.

### Board Game Questions

| | | |
|---|---|---|
| What is electricity? | Explain how a circuit works. | How do electric currents produce light, sound, and heat? |
| How does electricity produce light? | What is an example of how electricity produces heat? | Name a source of sound produced by electricity. |
| Who investigated electricity by flying a kite? | Name three conductors of electricity. | Name and locate the parts of a circuit. |
| How is static electricity produced? | What will happen if you rub a balloon against your hair? | Describe how electricity is used at school. |

motivation**science**™LEVEL 5

## Science Vocabulary Builder

In each empty puzzle piece fill in the correct vocabulary word that matches the definition. Then, cut out the puzzle pieces, and practice putting the puzzle back together.

Use the words in the box to fill in the empty puzzle pieces.

| work | pull | motion | pulley | force | push |
|------|------|--------|--------|-------|------|

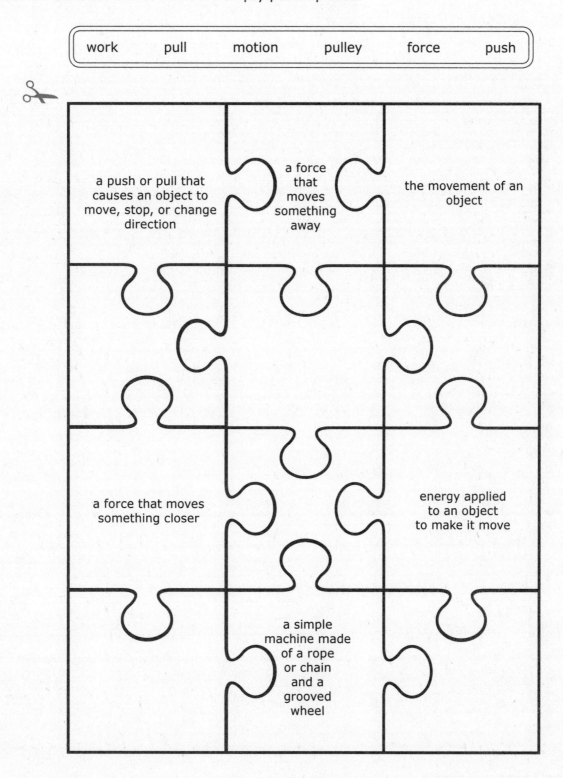

a push or pull that causes an object to move, stop, or change direction

a force that moves something away

the movement of an object

a force that moves something closer

energy applied to an object to make it move

a simple machine made of a rope or chain and a grooved wheel

motivation**science**™ LEVEL 5

## Science Vocabulary Builder

Create a bingo card using the words provided. Mix up the order of the words. Then, create word cards with definitions, questions, and sentences that describe each word. Cut out the word cards, and play bingo in groups or with the whole class.

| | | | |
|---|---|---|---|
| permeability | porosity | percolation | retain | sandy | loam | silt | clay | potting soil |
| gravel | sediment | humus | particle size | soil | texture | erosion | weathering |

## Bingo Card

| | | | |
|---|---|---|---|
| | | | |
| | | | |
| | | | |
| | | | |

## Word Cards

| | | | |
|---|---|---|---|
| | | | |
| | | | |
| | | | |
| | | | |

Name _____

## Science Vocabulary Builder

Unscramble each word below using the terms in the vocabulary box. Write the definition for each word in the space below the box.

| | | | |
|---|---|---|---|
| weather map | meteorologist | low pressure | cold front |
| forecast | warm front | high pressure | precipitation |

1. wol speerusr

_____

2. ramw nroft

_____

3. gmelotetsorio

_____

4. actsefor

_____

5. dcol ortfn

_____

6. gihh surperes

_____

7. iaetptprnoici

_____

8. eahtrew pam

_____

**Definitions**

| | |
|---|---|
| 1. | |
| 2. | |
| 3. | |
| 4. | |
| 5. | |
| 6. | |
| 7. | |
| 8. | |

motivation**science**™LEVEL 5

## Science Vocabulary Builder

Use the words in the box to create clues for each card. Write a word on the back of each card. Then, write 3 clues for the word on the front of the card, under the card number. Cut out the cards.

In groups or partners, compete to win the most points. One at a time, pick a number card. The opposite team members read the first clue. If the answer is guessed correctly, the player receives 3 points. If the player does not know the answer, the second clue is read. The player receives 2 points if answered correctly. Questions answered correctly after the third clue receive 1 point. Switch teams after each set of questions. The team with the most points wins!

| | | | | | | |
|---|---|---|---|---|---|---|
| Shadows | Tides | High tide | Low tide | Spring tide | Neap tide | Seasons |
| Winter | Spring | Summer | Autumn | New Moon | Waxing Crescent | Gravity |
| First Quarter | Waxing Gibbous | Full Moon | Waning Gibbous | Third Quarter | Waning Crescent | |

| | | | |
|---|---|---|---|
| **Card #1** | **Card #2** | **Card #3** | **Card #4** |
| **Card #5** | **Card #6** | **Card #7** | **Card #8** |
| **Card #9** | **Card #10** | **Card #11** | **Card #12** |
| **Card #13** | **Card #14** | **Card #15** | **Card #16** |
| **Card #17** | **Card #18** | **Card #19** | **Card #20** |

**Science Vocabulary Builder**

The object of the game is for a player to collect all the planets in order. The first card played is the Sun. Then, play the planet cards one at a time beginning with Mercury and ending with Neptune. The player who lays down the Sun and the correct order of the planets first wins.

Deal each player 3 cards. If Player One has a Sun card, he/she lays down the Sun card and draw another card. Player Two does the same thing. (If no Sun card is in their pile, they must draw from the card pile, and it is the next player's turn.) Players take turns laying down one card at a time.

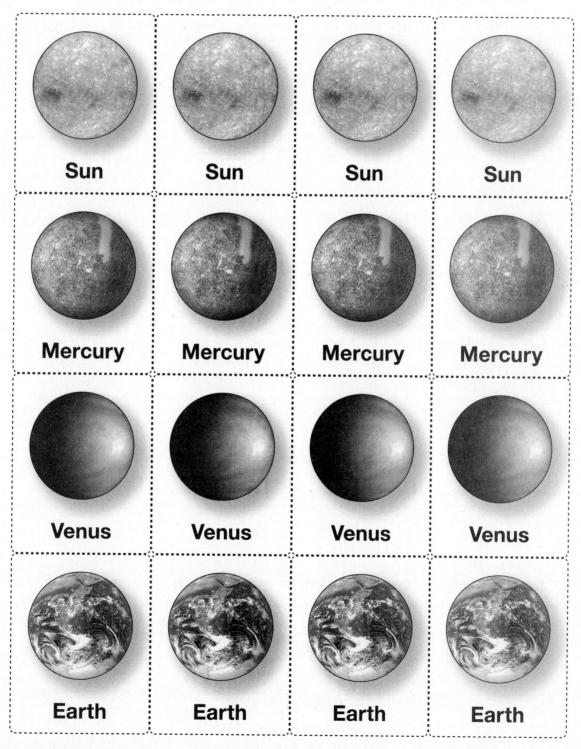

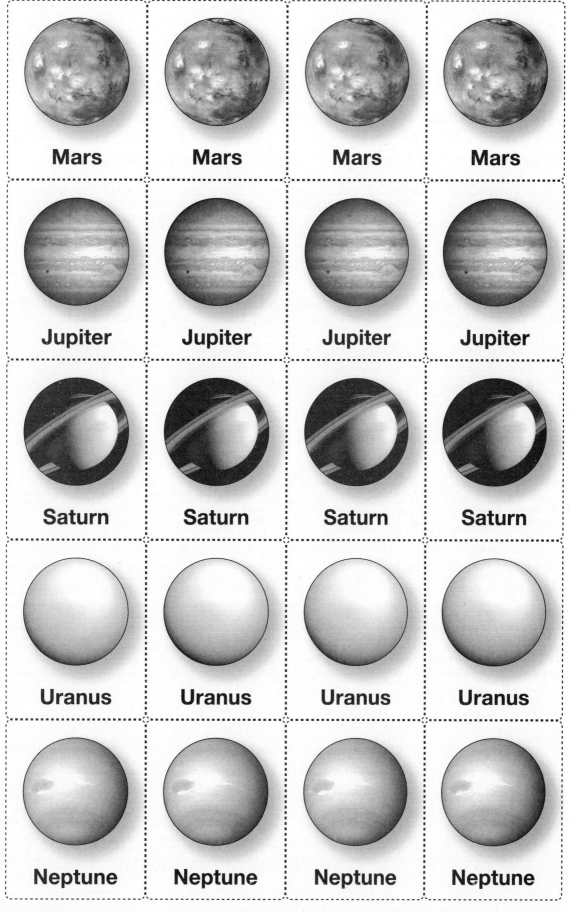

Mars    Mars    Mars    Mars

Jupiter    Jupiter    Jupiter    Jupiter

Saturn    Saturn    Saturn    Saturn

Uranus    Uranus    Uranus    Uranus

Neptune    Neptune    Neptune    Neptune

## Science Vocabulary Builder

Use the clues below to complete the puzzle.

carnivore

decomposer

energy flow

energy pyramid

food chain

food web

herbivore

omnivore

predator

prey

primary consumers

producers

secondary consumers

tertiary consumers

### Across

1. the movement of energy through the food chain
5. organisms that eat plants
7. overlapping and connecting food chains in an ecosystem
10. organisms that make their own food
12. an organism that helps dead plants and animals decay
14. a diagram showing the flow of energy through a food chain

### Down

2. traces food energy from producers to consumers
3. organisms that eat secondary consumers
4. an organism that eats only plants
6. organisms that eat primary consumers
8. an organism that eats both plants and meat
9. an animal that hunts other animals for food
11. an organism that eats only meat
13. an animal that is hunted and eaten by another animal

## Science Vocabulary Builder

Unscramble each of the clue words. Copy the letters in the numbered cells to other cells with the same number.

X O N E G Y     ☐☐☐☐☐ (2)

L E Y C C     ☐☐☐☐☐ (3)

N O R A B C   D O X D E I I     ☐☐☐☐☐☐ (13)   ☐☐☐☐☐☐☐ (5)

M A A N I S L     ☐☐☐☐☐☐ (9)

L A N P T S     ☐☐☐☐☐☐ (11)(6)

D Y A     ☐☐☐ (15)

R U H N O E G E E S   G S A     ☐☐☐☐☐☐☐☐☐ (12) ☐☐☐ (4)

P O S H E R M E A T     ☐☐☐☐☐☐☐☐☐ (14)(10)(8)

U S N     ☐☐☐ (16)

M I N N E N T O E R V     ☐☐☐☐☐☐☐☐☐☐☐ (1)(17)

T N H I G     ☐☐☐☐☐ (7)

☐☐☐☐☐☐   ☐☐   ☐☐☐☐☐☐☐☐☐
1 2 3 4 5 6   7 8   9 10 11 12 13 14 15 16 17

**Science Vocabulary Builder**

Cut the paper below on the dotted line. Fold lengthwise with the words on top. Cut each solid line so there are four flaps that can be lifted. On the underside of each flap, explain what each word means. On the solid flap, draw a picture of what the word means.

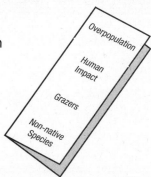

✂ - - - - - - - - - - - - - - - - - - - - - - - - - - - - - - - - - - - - - - -

## Overpopulation

## Human Impact

## Grazers

## Non-native Species

RR Donnelley/Owensville, MO USA/October 2014 – 16850